WITH ALL
ITS FAULTS

WITH ALL

A Candid Account o

ITS FAULTS

Forty Years in Advertising

by Fairfax M. Cone

with illustrations

LITTLE, BROWN AND COMPANY
BOSTON · TORONTO

Published simultaneously in Canada
by Little, Brown & Company (Canada) Limited

PRINTED IN THE UNITED STATES OF AMERICA

To G.K.C. and the O'Rileys

Contents

PART IV

Part I

The View from the Tower

THIS is a book about advertising that has the distinction of having been written by an advertising man.

During forty-three years of competition in behalf of a number of products and services that are widely accepted in American life, I have heard most of the complaints and read most of the articles of defense that are brought forth to argue the advertising case. Moreover, I have uttered more than a few of the complaints myself, just as, on other occasions, I have summoned up what I believe to be a reasonable response.

When I came into the business, the objections were almost all against specific advertisements or classifications of advertisements where the truth was violated almost as a matter of course; where, for instance, cures were promised for incurable diseases and fortunes assured from the purest of blue-sky investments. This has changed. Today a small coterie of economists and a somewhat larger number of well-intentioned government officials and their advisers on what are called consumer affairs see advertising as an instrument of moral as well as intellectual miseducation. They believe that insofar as it succeeds in influencing people's minds, advertising conditions people not to think for themselves and not to choose for themselves. It is hypnotic in its effect, these critics maintain, and mesmerizes consumers into helpless brand slavery.

Altogether, it is the view from the ivory tower that the manufacturers and distributors of consumer goods, and the advertising people who represent them, exercise their wills and their wiles over a public that is entirely unaware of what is being done to it. To which I can only reply that this shows an amazing contempt for the intelligence, the purpose and the wisdom of the great mass of men and women around us.

Also, it should be noted that when critics inveigh against moral and intellectual miseducation which makes people suggestible and docile, and against wants that are synthesized by advertising and shaped by the manipulation of hidden persuaders, they fail to explain how this miseducation is directed, what wants are synthesized, or how the manipulation is accomplished.

Advertising, of course, has no entity. It is something people do, and they do it according to their own interests. Since their purposes are many, there are few elements in our daily lives that are more ubiquitous, and since this means also inescapable, advertising can be extremely abrasive.

I suppose this is nowhere more true than in the repetition of an ugly advertisement for a mouthwash or dandruff remedy or deodorant, or whatever, that imposes itself on our television viewing at inappropriate times and with maddening frequency. Or when the peace and beauty of the landscape is interrupted and, in effect, violated by jungles of unsightly advertisements for wayside fruit stands and eating places and motels.* Under either of these circumstances, one's contempt for advertising as a means of attracting customers for any business enterprise must stiffen, for it is both intrusive and impertinent.

Nor is it only certain broadcast advertising and certain outdoor advertising that I find distressing.

I am offended by much of the advertising of motion pictures in our daily newspapers. The promise of so many theater owners that what they have to show stretches sophistication to its limits, which may be quite beyond the limits of decency, seems to me disgraceful to both the exhibitors and the publishers of the newspapers that carry the lurid announcements.

Perhaps it could be argued that the moving picture people are no worse than certain book publishers; that their advertising is in exactly the same pattern as the advertising for novels in which the erotic appeal is so thinly disguised as to be transparent. But this is hardly an excuse. The movie producers and exhibitors and the publishers have simply gone into the gold-filled gutter together.

Under the circumstances, it should surprise no one that the use of suggestive text and illustrations in the advertising of health and

---

* California leads in this pitiless abuse of the natural scene. U.S. 101 between San Francisco and San Jose should be an object lesson to the world not to permit indiscriminate signing by roadside or any other businesses.

Only you can prevent forest fires.

Smokey the Bear is a continuing reminder that advertising has many uses.

beauty aids in magazines and on the air should follow in their foot-steps; the promise the latter imply in only faintly veiled terms is the promise of seduction.

I am equally distressed by people who persistently use advertising with a cynical disregard for truth. For the most part these malefactors are prevented from engaging in outright fraud. But there is a kind of scrupulous dishonesty that is possible in advertising that is called the weasel — a flaw in the promise that makes the proposition fuzzy. For example: *XYZ tires are the largest-selling tires in the world with their exclusive nonskid tread.* This seems to say that XYZ tires have overtaken all other similar tires in popularity and in use. But does it? It does not. It actually says that these are the only tires with their par-ticular tread; thus, they are the largest-selling tires in their own indi-vidual category as a matter of course. The weasel rests on a slippery claim that is technically correct.

Altogether, I am mortified by a number of things that go on in ad-vertising, not the least of which is the current fad of irrelevancy by which it is hoped to attract the maximum of attention through pure advertising invention or by irrelevance depending on whether or not the stated proposition contains a double meaning. *People who drink Old Fitzgerald bourbon don't know any better* is a fair sample of this foolishness.

However, these things that bother me most in advertising are largely overlooked by the highbrowed critics of the business who hold it to be a planned and persuasive and precise means of deceiving and defrauding a trusting if not simpleminded public.

This is both faulty evaluation and wild generalization. Advertising is not a science that can be mastered and applied with success in any given circumstance, either honorable or otherwise. And the public, which is largely hardheaded and wary, particularly when it comes to parting with its money, has an almost uncanny ability to know when it is otherwise.

No one who can remember the Edsel automobile has any right to doubt this. Advertising, together with a vast program of publicity that included such heroic exercises as enlisting the poet Marianne Moore to invent a sprightly name for the new car, brought three mil-lion people into showrooms across the country when the drumbeating was loudest and the car was introduced. There, completely unmoved by the noise, they turned thumbs down on it. Why, no one exactly knows.

This is something about the American public that no advertising yet has overcome: its ability to make up its own mind for reasons that are entirely its own, and to disclose these to no one. All anyone knows about the classic failure of the Edsel, which was a $400 million failure — the most traumatic in this country's business history — is that the public didn't like what it saw and wouldn't listen to any argument.

The Edsel, which, as we shall see, my company helped to introduce, and for whose life I prayed since nothing else could save it, was four years in planning, and dead in a matter of days.

When it comes to downright evildoing in advertising, the catalogue grows thinner every year.

Most of the instances of deceit and deception cited by fearful onlookers are matters of record wherein the culprits have been caught and punished, or at least made to desist from their wickedness, just as evildoers elsewhere are arrested and restrained. For while advertising is something anyone can do, most people are honest and so, consequently, is most advertising.

When it isn't, there is considerable recourse, for we have the Federal Trade Commission and the Food and Drug Administration to guard the public interest at the national (or manufacturers') level, and we have a network of Better Business Bureaus to guard against unscrupulous retailers at big-city neighborhood levels. The more closely knit smaller communities maintain a close and effective personal watch. Over and above all these, there is the vigilant and intrepid Post Office Department to see to it that the mails are not used to defraud, and if its pursuit is sometimes obstructed by legal devices, it rarely fails to bag its quarry.

While I am not at all sure that any of these agencies is as adequately financed or as completely programmed as it might be, I do believe that the machinery for dealing with dishonesty in which advertising plays a part is properly conceived, and with the aid of the media of advertising, generally effective. Newspapers and magazine publishers and radio and television broadcasters try to see to it that the advertising they carry is honest. When this turns out not to be the case, when someone is lied to, it is a rare medium that doesn't insist upon immediate compensatory action.

As to the time-honored charge that advertisers and advertising suborn our media of mass communications, let me quote Henry R. Luce, the late great editor in chief of *Time, Life* and *Fortune*. When asked how much it would cost to get a story about a certain company in *Fortune*, Luce replied, "Five million dollars — and along with the article we would throw in the whole magazine, lock, stock, and barrel."*
While the quoted price might vary according to the size of the op-

---

* *Time, Inc.* by Robert T. Elson (New York, 1968).

eration, I have no doubt that the vast majority of American publishers and broadcasters would answer the same question in identical terms.

Advertising follows circulation; it does not dictate editorial content; and modern advertisers have learned better than to try.

It is one of the favorite ploys of the critics in the tower to lump advertising with such contemporary social sicknesses as urban blight, air and water pollution, juvenile delinquency and even the machinations of the Mafia in an indictment of our times. But these are only a few of the unlovely things in our lives with which advertising has nothing whatever to do.

Murder, rape and armed robbery have never had the benefit of a promotional appropriation. No advertising of which I am aware has ever sung praises to auto-stealing, purse-snatching, shoplifting, mugging, party-crashing, tax-dodging, cop-hating or the juice racket. Sit-ins, laydowns and dropouts are as foreign to promotion through advertising as mononucleosis, drug addiction or child abandonment. Farm surpluses and the high price of haircuts, doctors' prescriptions, hospital beds and downtown parking all have come about without any use of advertising space or time.

Advertising has yet to be written to drum up attendance at race riots or to promote teachers' strikes. The hippies and the flower people have made it entirely on their own, and so have black humor and pop art. There is nothing in the annals of advertising that could have served as a model for Bobby Baker, Billy Sol Estes or Senator Dodd or Justice Fortas. There has never been a line of advertising to support the arrogance of James Hoffa or Maria Callas, or the tantrums of Cassius Clay or the average U.S. amateur tennis star. And insofar as advertising is concerned, neither Lee Harvey Oswald, James Earl Ray or Sirhan Sirhan could have found inspiration in it.

Most of the viewers who fear advertising as an evil force give it too much credit. About all it can do under the most skillful direction (and by skillful direction I don't mean either hidden or otherwise undue persuasion) is to exploit a given interest, predilection, disposition, prejudice or bias and bring this to bear on a buying decision. The thing to remember is that the given interest, predilection, or whatever usually has to be there first. It is quite true that probing by advertising people sometimes uncovers prejudices, for or against, not previously known to exist, but they rarely manage to invent such prejudices.

The effect of advertising upon most of us is to help resolve the choice of buying alternatives that confront us in the normal course of every day. What the hardworking critics forget is that they and only they undertake to look at *all* advertising; the rest of us sort out automatically what we find useful and pay little or no attention to what is left.* One of the most highly developed functions of the human brain allows it to close instantly to advertising that is unnecessary or uninteresting, and neither sound nor fury can open it except at the advertiser's own risk; he can shout himself from mild apathy to sharp disapproval in a single thirty-second television commercial.

The power of advertising is greatest when it helps to answer questions. Shall we buy a new car or install a backyard swimming pool? Will the old refrigerator do, and if it will, shall we save for a color television set or shall we make over the family room? Or would a boat mean more lasting pleasure? These are large buying questions.

And there are many small ones: what kind of shirt, socks, shorts, slip, bra, sheets, towels, cold cream, toothpaste, razor blades, light bulbs, frozen foods, canned meats, coffee, soup, soap, detergent, facial tissues, floor wax, greeting cards or diet cola should we choose this time? These are choices advertising helps make every day.

The woman in the supermarket with her shopping list in one hand and her purse clutched tightly in the other has rarely been blinded by anybody's blandishments. However sweet her smile may be, however disingenuous her getup (even to tight velvet stretch pants and aluminum hair curlers) she is one of the world's most astute purchasing agents.

One of the things her eager protectors forget is that there is no power on earth that can make her buy a product a second time that fooled her once; nor can anything keep her from telling anyone within range of her voice when she feels victimized. That the advertiser knows this, too, is her constant guarantee. The marketplace is no place for lies.

What follows is an account of a lifetime in advertising that began by the merest chance in San Francisco, punctuated itself twice in New York and culminated in Chicago. Here I have followed it sometimes with amazement and sometimes with dismay, but with a growing conviction that with all its faults advertising is as necessary in our times as the power that turns the wheels of industry.

It is our sole source of information about most of the products of that industry. Word of mouth could hardly keep up with the speeding wheels. In fact, the only substitute that has been suggested is a system

* Research shows that the average American is exposed to some sixteen hundred advertising messages each day, is moved pro or con by no more than fifteen of these.

of consumer reports compiled by the government to inform the public and protect it — presumably from both the advertisers and its own irrepressible folly.

Here I must object. Surely it has yet to be proved, as my friend James Lorie, a professor in the Graduate School of Business at the University of Chicago, points out, "that consumers may be competent to select presidents, wives and husbands, and schools for their children, but not to pick breakfast foods; and that only the federal government can make such decisions soundly."

It must be clear now that mine is an old-fashioned point of view. But I make no apology for this. For one thing, I have had a wonderful time overall, and the total of my earnings in advertising has made it possible for me to contribute beyond my wildest dreams to a number of intellectual and artistic endeavors that I otherwise could have supported only with my voice.

It is the essence of my argument that I think voices are insufficient. I wish I could believe that the principal critics of advertising had ever accompanied their wives on a week of shopping tours. If they had, or if I could take them, I am sure they would be less concerned with the hazards they see in the path of the consumer, and much more understanding of a career like my own that has been dedicated to the distribution of all manner of goods to a world that doesn't *need* any of them.

It is said that people only want most things because others have them. The question I would ask is why shouldn't they? Why shouldn't they want the mildness and the efficacy of a Dial soap, or the soft efficiency of Kleenex tissues or the pleasant artistry of Hallmark greeting cards? These and the other non-necessities with whose advertising the following pages are concerned are no longer the prerogatives only of the few. They are everyone's.

It would be totally wrong, as I have suggested, to maintain that all advertising is good. I am frequently disappointed by it, as when it doesn't tell me all I want to know. I am also, not infrequently, discouraged by its uses, for when it is designed, for example, to sell political candidates (even my candidates) with gaudy words and pictures, like beer or breakfast food, and with intimations and implications that would not be acceptable in product advertising, then I think it is misused.

Disappointment and discouragement are different from disillusionment, however, and I have found no disillusion in advertising. With all the shortcomings to which it is liable, advertising continues to be only a *means* of communication, and I believe that its value to the public at large outweighs any wages of its venial sins.

Part II

Sternberger

THE want ads department was where the San Francisco *Examiner* made most of its profits. The gross was enormous and the net was large. For one thing, the clerks who took in the classified advertisements were hardly more than slaves.

I know this because I was one of them. My pay was seventeen dollars and a half per week, and a week was made up of six eight-hour days. Actually, I was released from behind the marble counter on the first floor of the Hearst Building in Market Street at one o'clock each Saturday afternoon, but the *Examiner* made up for this beneficence by requiring me to work a full shift every other Sunday. This was in 1926.

The Sunday exercise was a Sternberger invention, and my only question about it was whether the classified manager had planned it to make money or merely to confirm his contempt for the clerks. This bald, bitter little man never spoke to any of us, even when he came down from upstairs to look over his domain in the quiet gloom of a Sunday.

The only activity on Sundays was taking in funeral notices, which for convenience were handled as want ads, at extremely high rates. As I recall the scale, theatrical announcements, political advertisements and death notices all were in the highest bracket. The advertisers could not dispense with such advertising and the newspaper priced it accordingly.

The death notices were brought in by the undertakers or their runners, and a happier man never came to the classified counter than one who had just landed the remains of a bigwig. However, there was one tall, cadaverous mortician whose special place was acknowledged above all others.

"We got him. We got him," he had fairly shouted as he ran into the *Examiner* office one Friday morning several years before my time. Warren G. Harding, twenty-ninth President of the United States, had died of pneumonia the night before in San Francisco's Palace Hotel, next door but one to the *Examiner*, and the cadaverous mortician had, indeed, got him. Even the uncompromising Sternberger treated the undertaker with a certain respect.

The saddest people who came to our marble counter, the people who made it seem even colder than it was, were the aging, shabby, more or less hopeless men and women who placed two-line advertisements under the heading Situations Wanted and rarely received a reply. Later, of course, they would answer an advertisement for Help Wanted, and life would go on. But the Situations Wanted advertisers were one-time hopeful customers and they were almost always disappointed.*

For other advertisers the counter often yielded a harvest of results. Lost and stolen animals were returned to their owners; if lost, usually for small rewards and many thanks; if stolen, for rewards that might be sizable, with no questions asked. Fences advertised fur coats and jewelry under an endless stream of aliases. Men and women divorced or separated stated tersely that they would no longer be responsible for debts other than their own. Rooms and apartments were offered for rent, and houses for sale. Trade schools and the suppliers of materials for making signs and bronzing baby shoes promised new careers. Stamps and coins were advertised for sale or trade, and some of the same advertisers offered money to loan, with no rates stated. The world's oldest profession was represented by massage parlors that featured new operators and new methods, and guaranteed satisfaction.

Dental plates were promised in eight hours, with six months to pay. There were always doctors who could (or said they could) cure psoriasis, and Chinese herb doctors who ran full pages of vivid testimonials. Also, you could take your choice of cameras and musical instruments, acoustic ceilings and seamless linoleum, porch furniture, modern furniture, antique furniture, baby furniture, even doll furniture; refrigerators, sewing machines, washing machines, and kitchen ranges; motorcars and trucks and motorboats; horses and dogs; and a thousand different businesses.

The businesses were always heralded as doing well (just as the rooms and apartments were always sunny and newly decorated, and the

---

* One of my earliest experiences at the counter concerned a desperate man for whom I helped write a Situations Wanted advertisement. When he turned his pockets inside out, and they were empty, I paid for the ad myself. But that was the last I ever saw of him, which was just as well, for there were no replies.

used automobiles in showroom condition); selling out was invariably tied to ill health. But the variety of businesses was infinite. Restaurants, coffee shops, cigar stores, poolrooms, bowling alleys, doughnut shops, bakeries, dry-cleaning plants, grocery stores, meat markets, chicken farms, fruit orchards, miniature golf courses, nursing homes, pharmacies, candy stores, stationery stores, gasoline stations, garages, machine shops, haberdasheries and hotels were part of the miscellany.

The only things that weren't for sale in the *Examiner* classified columns were bars, taverns, cocktail lounges and liquor stores. Prohibition was at midstage in 1926, and speakeasies and bootleggers didn't exist in advertising.

There was one column in the *Examiner* classified section that was filled every day with heartache and hazard. This was the Personals column, and the advertisements were handed across the counter by the unsteady hands of furtive, frightened people, and by some who were furtive and fearless. The frightened people were tearstained or frantic men and women whose mates had disappeared or whose children had vanished mysteriously or who were fugitives from the law. The fearless ones used the columns for clandestine messages that were undecipherable to the clerks and presumably to the police.

Gordon. We were there. Where were you and Joe. LORRIE could mean that a hoped for reconcilation had broken down. Or it could be a message in code from a band of burglars, or a rum-running gang. You never knew; although I always suspected that Sternberger did. What none but the advertisers knew were the specific actions or events that caused hundreds of individuals to purchase two-line personals that read: *Thanks to St. Jude for favors received.* To complete the mystery, these were usually signed only with initials.

Still, the most puzzling advertisement I ever took over the counter was handed to me typed on a piece of yellow paper to be pasted on a standard want-ad blank. The woman who gave it to me together with a two-dollar bill and left without waiting for her change, was an unusually tall, thin-nosed woman of middle age, dressed stylishly in a tailored suit of banker's gray, decorated with a heavy gold watch chain looped from the breast pocket to some hidden place inside the suit jacket.

The advertisement read: *Formaldehyde on fish.* And it was signed FRED.*

---

* Perhaps the most famous of all want ads appeared in London newspapers in 1900. It read: MEN WANTED for Hazardous Journey. Small wages, bitter cold, long months of complete darkness, constant danger, safe return doubtful. Honour and recognition in case of success.

It was signed ERNEST SHACKLETON, and it is believed to have produced hundreds of inquiries.

If I ever knew Sternberger's first name I have forgotten it now. But it doesn't matter.

He had no reason to like me more than the other clerks, and he didn't. In fact, he liked me somewhat less, for I had been foisted upon him. My entree to the *Examiner* had been to the general manager, a man named Callahan, to whom I was directed by a member of my class at the University of California who happened to be the son of the publisher, William Randolph Hearst.

The general manager was a formidable figure, even sitting down. He was a large, heavily jowled man, behind a large untidy desk. It was obvious from the piles of papers that he shuffled and the deep furrows in his forehead that he was troubled by vast responsibilities and gross exasperations.

It didn't take long for me to deduce that I was one of the latter.

"So you want a job," he said. "So you want to be a newspaperman."

These should have been questions. Instead they were lamentations, and I was stunned. The man waited. "Goddammit," he said, finally, "if Bill Hearst wants you to have a job, I suppose there is nothing I can do but find you one. But *where*? That is the question."

Here, I thought, was my chance to bravely clear myself of the charge, implicit in the general manager's tone, that I foolishly and boorishly expected nothing less than appointment as night city editor. I remembered the tumultuous city room of the San Francisco *Bulletin* where I had worked one summer years before as a copy boy; I remembered that advertising people were not welcome there and that classified advertising people were positively prohibited. These were the most despised of the species. And although I was not yet a novitiate in the exalted order of the press, I was ready to do penance.

"Could you," I asked the general manager, "put me in the want ads?"

That he could and that he did, with an alacrity that said he only hoped I wouldn't change my mind. "Get me Sternberger," he said quietly into his telephone; quietly as if otherwise he might break the spell. And then, "I'm sending you a fellow. Put him on the counter."

That is how I got into advertising.

Naturally, I think, Sternberger resented my intrusion in his life.

This was coupled, unfortunately, with another intrusion that he couldn't avoid. Charles Mayer, a Hearst cousin, started to work behind the counter in the classified department the same Monday morning that I did. This was almost too much for the classified manager.

As long as Charlie Mayer was there he said "Good morning" each day to us both. But that was all. And when Charlie was moved to another department, which was his first step up the ladder that took him eventually to the office that he filled for many years as publisher of the *Examiner*, the classified manager stopped speaking to me at all. Never again did he pass the time of day, or anything else, except once.

No one ever worked very long for the classified manager, if he were even mildly ambitious. Sternberger knew that Mayer would quickly move on and he resented him for this. Plainly he resented me for the same reason. He was aware of my introduction to the *Examiner* by a Hearst, and that made him contemptuous.

Eight months went by without a word or a nod from this man against whom I brushed in the narrow space behind the counter several times each day. For a long while I had it in mind to dramatically quit the minute he spoke but never did he open his mouth to me until one day when I could stand my stupid job no longer, I went to his office and told him that I was through.

"Well, I should hope so," he said, almost with a sigh, "I've been waiting to see how long you would stay behind that goddam counter."

I was sure the classified manager would not understand how I had got there. This little man was as hard as the gray rock he looked like, and my abject performance with the general manager would have made him ill. As it was he simply couldn't fathom a Hearst family friend in such a position. There were ex-coachmen and ex-gardeners and ex-butlers from the Hearst estates at Pleasanton and San Simeon and Wyntoon all over the *Examiner*, well-preserved men in derby hats and vests with white piping whose only visible activity was the collection of their fat weekly retainers. And there was I, actually working, slaving behind a counter. It didn't make sense to Sternberger.

What did I propose to do? The classified manager was about to be rid of me, so he could afford the question. But I hadn't the slightest idea, and I told him so.

"Look," he said. "I've noticed you drawing things, making sketches, cartoons, when the counter is empty, and on Sundays. Fact is, I picked up a drawing you made of Charles Lindbergh out of the wastebasket, and showed it to Bailey, in promotion.* Why don't you talk to Bailey, he's the manager. I'll tell him to give you a job. And he will."

Which is exactly what I did and he did, and Truman Bailey did.

It would be nice to say that I had a great success in the promotion

---

* It was while I worked behind the counter at the *Examiner* that Charles Augustus Lindbergh made the first transatlantic crossing by airplane, and his triumphant tour had brought him to San Francisco.

department, where the *Examiner*'s own advertising of its various features and its departments, such as the want ads, were made, and that as a result the classified manager and I shared a series of mutual triumphs. But Sternberger never spoke to me again.

The classified manager had gone out of character as far as he could. Even if he had guessed it, I doubt that he would have cared that he had launched a young man on an advertising career.

The Young Man as an Artist

THE manager of the *Examiner*'s promotion department was as open and outgoing as the classified manager had been shut and forbidding. He welcomed me to his staff, and I became his backup artist. He had two good writers and a lettering man who was really a virtuoso, but Truman Bailey was the only artist until I arrived.

Bailey was a tall, aesthetic-looking man of thirty-two who had come to the newspaper as an artist in the editorial department several years before, straight from art school. When it turned out that he was capable of direct, uncomplicated argument as well, and in print, he was shifted to the promotion department. There he quickly established his authority, and soon afterwards he was made manager.

This was fortunate for me. Advertising was something I had given little thought to. I had failed entirely to connect it with the small sign and show-card business that I had had in high school. That I had thought of as commercial art. But Truman Bailey made me realize for the first time that commercial art is part of the business of advertising. It is art with a purpose that is not artistic.

"Commercial art is strictly business," he insisted. "And the business in our case is advertising the *Examiner* and everything in it. Advertising can never be an end in itself, either; although you might think so, the way some of it is done. So bright. So ingenious. So foolish. Beware of the advertisement that someone calls beautiful or clever. If someone says 'look at that beautiful cake or that beautiful house for sale,' that is different. That is what advertising is all about, the *what* and not the *how*. As for a clever advertisement, I have never seen one that I thought was worth a damn."

I didn't know it then, but what I was hearing from Truman Bailey would be repeated during the years by every important figure that I would know in advertising.

Bailey was careful about my drawing, too. "Draw with your head," he kept repeating. "Your hand will take care of itself."

"That is exactly what I am doing," I would reply.

But Bailey wasn't fooled. "Forget what you are trying to draw," he would say patiently. "Think only what you are trying to say."

I had been drawing ever since I had been able to hold a pencil. Beginning with horses, I drew everything I saw. Not very well, but not entirely badly either. No one ever had to ask me "What is that?"

Shortly after I opened my business in signs and show cards, I managed to win a national high school poster contest, and I determined at once to follow in the footsteps of the great poster artists — J. C. Leyendecker, Adolph Triedler, and James Montgomery Flagg, whose World War I posters had brought the whole nation up short. (The most famous of these was Flagg's vigorous Uncle Sam pointing at the viewer, saying "I want you!" You knew he meant business.)

When the war was over, my ambition took a slight turn. But this it did frequently. To become an illustrator instead of a poster artist was only a small bend in a fickle imagination.

I practiced what I conceived to be the sophisticated techniques of Henry Raleigh and Wallace Morgan, and the somewhat softer penciling of Frederick R. Gruger and Arthur William Brown. These were the stars of the big magazines, together with James Montgomery Flagg, who worked in pen and ink; and I doted on them. Years later, when I lived in New York City and belonged to the Artists and Writers Club and the Society of Illustrators, I came to know both the diminutive, tranquil "Brownie" and the tall, tempestuous Flagg, and they were pleased that anyone could remember having wanted to walk in their path. Time and the photographers' advancing techniques had all but ended their careers.

My drawing was put aside temporarily in the spring of 1920 when I became a seaman aboard the S. S. *Haxtum* bound out of San Francisco for the United Kingdom.

It would be wrong to say that eight months on the freighter had anything to do with my ultimate choice of a life in advertising. Still, it would be equally wrong not to say the voyage of more than half a year had a good deal to do with changing my dream world into a world of real people. And what people! In place of my middle-class Protestant neighbors living happily in a university community, I suddenly found myself part of a small universe of unkempt and un-lettered Catholics and Jews, Italians, Portuguese, Lebanese, English, Irish, French, Dutch, Swedish and Finnish, and men of no clear nationality, no formal religion, no homes, no ties.

Most of the talk on the deck between shifts was about sex (although I can't recall that anyone ever called it that). Reading had an entirely different focus.

The *Haxtum's* small library, a shelf of tattered books donated by some seamen's aid society, contained almost nothing but Western stories, and these were read and reread by all the members of the crew who could read. Zane Grey was their favorite author. *Riders of the Purple Sage* was their favorite book. Except for the lone Frenchman aboard and one of the Finns, every member of the crew was determined to live someday in the desert — as far away from the sea as he could get. It was something that no one of them would ever do.

The crew of the *Haxtum* was, I am sure, like every crew. They were a curious lot of lonely men. Here I shall mention just three. The first, the captain, a rugged ape, drank hair tonic with relish. He was an Annapolis dropout, predestined for trouble. But he was a fine navigator. Several years after he was relieved of his command of the *Haxtum* for insubordination, he piloted a tiny plane, the *Southern Cross*, in the first Pacific crossing to within a few hundred miles of Australia, whence Sir Charles Kingsford-Smith, a proper Australian, took her in from Suva. The captain was a brave buccaneer, but he lived in the wrong time and died in his bed in a skid-row hotel fire. The second and third of these lonely men are probably dead too.

Action on the *Haxtum* was apt to be direct. One night in Dunkerque, where we put in before making Liverpool, one of the Finns killed one of the galley help. The fight began when the Finn jumped on the fat old Englishman who was second cook and waiter in the crew's mess. The Finn said the Limey sweated into the food.

"I'll kill you some dark night," the Limey muttered.

I doubt if he meant it. The only fierce thing about the man was his walrus moustache. Otherwise he was almost effeminate.

Nevertheless, he had threatened the Finn, and two or three mornings later the waterfront police found the Limey's body floating in the quay. After that everyone left the Finn pretty much alone.

The third memorable character on the *Haxtum* was the second mate, a square-jawed fellow with the soul of a poet. I stood the twelve-to-four watch with him, and in the long dark hours of the night, he recited the lines of the *Rubaiyat* of Omar Khayyam, from beginning to end, and then began again, and again. It was his religion.

That is how it was on the *Haxtum*. Except that I was graduated from high school while I was abroad — in absentia. The rather original principal of my school, knowing that I was itching to be away, apparently thought that a few months before the mast, so to speak, was a good trade for part of my final semester; and he handed me my diploma when I returned.

Many a time in writing advertising I have asked myself whether everyone on the *Haxtum* would know what I was trying to say. If I thought the answer might be no, I changed the copy.

At my father's insistence, I entered the University of California at Berkeley in January of 1921. I had wanted to go back to sea. As a compromise I went back to drawing. Only now I was drawing cartoons for the *Pelican*, the monthly campus humor magazine. Sometimes there would be four or five of my drawings in a single issue. But I didn't do these either easily or quickly. And my painstaking efforts were my undoing. They left me so little time for study that I failed to pass the required number of class units, and the dean sent me home for six months to meditate my sins.

This I did in the attic of my family's house — between drawings.*

When I returned to the campus, it was to the *Pelican* and not to classes, and once more there occurred a hiatus in my college career. This time I put aside my pencils and my pens and my illustration board, and read. To my astonishment and my delight I discovered the English novel. By the time I had devoured *Moll Flanders* and *Tom Jones* and *Robinson Crusoe* and *Gulliver's Travels* and *Fanny Hill* and contemplated some other wonders of English literature, I decided that here was a delectable life's work: I would become a teacher. I would live with Defoe and Fielding and Swift, with Shakespeare and Marlowe, and Samuel Johnson and his circle. I worked hard at this, too. The result was that I compiled a record in my final two years at the University that would have been close to perfect except for one thing. I never quite got inside the gymnasium.

Of course I knew that gymnasium work was required. But my hours with the English writers and the professors who were my new friends blinded me to everything else. Somehow, I was under the delusion that my string of excellent grades, together with a tentative invitation to become a teaching fellow in the English department, would outweigh any small deficiency.

---

* Every drawing I ever made for the *Pelican* was bought and republished later in a popular magazine called *College Humor*, but the money went to the editors. I got nothing for my pains.

But I had made a miscalculation.

"That fellow will be graduated over my dead body," the head of the hated physical education department bellowed at the dean when my old friend, who had rescued me twice from expulsion, sought some kind of compromise.

"That is that!" the man said, banging down the telephone.

And that it was. The gymnasium man died in the spring of 1947 and the parchment that might have made me a teacher arrived in the mail in Chicago in a matter of days. I have never found out who arranged it. I only know that the diploma arrived twenty-one years too late. By this time I had lived half my life.

The part that began with Truman Bailey is still going on.

The want ad counter and the people who came to it with so much hope and so much despair and so many diverse problems had constituted a different world from Bailey's. Even so, I had learned some important things about advertising. I had learned, for example, that even in a two- or three-line want ad, the confidence of the advertiser in what he has to sell, the real value of his proposition to the right prospect, usually makes the difference between success and failure. It also keeps him honest.

There were numerous occasions on which the clerks helped write the want ads and we made them very simple. Clutter of any kind cost money, and the want ad advertisers were a frugal clientele. Although we didn't know it, we were doing the purest kind of advertising. There was no place in it for more than mild puffery. Adjectives were simply too expensive. Except for the time-honored *clean* rooms and apartments and houses and the used cars that were always *like new* (and the fantastic Personals) the advertising went straight to the point and stayed there.

Now Truman Bailey began to add to what I had learned. For while I had been hired as an artist, he forced me to pay attention to the whole advertisement.

"The classified has taught you the value of getting straight to the point," he said. "How to start making display advertisements also begins with figuring out *what* you want to say, and not which of several ways you might say it. Many more advertisements are spoiled by technique than by lack of it."

Bailey was a practical man and a patient teacher, and I spent a happy year with him both during and after office hours. Most of our work, as I have indicated, was for the promotion of different *Examiner* departments and features. We were allotted large space, which meant large illustrations and high visibility for my efforts, and with Truman Bailey's constant, insistent help I developed a measure of competence that went considerably beyond drawing.

In addition to our work for the *Examiner* itself, the promotion department produced advertising for individuals and for groups of retailers that the newspaper's salesmen organized for various manufacturers and distributors for special selling events. One of the latter happened to be the introduction of the recording stars Moran and Mack, the Two Black Crows, who were the precursors of radio's Amos and Andy, and the caricatures I made of them brought me job offers from several of San Francisco's commercial art studios. It appeared that I was destined to keep on drawing.

I borrowed and adapted Whistler's mother in her rocking chair for Mother's Day candy advertisements and went from comedy to sentiment to pure romance for all manner of promotional products. This was fun and I enjoyed the work, but the salesmen let me down when they showed little concern with my growing interest in what I considered good advertising, and promised their customers anything at all that they wanted. Usually this was dull as ditchwater.

The upshot was my decision to leave the *Examiner*. I had designed what I thought was a magnificent full-page advertisement for a dental clinic. The illustration showed a silky brunette smiling widely above the caption *Your teeth are a part of your personality,* and the invitation was to our readers to have their smiles remodeled by our "painless, low-cost" client. But the salesman on the account was much more beholden to the dentist than he was to me.

That the client is always right is one of the sad untruths that undermines the advertising business, and I learned it then and there. Coming back early from a vacation to see my masterpiece the minute it appeared in print, I discovered that somewhere between my drawing board and the presses my smiling beauty had given way to a huge set of full dentures floating in space on a mechanical jaw above my headline. It was the ugliest advertisement I had ever seen.

That did it.

Truman Bailey and I were both dissatisfied with our jobs. He was really, as I have said, an artist and designer, and while he understood advertising very well, he had no great taste for it. The result was, he left the newspaper to become creative director for a large printing company in mid-1928. I left soon afterward.

Our last project together was an elaborate Christmas giftbook that we illustrated and colored by hand. This was "The Fountain of Gold," which Houghton Mifflin Company gave us permission to reprint

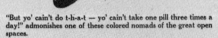

No one thought I was belittling anyone when I pictured Moran & Mack in this full-page newspaper advertisement exactly as they pictured themselves.

from *Fantastics and Other Fancies* by Lafcadio Hearn. We had plans for a whole series of such books, but this never materialized. Truman Bailey went off to the South Pacific to study Polynesian arts and crafts, and I went to work for a small advertising agency as an art director and freelance artist.

Magenta
Was the Name of a Girl

MY second employer was one I never saw, even though I worked for him for more than a year in the best-paying job I was to have for a long time.

The L. H. Waldron advertising agency had only eight employees, but they were curiously spaced at opposite sides of the country. Waldron and his secretary lived in New York, the other six of us in San Francisco. The agency's principal client was the E. T. Cunningham Company, a manufacturer of radio tubes for the scores of small manufacturers and thousands of amateurs who were caught up in the new craze. There was only one thing more exciting than radio in 1928. That was the stock market. And the L. H. Waldron agency was deeply involved with both.

A finely educated, white-haired Englishman named Winthrop Martin wrote the Cunningham advertisements in San Francisco. My friend Louis Hoen, who had got me into the Waldron agency, illustrated them. Printing plates were mailed to the publications. Then an astonishing thing took place. Invoices were sent to Waldron in New York. He presented them to the Cunningham company there. They were immediately paid, and the payments dispatched to L. H. Waldron in San Francisco to be deposited in the bank before the agency's checks to the publishers had been returned for clearance!

This way the Waldron bank balance was held at a maximum, to earn 3 per cent interest in the frantic scurrying for cash in the great bull market. This was more than anyone in the agency business could make on many times the Waldron company's volume of advertising. Waldron had helped Cunningham in the manufacturer's winning patent fight against the Radio Corporation of America some years before, and Cunningham never forgot this. The unusual banking arrangement that he supported was the result.

Martin, Hoen, the firm's treasurer, two secretaries and I made up the San Francisco staff. In addition to the Cunningham business, we had the account of the bank where the Waldron money was quietly at work, two or three small radio parts manufacturers, and a retail shoe store.

Only the Cunningham business mattered. When the bank acquired another, smaller bank which it operated separately, this was regarded as a nuisance by my employer, and it was put in my hands. The agency paid me for the layouts (the advertising rough sketches) that I made, and the bank, or any one of the other accounts, paid me for the finished drawings. Later I learned that layout men in agencies didn't make drawings for publication and that artists didn't get paid for sketches. But ours was a very unsophisticated agency, except in its financial operation, and I got paid for everything I did.

My weekly pay went up from the thirty-five dollars that I had been earning in the *Examiner*'s promotion department to a drawing account of fifty dollars a week at the L. H. Waldron company, and never did I take home less than double this amount. Sometimes it was substantially more.

I was able to buy my first automobile. It was a secondhand Buick roadster, painted fire-engine red, that I bought from Louis Hoen when he bought himself a fine Packard. There have been a good many automobiles in my life since. But no other automobile ever thrilled me the way that first red Buick did; I can still see myself, as I saw myself then, reflected in store windows, driving nonchalantly as though it had always been thus.

The Waldron year was good in every way. But all good things come to an end.

Through my friends at the bank whose advertising I wrote and illustrated, I was offered the fairly large account of a successful, growing manufacturer of building materials. "The bank has recommended you," the man said. "If you want it, the account is yours."

Did I want it?

"More than I can tell you," I told the man.

There was only one drawback. While it was perfectly true that I could draw well enough for the proffered job, I was hopelessly color-blind. The building materials company was a maker of roof tiles in a hundred different shades, and I couldn't possibly tell which was which. I could tell blue from red; but I couldn't always tell blue from green or blue from purple, or red from pink or orange. Brown was utterly beyond me. Magenta was only the name of a girl I knew.

What to do?

Working at the newspaper and working at the agency on newspaper advertising, I had simply not given color a thought, except to have my wife buy my neckties. Truman Bailey had mixed the colors for our Christmas book; and I was doing all my business in simple monochrome.

People have asked me many times since how color looks to me, whether it is all gray. I tell them it isn't. Anything but. But the colors are not constant. They change. They defy definition and they defy my memory, and they sometimes disappear right before my eyes. When I tried to play golf with red tees, years ago, they were always lost in the green grass.

I suppose I could have arranged to have someone mix colors for me. I believe Maxfield Parrish was color-blind, and there have been other well-known artists who were similarly afflicted. But I wasn't that good a draftsman.

"I am sorry," I told the tile man. "I can't take you up on this. I am going into another business." I had made up my mind in that instant. If he was puzzled, and he was, I couldn't help it. I couldn't spend my life doing something in which I was so spectacularly limited.

I left the Waldron company the next week. Martin and Hoen were puzzled, for I never told them why. I suppose they thought I was crazy.

Walter Doty

NOBODY but my family and I knew that I was color-blind.

At the same time that I was offered the tile assignment I was invited to join one of the leading commercial art studios in San Francisco. The people who ran it assumed that my color sense was normal, and I didn't tell them anything different. I planned soon to be married and the money that was offered was attractive.

But my conscience bothered me. I was no good at bluffing. And I couldn't ever be a first-rate artist.

Because I had done a little writing at Berkeley, and because I had become interested in advertising at the *Examiner* and in the Waldron agency, I decided to try my hand at advertising writing. Through one of the friendly art studio men I was given an introduction to the San Francisco manager of the large, old advertising agency of Lord & Thomas, which was owned by Albert D. Lasker, of Chicago, who was the richest and most powerful individual in the business.

Shortly after I presented my introduction I was hired as a copywriter on a trial basis. The manager wanted to put me on as an artist. But I insisted that I could be a much better writer; I didn't tell him why.

Even though the only writing I had ever done had been overshadowed by my drawing, I thought that if I had the chance I could write acceptable copy. I was sure that I knew how to approach advertising. And I did. My approach was crude. But it was also right; Truman Bailey, in talking about advertising art, had set me on a well-charted writing course.

Also, I loved the work; I couldn't get enough of it. I wrote day and night. Five years later, when I left Lord & Thomas temporarily in 1934, the agency found it necessary to recruit four writers to take my place.

It had been Truman Bailey's concept that advertising is the language of business that is used to tell someone something of importance. This is entirely different from "making ads" which is a favorite expression of advertising people. It is a matter of being as direct and as simple as you can, of honest promises explained sensibly. And I found these easy to make.

Most of the copywriters in the Lord & Thomas office spent restless hours trying to decide how to say something brightly and catchily. I spent my time deciding what to say, then saying it as plainly as I could. In part this was possible because my first assignment was advertising for the Southern Pacific Railroad, and this was devoted to facts about fares and schedules; about getting from here to there and back by a choice of trains. Perhaps I would have started out differently had I been writing advertising for coffee or beer or gasoline, which were our other large interests in San Francisco.

As it was, I was held to a rigid approach to my job by one of the ablest advertising men I can imagine. He later became a famous editor. Like Truman Bailey, Walter Doty was firm in the belief that the best way to move people is reasonably. He made *Sunset* magazine one of the outstanding editorial (and business) successes in American publishing history by the depth and the breadth of his understanding. He knew people instinctively because he knew himself, and he planned accordingly. Also, Walter Doty was impervious to what anyone else in advertising was doing. He was influenced not at all by the fads that infested the business.

Next to being gossipy, the advertising agency syndrome is most noted for its inability to withstand the temptation to follow the leader. Let someone design a new approach or a new format in print or in television, then much of the industry follows suit. Advertising people sooner or later become completely fed up with anything they are doing. They have looked at it through months of development and redevelopment and it is old stuff to them before it ever breaks into print or appears on the television screen. Hence the rush to follow any leader into any new form or new method of expression.

Today one sees this at its most absurd on television, where incredible knights on horseback vie with even more improbable white tornadoes to challenge each other in household cleaning, and women who use a new detergent may be warned to protect their eyes against the resulting blinding brightness of the family wash!

In 1929 advertising was a little less eccentric. Theodore F. Mac-

Manus had written *The Penalty of Leadership* for Cadillac almost fifteen years before, and a whole generation of advertising writers had been trying ever since to top it. Raymond Rubicam had come close with *The Priceless Ingredient,* which was what he termed the integrity in the pharmaceutical products of E. R. Squibb. Rubicam also called the Steinway piano *The Instrument of the Immortals* in an extraordinary flight of imagination. Edward S. Jordan had written an advertisement for his Jordan Playboy automobile entitled *Somewhere West of Laramie* which was almost pure poetry; the romance of the windblown Wyoming scene couldn't prevent the death of the Jordan, but the advertisement had become a classic anyway.

And in the summer of 1929 it was Philip Lennen's campaign for the Scripps-Howard newspapers that had the advertising people jumping up and down. *Kill my cow for an editor? Never!* dramatically interpreted the newspapers' fight for the tuberculin testing of dairy cattle. When this advertisement won a Harvard University advertising award the industry took immediately to narrative.

Most of this advertising appeared in the *Saturday Evening Post. Life* was still a slim comic and satirical weekly, and the *Post* was studied each Thursday morning when it went on sale to see who had done what and what we all thought about it.

All, that is, except Walter Doty. He was only interested in what *we* were doing.

My starting salary as Doty's assistant was less than half what I had been making at the Waldron agency. Then came the stock market crash, in October of 1929. Business was bad generally, and the advertising business was no exception; my salary was cut 15 per cent in 1930 and another 15 per cent in 1931. On the first cut I sold my red Buick. When the second occurred, my wife and I moved from our pleasant house in a pretty walled garden in Vallejo Street to a small, plain flat on the steep side of Russian Hill.

But I stuck with Walter Doty. After World War I, when he had been a slender young captain with a wispy moustache in the United States Army, he was briefly in the lumber business with his father in the state of Washington. Then he worked as a salesman of advertising space in newspapers, calling on advertisers and advertising agencies in San Francisco.

Walter Doty was very popular. It was part of his disposition to become involved; he was never an onlooker. And people whom he met in even the most casual way found him sympathetic to their problems and more than willing to help solve them. This was particularly true where money was concerned, and he had a small army of retainers whose demands he accepted and paid off simply because he understood their needs. It was a typical item in the Doty legend that if he should be locked alone in his office with a ten-dollar bill in his hand, he would have only small change when the door was unlocked an hour later. To be sure, the army performed all manner of small deeds, in looking up data and making experiments, for, although he didn't know it, Walter Doty was one of the first copy researchers; he used his motley troops to check his instincts.

One of the agencies that Walter Doty had called on as a space salesman was Lord & Thomas, and it was only a short time before the agency hired him. When I was dumped into his office to sit across the desk from him, to see what I could do, he was in charge of the railroad account.

If writing advertising was an art, no one had ever informed Walter Doty. Like Truman Bailey, he saw it solely as a means of communication, and he kept me looking at it that way, too. Its purpose was to deliver a message, presumably a worthwhile message, he said, to a specific audience of one. "Write to one person," he insisted. "Aim what you have to say at someone who has every reason to be interested. If the message is clear, then everyone else who has any reason to be interested will get it too."

I wish I could say that I always remembered this. But I didn't. There were times when lacy words and phrases caught my fancy and Walter Doty had to pull me up short. Gradually, however, his admonitions to beware Art and Poetry in advertising became a part of me.

For two years I labored on the Southern Pacific account and I couldn't have learned in a stricter school. For in addition to Doty's disgust with any kind of advertising extravagance, or with ambiguity, the railroad's schedule of advertising was so heavy that there was little time to correct either fancy or faulty writing. Southern Pacific advertised in every newspaper in every town along its lines in the five westernmost states and Texas and Louisiana every week (unless, for some reason, the railroad was unhappy with an individual paper; then that paper was omitted from the schedule until the unhappiness was resolved). Every advertisement carried fares and timetables that were different for each town. Some of these were filled in locally, but every newspaper had to have a suitable ad to fill in. And we had to make these ads, too.

In addition to the hundreds of newspapers in on-line towns, there were scores more off-line newspapers that had to have copy on a

To California!

Across horizons where rose the seven cities of Cibola

Was it only a prank of the western sun...the fleeting silhouette men thought they saw of cities of turquoise, pearl and gold? Was it only a prank *or was it prophecy* ... that flashed to gold the cold steel helmets of Coronado's soldiers of Spain when they searched for the fabulous cities of Cibola . . .

Today in this same western sun a new steel flashes in many a league of Coronado's path. Steel rails of Southern Pacific's SUNSET ROUTE.

And the cities that edge its glittering miles out-fable the cities the Spaniards sought. New Orleans, the SUNSET's source. Houston. San Antonio. El Paso. Tucson. Phoenix. San Diego. Los Angeles. San Francisco. These shine today in the bold reality of sky-thrust stone and steel and reclaimed desert that is become acre upon acre of agricultural wealth.

As your train speeds into the golden evening you can forget, if you like, the world that is new and the one that is gone ... you need only a mind to good living. "Sunset Limited" is a kingly train ... and yours to enjoy as you will —a diner the hospitable

south has sponsored.— club a observation cars with skilled tendants waiting for your wi

Sunset Route is not Southern Paci only way to California nor is it the one that lifts horizons. Overland Ro Golden State Route and Shasta Ro have stories of their own to tell ... blue-blood trains for you to travel

To go West one route and return other is Southern Pacific's way of mal the whole Pacific Coast and half United States a part of one regu roundtrip ticket. A ticket that finds interprets the West. For Southern Pac rails follow natural pioneer pathways It is close to the spirit of the West you to see. Its vast network of lines exp the whole Pacific Coast. Southern Pac is the only railroad offering choice of f routes. Go one way, return anoth Stopover anywhere.

Southern Pacifi

Four Great Routes

Write to O. P. Bartlett, 310 So Michigan Blvd., Chicago, or H. H Gray, 531 Fifth Ave., New Yorl City, for copy of illustrated book "How Best to See the Pacific Coast."

For two years I labored on the Southern Pacific account, where Walter Doty and I had all the West to write about, without limit to our enthusiasm.

biweekly or monthly basis. Finally, there were the national weekly and monthly magazines, and the railroad's advertising appeared regularly in dozens of them.

Riding airplanes was still very much a sport, and a dangerous one, in the early 1930's. The yellow streamlined trains with their diesel locomotives that were operated jointly by Southern Pacific, Union Pacific and Chicago & North Western were the newest thing in speedy transportation. They made it via the mid-continent route between San Francisco and Chicago in 39¾ hours! Or if you chose you could go East on another one of Southern Pacific's four routes (through Oregon; through Arizona and New Mexico; or through Texas and New Orleans), then return by still another — at no increase in fare. In this way, the railroad had something very attractive to offer against the single routes of the Western Pacific and the Santa Fe, and we offered the four choices with enthusiasm.

Under Walter Doty's tutelage you learned advertising by making it. When it was right, when it met his requirements, when it was clear and complete, when it presented the railroad's whole promise, you moved on to the next assignment. When it didn't, you got it back across the double desk with a pained sharp comment.

"I don't understand you," Doty would say. "You're taking too much for granted. Tell me so there will be no mistaking what you mean"; or "Remember, late trains and dirty coaches, and tired, grumpy conductors are something we can't do a damned thing about. But we can make the advertising interesting and useful; and useful starts with being clear."

If I tried to argue for a pretty phrase, which I did on occasion, Walter Doty would listen, frowning. Then he would say, "Look. I've told you before and I'd like to remind you again: you can't stand behind any reader of any advertisement and tell him what you *meant* to say. He either gets it in a second, or you have failed. The reader is rarely seeking you out. You're seeking *him*. Furthermore, he has no time to waste.

"He never reads advertising for fun. Next time you ride a train watch him turn the pages of a newspaper or a magazine. You'll wonder how advertising is ever effective, the way people turn those pages. When someone stops and reads your ad, that is an accomplishment.

"There is nothing easier to do in this world than turn a page or tune out your ears to advertising that doesn't make its promise clear. It isn't like trying to tell someone something in person. There, if you don't make it on the first try, you can back off and try again. In an advertisement you have only one chance; the first. If you fail, you fail entirely."

All this, of course, was before advertising had made its mismatch with television. Radio was still in its crib. Advertising was not yet concerned with entertainment. It had no captive audience. You had to go and get your public.

Substance was Walter Doty's aim in everything he tried to do. In advertising for the Southern Pacific he insisted that we talk not only about transportation, about getting from here to there and back again, but also about the wonders of the land. To him these were all-important. Seeing Crater Lake in Oregon, visiting Lake Tahoe or Yosemite National Park, stopping off on the Monterey Peninsula, or exploring Carlsbad Caverns in New Mexico, were all experiences along the Southern Pacific that Walter Doty had enjoyed and wanted to share. He felt the same way about the railroad's excellent dining cars. The crisp salads rustled from his copy, and you could almost smell the savory, steaming casseroles.

This involvement, which I shared, resulted one sunny day, in a request for more information that almost turned the railroad inside out. It came in the cramped longhand of President Calvin Coolidge in response to an advertisement subtitled *The Seven Cities of Cibola,* the legendary golden cities that are part of the lore of the Spanish Southwest, and President Coolidge wanted to know all about them. I doubt if an inquiry from any other advertisement ever resulted in more immediate action. The railroad mobilized as if for war. A huge presentation was put together by K. C. Ingram, the advertising manager, and Fred Tredway, his assistant, and it was arranged that the president of the railroad should deliver it.

But it turned out that the saturnine Coolidge wasn't going anywhere; he was merely curious. This made it much less important to know whether Walter Doty or I had actually written the advertisement. The headline, I know, was his — and the credit for the inquiry. But often as not, he would write a headline and a few words of introductory text, then toss this across the double desk for me to complete. So similarly had Walter Doty taught me to think that after only a few months it would have been difficult to tell which one of us had written any of the huge flow of advertisements for the railroad.

The pressure to move into the agency's art department continued, but I wasn't interested. One picture might, as the old Chinese proverb has it, be worth a thousand words. But I was devoted to the words and to Walter Doty. Besides, at the end of two years I had an office of my own and a new, additional assignment.

Walter Doty was breaking in a new assistant, a quick-witted graduate of Stanford named Herbert Kittredge Reynolds, who, from the be-

ginning, wrote exactly the way Doty conceived advertising, lean and
hard and straight to the mark; and I was relieved of the newspaper
part of the railroad assignment. Still, happily, in the Doty group, I
became responsible for the advertising of San Francisco and northern
and central California, for a group called Californians, Inc., that had
been gathered to finance advertising competition against Southern
California for tourists.

When Walter Doty insisted that advertising should always be addressed to one person, he was making a case that is often overlooked.
In trying to write to everyone the chances are that the writer will
reach no one.

The result of these admonitions was that I attempted to invent and
characterize individuals to whom I could direct all my arguments.
I tried to figure out how they would react to whatever I had to say, and
I was strict with myself. But this was hard work, and I struggled with
it only until I realized that I had two perfect adversaries to overcome
with logic right in my own family.

The first was my wife. This was someone I knew very well. I first
saw Gertrude Kennedy when we were both in the same first-year
class in high school, and I saw a great deal of her. After she transferred
from that public school, which was a teacher-training school for the
University of California, to the Dominican Convent in Marin County,
California, I made the long trek there by a combination of train and
ferryboats and back again so many times that a good part of my weekends for four years were devoted to this exercise.

It was a good one. By the time this small, bright, even-tempered,
exceptionally pretty girl transferred back from the convent to the
university at Berkeley, in what was the junior year for both of us, I
came completely under her spell. She encouraged me when I wanted
to become a professor, and later accepted me as a full-fledged newspaperman when I worked behind the *Examiner*'s marble counter; and
we were married in 1929, two months after I joined Walter Doty and
Lord & Thomas.

Gertrude Kennedy Cone is extremely, though not belligerently, in-
telligent. Under these circumstances she is a hard critic of advertising,
particularly when it is foolish (which wastes her time) and when
she deems it to be exaggerated (which is an affront to her credulity).

For many years now I have subjected almost everything I have written to this simple test: *Could I say this to my wife without blanching,
or without sounding like an idiot?* Too often have I heard her uncon-
sciously argue with an advertising headline or a promise hurled through

the air, to take a chance. My wife is a member of the All-America team that I have described as the nation's most astute purchasing agents. There are times when she will try nonessentials, even nonsensicals, just for the fun of it, but she knows what she is doing when she does this (usually for one or another of our grandchildren). It is a mild form of revelry, an incident in a passing mood to which she has earned the right. For the most part, when she has her purse in hand she is strictly business. To plot to take advantage of this woman is something I would never venture, I only want to reasonably tell her *why* it is in her own best selfish interest to choose what I want her to buy.

This, by the way, is an entirely mental project. I never talk about advertising to my wife, for this would spoil the usefulness of the image. My wife is on my side. She is conditioned to like what I like and what I do and how I do it. Her critical faculty is no match for her partiality. I want her reactions completely uninhibited, and these I can have only in the limbo of past experience and what I know.

The second of my mental adversaries was a tough-minded spinster aunt, my mother's sister and a born enemy of the Establishment on every issue. She had been a supporter of Eugene Debs, five times Socialist party candidate for President of the United States, and she was not about to be sold *anything* by the capitalists she imagined to be lurking behind every advertising proposition. This independent soul, whom I love dearly, is a stony foe. She has made it a cardinal rule in her life not to be moved by advertising, and if she could, she would penalize all advertisers. "If advertising intrudes itself upon me," she says, "then I make it a point not to buy the brand advertised under any circumstance."

When television came to be, she purchased a set in which the sound could be turned off at the flick of a switch, thus eliminating the hateful promises. You might have thought this a poor return on my devotion, but the fact is that I was getting a large and useful one. For I had only to write with my Aunt Sarah firmly in mind, and convince myself that she would be motivated by what I had to say, to know that my copy was probably right.

The tipoff came one day when I happened to go to her kitchen for something or other, and opened both her cupboard and her refrigerator. There I found Kraft mayonnaise, Heinz vinegar, Borden's milk, Libby tomato juice, Campbell's soup, Dole pineapple — a monumental assortment of advertised brands.

My aunt had simply not realized that the information she had received and accepted about these products had anything in common with advertising that she found offensive for products in which she had no interest.

My Aunt Sarah is eighty-three years old now, but she remains an object of my fondest intentions, for only when I feel sure that she would not scoff at my advertising promise, that she would accept it as useful information, am I satisfied. Only then am I willing to leave her to her chess, which she plays exceedingly well, and to digging for clams on the foggy beach of California's Morro Bay.

In a most important way, when Walter Doty went away to edit *Sunset* magazine my Aunt Sarah took his place.

Are You Doing Any Writing?

WITH the advertising of Californians, Inc., and the magazine advertising for the Southern Pacific, I was responsible for two national campaigns and my copy appeared in a dozen or so magazines every month.

One of my grandfathers had come to San Francisco from Virginia in 1849.* Both my mother and my father had been born in San Francisco. And so had I. I was steeped in the history of this city that defied any tradition but its own and dared anyone to change it. San Francisco is beautiful and spirited and feminine and capricious, and I wrote about it in what turned out to be a long series of love letters.

Once, when I was away on a trip for the railroad, Walter Doty wrote an advertisement for me for Californians, Inc., under the title *The Chapter in Your Life Entitled San Francisco.* This seemed to me to hold so exactly the promise I had been trying for that I appropriated it as the continuing caption in a series of color pages that ran in the *Saturday Evening Post,* and later in *Time* and *Newsweek,* for eight years. It was an experience that I wanted for everyone, for I couldn't imagine anything more exciting.

I showed San Francisco to countless editors and publishers who came our way, and they were enthralled by it. Some, like Edna Woolman Chase, the petite editor-in-chief of *Vogue,* had expected to see shirt-sleeved San Franciscans panning for gold in the city's gutters by day and shooting up the town at night; but once they got over their surprise they loved the place.

* One of the reasons why I was so devoted to the Southern Pacific Company was because my grandfather had been one of its original right-of-way agents, and knew Leland Stanford and Collis P. Huntington of the incorporators intimately.

John Sterling, publisher of *McCall's* (and later of *This Week*) held court in a balcony suite at the Fairmont Hotel, high above Chinatown and the Bay, while his loyal assistant, Tom Cathcart, mixed drinks with royal aplomb. San Francisco made the perfect background.

The editors came from all the weeklies — the *Saturday Evening Post, Collier's, Liberty,* the *Literary Digest* and *Time;* and the general monthlies, *Cosmopolitan, American, Redbook, Atlantic, Harper's, Scribner's,* and the six big women's magazines, *Delineator, Good Housekeeping, Ladies Home Journal, McCall's, Pictorial Review* and *Woman's Home Companion.* I put them all down to show how times have changed, for eight of the seventeen are gone.

Gilbert Grosvenor, editor of the *National Geographic,* was another frequent visitor. And Charles Douglas Jackson, a delightful gentleman who at one time or another published all of Henry Luce's Time, Incorporated, magazines, came regularly to my house to astound my daughter by standing on his head! These people came in droves, and they found San Francisco all that we said it was.

My clients at Californians, Inc., were a group of the city's leading businessmen, and I had my first experience in making advertising for non-advertising people. The majority of these men had the same extravagant feelings about the city that I had. But instead of allowing me to exaggerate San Francisco's claims, as I am sure I was bound to do — as advertising people were supposed to do — my clients held my enthusiasm in check. Despite the purpose for which Californians, Inc., had been formed, the board of directors were morbidly afraid we might attract a kind of visitor they didn't want — a wide-eyed tourist in a celluloid collar who might later return to San Francisco to live. The city, they thought, had population enough of any kind.

During the years that I worked for these men a number of them were active behind the scenes in opposing the building of the Golden Gate Bridge. It was generally believed that this opposition was directed by the Southern Pacific Company, whose large fleet of auto ferries would be replaced by the bridge. But this was not true. The dissenters were against anything they thought would detract from a famous view.* As it turned out, when the Golden Gate Bridge was completed it made the scene even more spectacular. But I don't think the majority of the directors ever looked at it with anything but loathing. They hated change.

Under the circumstances, it wasn't strange that they were a little bit

* There was one vigorous supporter: the late S. F. B. Morse, president of the board of Californians Inc., and creator and conservator of the Monterey Peninsula fiefdom that includes Pebble Beach.

The Chapter in Your Life
entitled
SAN FRANCISCO

Adventure: Five Cents!

Around goes the car on the turn-table, bell ringing: *Ding, de-ding ding. Ding. Ding!*

People rush and you rush too, to get a seat outside. To pay your nickel and be in your place when the gripman's giant lever grabs the cable in the slot.

Now the bell rings out again, singing its little tune. And *now*, you're off!

Wheels click. People smile. There's a breeze in your face as you climb Nob Hill...and with it comes the realization that this city will be different *endlessly!* As different and as much fun as the cable cars. Thrilling as the towered hills they cling to.

Today you will explore the storied water-front. Ride the upturned arches of the world's two greatest bridges, high above the highest masts of ships.

You'll buy a teakwood idol in a shop in Chinatown; and see old Spain's *Presidio* that guards the Golden Gate!

And later, when dusk purples all the city's fourteen hills, you will join with San Francisco in welcoming the night. You'll whisper a toast, and dine and dance. And, finally, sleep in a hotel room that is cooled by tradewinds from the whole Pacific ocean.

And for tomorrow, and as many tomorrows as you can stay, San Francisco promises new, unforgettable experience...in the city, and in the varied outdoorland it centers.

At nearby Santa Cruz, Del Monte, Monterey, Carmel—on the ocean's sandy shore. In the Yosemite Valley and at Lake Tahoe. In the Gold Towns of the 'Forty-Niners. On Russian River and Feather River, on Mt. Shasta and volcanic Lassen Peak...in forests of giant Redwood trees.

Send the coupon for the free, illustrated book: *The Chapter in Your Life entitled San Francisco.* Get travel details from your auto club, or any railroad, airline or travel agent.

★ **CALIFORNIANS INC.**

Dept. 104, 703 Market St., San Francisco. Please send your free book and Official Tourist Map.

*Name*_____

*Street*_____

*City*_____

*State*_____

This was one of the long series of color pages that ran in Time *to salute almost everybody's favorite city. Note the cable-car fare: Five Cents.*

uneasy with their imported advertising manager. John Cuddy was a middle-aged, slightly bald, experienced advertising man, a transfer from a New York advertising agency, who had been introduced into the picture by a director representing the petroleum marketers. Quite naturally, the petroleum man wanted our advertising to stress the low cost of a vacation in San Francisco and Northern California; the other directors, for the most part, couldn't have cared less. While Cuddy wanted only to increase the tourist flow, the job he had been hired for, most of the directors were afraid he would open the gates to unwanted hordes, come to stay.

I was in between. But once again I was receiving instruction in advertising — this time with alternating treatments of hot and cold criticism. John Cuddy had been a copywriter himself. Now he assumed the role of critic. I was at once his public and his pupil. Sometimes he flattered me; sometimes he tore me to pieces. The real trouble was, I suspect, that he thought teaching me was all he had to do. He was miscast as a promoter, and he took refuge in advertising.

The routine usually began the same way. "Will you have a cigar?" John Cuddy would ask, beaming.

"No, thank you, I think I'll just have a Lucky Strike," I would reply. Thus were established the senior and junior roles. The lesson could now begin.

"Are you doing any writing?" Cuddy would ask about half the times when I brought him a new piece of copy.

"Of course," I always answered. "I wrote this."

"No, no," he would say. "I mean writing for the periodicals? Or, perhaps, a book?"

"Look," I would say. "It takes all the time I have just to write advertising."

"I only asked," he would counter, "because this is so beautifully done."

The words were not always exactly the same, but the pleasantries were. Except when there were unpleasantries. These seemed inevitably to be the result of my best efforts; when I tried to interpret San Francisco instead of merely describing it. In his own way John Cuddy was as little interested in innovation as were the directors. He would allow change only within certain limits. He accepted only certain ways to say things. When I attempted others, he was impatient. He would shoot his hard cuffs, and shake his large head sadly as if to say, "My boy, you'll never, never make it." Then, as if to give me one last chance, he would attack my copy line by line, then word by word, until it was either utterly destroyed or completely unrecognizable. Finally, he would hand it back.

Altogether, I must have paid Cuddy a thousand visits. On perhaps half of them I received all the paeans of which he was capable. On the others, I was a shallow thinker whose writing hand had become all thumbs.

The Doty method of writing called for the sparest possible prose written on the shortest line between two points. Even *The Seven Cities of Cibola* gave way in a single short paragraph to positive, provable facts of the modern Southwest. The Cuddy pattern was one of embellishment bordering on jewelry. Doty threw you into a clear stream of advertising opportunity to sink or swim. Cuddy put a rope around you and dragged you through the lily pads.

This was time-consuming and messy. Long before it was all over I knew pretty well what this man wanted. But he never changed his ways. And whether my work was praised or condemned at the outset made no difference. It had always to be painfully revised. Finally, when I realized that this was the way it had to be, it became a game, and eventually we always got back very close to the original copy. Indeed, there was a period when my most exacting client and I were rewriting advertisements that had already been set in type and plated and shipped off to the magazine publishers! As it was, I have been told that I had the worst record for deadline extensions of anyone in the agency business. But had I ever confessed to John Cuddy that a deadline was close he would have canceled the insertion, for he wouldn't be pushed. Luckily, I made every scheduled issue and my withholding was never discovered.

Writing about San Francisco was easy because you had your audience with you from the start of each advertisement. The only problem was not to lose that audience by getting mixed up in things of purely local interest, however colorful they might have been. John Cuddy insisted that everything I described be relevant to something in our reader's experience. He refused to approve any reference at all to a colorful and meaningful annual event in the countryside near Monterey that was his pride and joy.

Nowhere else in California was there anything like the fiesta and pageant at the Mission of San Juan Bautista in the brown hills that separate California's Santa Clara Valley from the valley of the Salinas River. The two valleys are almost equally rich and prosperous, but the old adobe mission in the hills is lonely and poor, and it appealed to John Cuddy's sense of charity. The two-day fiesta and the pageant were the mission's principal means of support beyond the barest necessities and my client wanted them to succeed for that reason.

Also, Mrs. Cuddy directed the pageant. She was a professional and did her job well, adding a sufficient number of performers from San Francisco to fill out the mission cast, which was made up largely of children. Altogether, it was usually a fine show. If its lines were somewhat lofty for a scene that was dominated by a crumbling and decrepit church, this may have been because Cuddy wrote them without our usual collaboration. This was an exercise from which he barred me. He was a fair man and he said that working on the pageant was not part of my job for him.

I have wished many times that some of my other clients had the same solid precept. It is part and parcel of the advertising agency business to write scripts, speeches, leaflets, folders, broadsides, booklets, brochures, letters and other mailing pieces for Catholic, Protestant and Jewish charities, for hospitals and clinics, colleges and universities, libraries and museums, day nurseries and summer camps, and so on through a list of hundreds of different jobs for which the agencies' services are generously donated by their clients and paid for with thanks. To be honest, I have profited out of all proportion from some of these contributions, and I shall have more to say about this. However, it will not change my appreciation for John Cuddy's attitude.

He was a difficult taskmaster. There were times when I hated him. But he was a gentleman of a strict old school. His manners were perfect, even if they were stiff. I worked with him closely for eleven years, and so fearful was he of bending that he never called me by my first name when we were alone. With other people present we put on a show of intimacy, first names and all, but when we were alone again ours was strictly a formal relationship, even to the extent that once when I invited the Cuddys to my house for a simple home dinner he insisted upon wearing his tuxedo. "This is an occasion I have looked forward to," he said. "And I couldn't think of not dressing for it." The dinner was delicious because my wife is a superlative cook. Also, in my dinner suit, I proved to be an admirable waiter. However, the dinner was not repeated.

Shortly after that stately occasion, our steamship lines account was added to my assignment, and I set off on a trip to the Orient. When I came back I picked up where I had left off with John Cuddy and the lessons were resumed. The book that he asked me about and poked me about so many times has had to wait until now.

Round the World for $749

No other client could have been more different from John Cuddy than the bandy-legged, dour Scotchman whose name was Hugh Mackenzie and who was vice president of the Dollar Steamship Lines in charge of passenger traffic. Mackenzie was an expert hunter and fisherman, and he loved to talk about his exploits in the wilds. He recounted these in minute and unvarying detail and at length. But when I tried to bring him to the business at hand he had no time for me. He refused under any circumstances to read the advertisements I prepared, or to approve them. This, he insisted, was up to me!

Almost everyone who traveled on the Dollar Lines wanted to see Hugh Mackenzie in person. This was particularly true of the old China hands, who knew to the number which staterooms they wanted and insisted upon having. It seemed that the only travelers who didn't want to see the vice president for passenger traffic were those people who were down on their luck and had tourist-class passage to Yokohama or Kobe, where they would purchase first-class tickets for the remainder of their voyage and arrive at Shanghai or Manila in proper style.

These travelers would have lost face if Mackenzie had seen them.

Mackenzie had no time for advertising. He refused to read the advertisements I submitted, and he wouldn't sign the estimates for their insertion in magazines or newspapers.

"If you wrote the copy, you okay it," he said. "And you sign the estimates. You know what the advertising budget is. You know how far it has to go. Only don't you put any ads in *Time* magazine.".

Hugh Mackenzie never forgot a favor and he never forgave a slight.

Once *Time* had mentioned in a piece about China that there were cannibals at large on the Chinese mainland. Mackenzie took offense at this and fired off a denial to the editor. There the matter probably would have ended had not *Time* in its infinite wisdom published Mackenzie's letter together with a map showing just where it insisted the outrages were occurring. This was no way to make friends, and for ten years *Time* received not an inch of Dollar Lines advertising. Mackenzie, I hasten to say, had no thought at all of influencing the press. He was quite satisfied to mete out punishment.

The San Francisco *Call-Bulletin*, the city's leading afternoon newspaper at the time, also felt the steamship man's wrath. Hugh Mackenzie had figured in a colorful divorce case. The melodramatic highlight was a pitching contest in which Mackenzie was alleged to have fired a roast leg of lamb at his wife.

"If I ever threw anything, it was a napkin," Mackenzie said. "And if I ever threw a napkin, I threw it down on the table."

But the *Call-Bulletin* went off the newspaper advertising list, never to be returned despite the best efforts of Hearstlings, large and small. The "large" in this instance was the imperious Mortimer Berkowitz, publisher of the *American Weekly*; the "small" was the wise and wily Clarence Lindner, publisher of the *Examiner*, and they tried every angle they could think of, to no avail. Not even the Dollars could budge Hugh Mackenzie against his will.

The Dollar Steamship Lines (with the American Mail Line, a subsidiary), will go down in U.S. maritime history as a remarkable institution. It was founded as a lumber carrier by a doughty old sea captain named Robert Dollar who was the model for the audacious Cappy Ricks in the sea stories that Peter B. Kyne wrote for the *Saturday Evening Post*. Cappy Ricks was forever the prey of sharpies and hoaxers and plain and fancy buccaneers, but the crafty Scot was never bested; he not only escaped every plot to do him in, but he made the tricksters pay handsomely for the stern lessons he taught them.

The real Cappy Ricks was reputed to be no less ingenious and astute. And when Robert Dollar died in 1928 it was the largest American steamship company that he willed to his three sons.

When Albert Lasker took leave from the advertising agency of Lord & Thomas to serve as chairman of the United States Shipping Board in 1921, primarily for the purpose of liquidating the wartime merchant fleet, his largest sale of ships was to the Dollars. They bought seventeen combination cargo and passenger liners and renamed them after Presidents of the United States, from the Adamses to Woodrow

Wilson, and a unique trans-Pacific and round-the-world service came into being.* It was appropriate that when Albert Lasker returned to Lord & Thomas, in 1923, after his Shipping Board job was done, the Dollar Steamship Lines advertising should come with him.

It was this advertising that I was assigned in the fall of 1932, and in addition to the unusual status with which Hugh Mackenzie vested me, I found the promise of the President liners, especially during the depression, irresistible. I felt that I was doing anyone a favor if I could lure him aboard. For one thing, the price of a first-class round-the-world ticket when I began to write the Dollar Lines advertising was $749! Since the trip took 110 days, this worked out to just over $6.80 per day for board and room and entertainment, and it wasn't surprising that a number of frugal people lived on these ships for periods of many months. The price was right, and the depression that was everywhere seemed mostly foreign, and to that extent remote. The President liners were immune to the economic illness of eighteen of the ports they visited in thirteen different countries, and so were the passengers they carried.

How I came to be one of the latter was Hugh Mackenzie's doing. While I was at work on the Southern Pacific and the Californians, Inc., advertising, the man in charge of the Dollar Lines account was a journeyman advertising man of the old school, named Bolton Mallory, a man with a heavy black moustache and a slightly evil leer. He claimed to have been almost everywhere and, among other things, he was an expert on the Orient, which was where the President liners touched first on their way westward around the world. Whether Mallory really had been out there I never knew. He had a way of making even a simple statement of a fact we all knew sound dubious. On the other hand, he could give a wildly improbable proposition the fine ring of truth. Mallory was a handsome fellow, despite the dark face that wore such a sardonic look, and it was generally accepted in the office that he was responsible for the ribald songs that turned up regularly on the pretty dictaphone operator's black cylinders. Since the girl couldn't tell what any record held until she played it, the prankster had her suspended between proper frenzy and utter fascination on many a morning, and Mallory got the dubious credit.

---

* Trans-Pacific President liners sailed every other Thursday from New York through the Panama Canal to Los Angeles and San Francisco, thence via Honolulu to Yokohama, Kobe, Shanghai, Hong Kong and Manila. Round-the-world President liners followed the same route in alternate weeks and continued on from Manila to Singapore, Colombo, Bombay, Suez, Port Said, Alexandria, Naples, Genoa, Marseilles, and home across the Atlantic.

The great advantage was that passengers could stop over anywhere, continue on the next or a later President liner at their leisure.

The Lord & Thomas office in San Francisco was two thousand miles from the company's sedate headquarters in Chicago, and the office had few inhibitions. It did sound work, but its ways, within certain bounds, were unrestrained. The office boy, who had been discharged by the manager in order to reduce expenses, was rehired by the staff on a personal basis. The manager was denied any access to his services, until finally, reluctantly, he gave in, and the office boy, who was known as Boojum, was reinstated to work for everyone. The plump, red-haired receptionist had an eager stag line at her desk every hour of the day. More than a few of the large file drawers in the flat-top desks held fat gallons of bootleg gin, the understanding being that this should be drunk only after hours and according to strict men's-club rules. Ladies might not be invited.

Mallory, for some reason, rarely attended the club sessions. He was suspected of preferring high-priced whiskey to low-priced gin — and of being more interested in girls, anyway. Perhaps he was, for, late in 1932, he left Lord & Thomas to become editor of the old *Life* magazine and to marry the actress Nancy Carroll, after which he went to live, and die, in Mexico.

When Bolton Mallory departed there was no one in the agency who had any idea what the Orient was like, or about any of the President liners' ports of call beyond Hawaii; and I was sent to find out. I was Mackenzie's choice to take Mallory's place. As it turned out, Mallory had written very little of the Dollar Lines' advertising copy. This he had purchased from a freelance writer who had lived for a number of years in China and the Philippines. Unfortunately, she had a poor memory and as a result she suddenly was lost to us, too. When she quoted an old South Seas chantey, "Oh, the monkeys have no tails in Zamboanga" as the headline for an advertisement that featured excursions from Manila to Iloilo, Zamboanga and Cebu, all hell broke loose. Our writer had forgotten that seamen the world over refer harshly to the agile, friendly Filipinos as *monkeys*. When the Filipinos threatened to boycott the Dollar Lines, the unthinking lady copywriter was promptly sacked to remove the blot on the Philippines' national escutcheon.

The reason, incidentally, why the Zamboanga monkeys have no tails is that they were bitten off by whales! Or so the chantey goes.

Anyway, I went on the job.

There was nothing chic about the President liners; no dressing for dinner, for example. But those heavy-laden cargo vessels rode the seas comfortably. The staterooms were large enough, and all had outside ports. The meals consisted of almost anything you could dream

Away, Away!

Round the Globe for $749, First Class. 26,000 miles. 14 countries, 22 ports, 85 cities or more. Take six months; stopover anywhere, continue on another Round the World President Liner. Available until December. Every other week from New York or California.

To the Orient via the Sunshine Belt. In President Liner luxury to Hawaii, Japan, China, Philippines, Malaya. Living royally—for a song! Plan now with your nearest travel agent. Sail away from winter, any week from New York or the Pacific Coast.

To California via Havana and the Panama Canal. 5500 sunny miles. 16 days..or longer..if you care to stopover. First Class, from $175. Special Class on the great new President Hoover and President Coolidge, from $135. All outside staterooms. Sail any week.

Dollar Steamship Lines and American Mail Line

24 Providence St., Boston · 110 S. Dearborn St., Chicago · Union Trust Arcade, Cleveland · 514 W. 6th St., Los Angeles · 604 Fifth Ave., New York · 152 Broadway, Portland, Ore. · 311 California St., San Francisco · 338 E. Broadway, San Diego · Fourth at University, Seattle · 1005 Connecticut, N. W. Washington, D.C.

We tried to bring the Orient onto the printed page with rather formalized illustrations in black and white. This one was by Fred Ludekens.

of, anytime you wanted it; the corps of eager, cheerful Cantonese stewards appeared to live without sleep.

And in spite of their configuration as freight and passenger ships, the President liners had adequate outdoor swimming pools and pleasant lounges and card rooms. The only thing missing was a bar. These were American-flag ships; Prohibition was in effect. But the sympathetic (and enterprising) ship's doctors dealt out "medicinal" whiskey and gin with the world's most famous labels at little more than freeport prices. The mixers came gratis and so did the hors d'oeuvres.

Altogether the President liners reflected the hospitality of both San Francisco, which was their home port, and the inviting cities of the China coast, where both old and new China hands were delighted to share the customs of the Orient with Dollar Lines passengers. One of these was to make each incoming President liner a center of social activity for as long as the ship was at dock.

It was quite the thing, too, for Americans living in Japan and China and the Philippines to make the trip north or south through the China Sea once or twice a year just for the change, to get away from the high-pitched Oriental sounds and the smells in the oppressive shoreside air. In this way the ships were usually filled between Yokohama and Manila with China coast residents who were glad to be interpreters and guides for people from back home.

I soon learned a startling fact: most people travel for nothing so much as a brief change of scenery. It is not for adventure, except of the mildest kind. They want every important circumstance of living to be exactly what they are used to. Hot water for shaving, easily identifiable food, clean beds, cold beer and good barbers and beauticians are most important. These were things the President liners promised and delivered while sailing in generally sunny seas; and I presented them in print with a minimum of adjectives.

To be sure, all the voyagers on the President liners had a look at the Ginza and the moated Imperial Palace in Tokyo and the giant Daibutsu at Kamakura, outside Yokohama. They walked briefly through the shinto shrines and temples at Kyoto, and fed rice cookies to the sacred spotted deer at Nara. Leaving Kobe, they marveled momentarily at the beauty of Japan's Inland Sea. They were at once captivated and appalled by the hordes of beggars thrusting aloft baskets from their sampans in the muddy Whangpoo River at Shanghai, pleading for anything at all. They rode in the crowded ferries through the maze of junks between Kowloon and Hong Kong in Hong Kong Bay. They rode in Dewey Boulevard in Manila in horse-drawn carromatos, and walked through the old walled city, the Intramuros.

But all this was no more than a small excursion in person through the pages of the *National Geographic* magazine. For most visitors, the most noteworthy things in Japan were the eagle-eyed woman caddies at the golf courses, and a brazen young New Yorker named Burton Crane who was cleverly translating popular American songs into Japanese, who was the darling of the dance halls. Kikisui restaurant in Kobe was highly recommended because it wasn't *too* Japanese.

In Shanghai the important life for tourists was the night life, centered in Sir Philip Sassoon's towering Cathay Hotel on the Bund, a completely European establishment except for the help; in the French Club, and at the Canidrome where the greyhounds raced; at the jai alai fronton; at the famous Del Monte cabaret, aswarm with sultry White Russian prostitutes, with nary a Chinese in sight. Hong Kong was considered dreadfully dull.

Manila was lively. But again, few visitors to the Philippines climbed up to Baguio or Benguet where the Igorots live, or sailed south into the Sulu Sea. The open dining room of the Manila Hotel on the beach, where a great flock of varicolored birds made their homes, was simply too lovely to leave.

Because I learned these things and mixed a little romance with the facts of living that most people find most important, the Dollar Lines advertising was very productive.

Under Walter Doty and John Cuddy, I had developed as a plain and, I believe, conscientious writer. I knew the adjectives and the adverbs and I wrote them down. Then I crossed most of them out. I tried to write as I would talk; this is impossible, but it is worth trying in advertising, for the closer one comes to it the better one does. I tried to say what I had to say clearly and make my propositions complete. I also broke a number of accepted advertising rules.

The most successful advertisement I wrote for the Dollar Lines broke all the rules of brevity. There were twenty-five words in the headline. It read, *Take only 110 days! Spend just $1033 for this 26,000 mile World Cruise to 21 fascinating ports in 14 famed countries! Shore excursions abroad included.* The depression was easing when this particular advertisement appeared in the first issue of the new *Life* in November of 1936, and fares had gone up. Also, I was guilty of a little *Time*-style in writing the text. But the pattern was a good pattern, and the advertisement ran virtually unchanged for a number of years.

When I took over the Dollar Lines account I was relieved of any part of the Southern Pacific assignment, but it was understood that when I returned from the Orient, I would assume responsibility for the Hawaii Tourist Bureau advertising for which Lord & Thomas had been appointed in 1931.

With Hugh Mackenzie's connivance, I had hoped to lengthen the trip to the Orient into a trip round the world. But I was ordered home from Manila so that I might stop off for two weeks in Hawaii to prepare to take over that account.

Stop over I did, and my wife and I were treated regally. Unfortunately, after the great cities of Japan and China, and especially Peking (whither we had gone by train from Shanghai), Honolulu and the island of Oahu were something less than wildly exciting. The green island of Kauai, where my old friend Charlie Fern, publisher of the *Garden Island News*, held forth, and from which he had occasionally sent me a gallon of Hawaiian rum, was better. But Hawaii was something I was destined not to worry about.

On the day we returned to San Francisco, I was informed that the Hawaii Tourist Bureau had decided to dispense with the services of Lord & Thomas the day before we arrived in Honolulu. Our hosts had been too polite to tell us. Even Charlie Fern, who was a member of the bureau, had kept the secret.

Mackenzie was furious. Hawaii was something he didn't like anyway. By agreement with the Matson Navigation Company, Dollar did not solicit passenger (or freight) business between Pacific Coast ports and Honolulu. That was bad enough, but it was an arrangement made long before Mackenzie's arrival on the scene. Now, in what he considered a personal affront, the Hawaiians had fired his friend.

Hugh Mackenzie's friends were a special privileged group and I was one of them. I was also a handy fellow, for I relieved the steamship man of any responsibility for advertising. He had an advertising manager, an extremely adept young Japanese named Earl Tanbara, but Mackenzie fitfully refused to deal with him; he respected Tanbara but didn't like Japanese. So it was that in the course of our long association I wrote and scheduled hundreds of Dollar (and later American President) Lines advertisements involving millions of dollars without benefit of a single signed estimate or approved piece of copy.

My only disapproval from Mackenzie came one night at a retirement party given for another Dollar executive. There was crap shooting, and when I gave a young fellow who shouldn't have been in the game under any circumstance several opportunities to recoup his severe losses to me, which eventually he did, Mackenzie was disgusted. As a serious gambler, he played according to a strict code.

"When you shoot dice, you shoot to win," he said angrily. Then he stalked out of the room.

While he thought very little of me as a gambler, I continued to enjoy his faith and trust as an advertising agent as long as I lived in San Francisco, and when I went away the first time to work in New York, it was he who insisted that Lord & Thomas bring me back.

Fred Ludekens

IT has always seemed to me that the best luck anyone can have is usually not to have bad luck. I have seen what bad luck can do to people. Nevertheless, the best luck I ever had was a matter of sheer good fortune that occurred on my first day at Lord & Thomas, in Walter Doty's office.

It was then and there that I met Fred Ludekens.

Ludekens was the talented artist who illustrated our travel advertisements. He had ridden the Southern Pacific routes from one end to the other. He knew every rock and rill in the state of California, for he had hunted and fished over all of them. Because he had never been in the Orient and had to rely on his reference files for local color, Hugh Mackenzie undertook from time to time to correct one of his drawings, but no one else did. The Ludekens authority was early established.

Like me, Fred Ludekens had started drawing almost as soon as he could hold a pencil. We were the same age. There any similarity between us as artists ended. For one thing, he had a true and magnificent color sense. He also had sharp eyes and a photographic mind. Everything he wanted to see he saw; everything he wanted to remember he filed away in his mind for instant, total recall.

In addition to illustrating our travel advertisements, Ludekens was one of the stable of young artists who were to make the *Saturday Evening Post* the best illustrated of all magazines. Men like Ben Stahl, Al Parker, Steven Dohanos, Albert Dorne, Robert Fawcett, Austin Briggs, together with Fred Ludekens, gave the *Post's* rather drab pages a new lively look with drawings that were both skillfully designed and beautifully executed. There was only one flaw in the arrangement. The *Post* failed to find successors to the consummate story-tellers who had made its fiction the most popular in America: Joseph Hergesheimer, Thomas Beer, E. Phillips Oppenheim, Sophie Kerr, Alice Duer Miller, Mary Roberts Rinehart, Dorothy Canfield Fisher, Ben Ames Williams, Owen Wister.

In several issues, ten years later, in the summer of 1939, the only writer who was recognizable from the *Post*'s era of exciting fiction was J. P. Marquand. The illustrations were still superb. But the only stories that had the old excitement were the Westerns. Mostly these were illustrated still by Fred Ludekens.

Ludekens could draw anything, and draw it accurately. He was often called upon by other artists to help them with details; particularly in the drawing of birds and animals. He could draw a rearing, bucking bronco high in the air from the point of view of a fallen cowboy on the ground; and once that I remember he painted a detailed picture of a new large passenger ship for the Dollar Lines with nothing to go on but a set of blueprints.

The *Post* editors allowed him the unusual privilege of choosing the story points to be illustrated and designing the illustrations for their pages as he thought best. These he planned to be window displays for the magazine's fiction. They had to be correct in their promise and true to life. Editors took a dim view of letters from readers that pointed out inaccuracies of any kind, and Ludekens was guilty of none. The authors whose stories he illustrated invariably asked him for the originals.

To know that this superb draftsman had taught himself would have astonished the writers. To know that he was more interested in advertising than in art would have left them bewildered.

Like Truman Bailey and Walter Doty, Fred Ludekens's first concern in advertising was with clarity, and he helped me to develop a firm set of rules by which to make advertising and judge advertising that I have lived by for almost forty years. The difficulty is to convince other advertising people that the message is all that matters. The cleverest headline or paragraph imaginable, or the most striking illustration, is of no value by itself. It has work to do and if it doesn't do this it had better never have been made; it is sheer waste.

I hadn't been working with Ludekens long when I learned that every time I brought text to him to be laid out for a magazine or newspaper advertisement and to be illustrated, he was going to ask me three questions before he looked at what I had written.

"What is it you are trying to say?"

"What is it you are trying to sell?"

"What is your proposition?"

When I could answer these succinctly the advertisement making would begin. When I couldn't, I went back to my typewriter to try again.

Although it is never entered in the books of account, the right advertising proposition is often among a company's most valuable assets. It can literally be more valuable than a new plant or a new manufacturing process. This is what Fred Ludekens always looked for, and he refused to spend his time on anything else.

Advertising is something anyone can undertake. And many people do this without success. On the other hand, millions of men and women write want ads every year and most of these are effective; in renting apartments, finding workers, selling automobiles, recovering lost animals, and countless other personal transactions. The want ad is a direct and usually unvarnished proposition made by one person to another for the purpose of some important *individual* action: to rent a *specific* apartment to a desirable tenant, to turn up an *appropriate* employee for a *particular* job, to dispose of a *given* automobile, to arrange for the return of a *named* dog or cat, and so on.

When most people sit down to compose advertising hopefully to influence large numbers of prospects for what they propose, they lose this personal touch; they forget that advertising is something one does only when he can't go see his prospects and make his proposition face to face. The maker of any advertisement is simply developing the best substitute he can for personal solicitation and he should come as close to this as he can in both words and feeling.

When Fred Ludekens and I were first making advertisements in San Francisco in 1930, there was a rash of absurd advertising (which is something that breaks out periodically) and the public was exhorted to buy all manner of products by means of outlandish propositions. A used car dealer named Earl Muntz plastered the billboards of Southern California with pictures of a small raffish Napoleonic figure shouting to the world: *My wife says I'm crazy. I want to give them away.* A candy maker who went by the name of Awful-fresh McFarland signed all his advertisements *Nuts 2 You.* And radio advertising that didn't depend on a jingle was considered in the trade to be sadly out of date. I am sure that had I tried anything of the kind Fred Ludekens would have written me off for all time.

The travel advertising with which Ludekens and I were primarily concerned didn't lend itself to either comedy or exaggeration. And as we got into some of the product advertising in the agency we decided there should be no difference.

The result was the establishment of a discipline that can be set down in five cardinal rules. Rosser Reeves, the outstanding creative director of the Ted Bates advertising agency through many years, has written wisely on the subject and makes many salient points. David Ogilvy has put down some 120 rules having to do with every aspect of advertising production, and done this with characteristic aplomb. I haven't any argument with either of them, or with Claude Hopkins of Lord & Thomas, whose *Scientific Advertising* is probably the classic book about advertising. But I believe that every honest advertisement will be successful that meets the requirements of only five rules that Fred Ludekens and I tried to follow; and that no advertising can succeed that fails to meet any one of them; they are not divisible. These were not written down in this form until much later. But they were clearly understood in principle, and we followed them carefully. Fred Ludekens saw to that.

The first rule for good advertising as we saw it was that it must immediately make clear what the basic proposition is. Few if any people have either the time or the inclination to try to solve the puzzle of obscure advertising promises.

> *Raid hunts bugs down like radar,*
> *kills them dead*

Second, it is equally important to successful advertising that what is clear shall also be important. The proposition must express a well-defined value.

> *Kleenex towels absorb 50 per cent more*
> *because they are two layers thick*

Third, the successful advertisement will express the value of the offering in personal terms. It will be beamed directly at the most logical prospects for the proposition; no one else matters.

> *We want to help people who want to write for a living*
> (Famous Writers School)

Fourth, good advertising will always express the personality of the advertiser, for a promise is only as good as its maker.

> ***The quality goes in***
> ***before the name goes on***
> (Zenith radio and television sets)

New Kleenex towels absorb 50% more because they're 2 layers thick - not 1

DOUBLE LAYER

Kleenex towels

Most paper towels are only 1 layer. New Kleenex towels are 2 layers pressed together. Thicker. Stronger. The thirstiest towels you can buy. Choose either pink, aqua, yellow or white.

The rules that were clear to me in 1932 applied equally twenty years later in this Kleenex towel page. Values must be clearly expressed.

Finally, a successful advertisement will always demand action. It will ask for the order, so to speak, or it will exact a mental pledge, because its promise is not to be denied.

> *The closer he gets*
> *the better you look*
> (shampoo hair coloring by Clairol)

These rules are illustrated every day in many ways, for they apply equally to advertising in all media. Inevitably, taken together and carefully adhered to, they result in advertising that will command attention but never be offensive. It will be reasonable but never dull. It will be original but never self-conscious. It will be imaginative but never misleading. Because of these qualities it will make people act.

This is all I know about making advertising.

It is also all that anyone needs to know in order to judge advertising.

"The trouble is," Fred Ludekens says, "it's one thing to know the rules and something else again never to break one."

It seems so much more original to say: *This car is for people who don't like cars*, which is the headline in a recent Volvo magazine page than to say: *In Sweden Volvos are driven an average of eleven years. Wouldn't you like to have eight or nine years with no payment to make?*

Here the very first rule was broken. The headline in no way makes clear that trading in a car after only two or three years is an unhappy business from which the sturdy Volvo saves many people.

Simply to be different exposes advertising to the limits of absurdity.

As this is written, the negative approach, as in the Volvo example, is something of a vogue.

Within the course of a few weeks the world is offered a new Lucky Strike cigarette *that doesn't taste like a Lucky Strike*; Renault (no doubt spurred to excess by Volvo) headlines that *our customers are dissatisfied*; Ronson advertises *table lighters for people who hate table lighters;* and Lava soap is presented as the *world's worst bath soap.*

Now the fact that there is a new taste in Lucky Strikes may be an attractive gambit. It may be true that Renault owners think the manufacturer is overly modest in his claims. Ronson may indeed have produced a table lighter that works better than some other table lighters. Lava is strictly a hardworking, gritty hand soap, and there may be no better. But the advertiser's approach in each instance is indirect and undirected. It is like the koala bear who says *I hate Qantas* (because it brings people to disturb his slumber) as the best promise of the Australian airline.

There is little question that the people who made these advertisements found them offbeat and full of fun. The truth is, each one is ridiculous, and, worse than that, wasteful, for it cost as much to publish as a sensible advertisement.

Television is full of such foolishness. But the lack of sense in so much television advertising is in accord with the lack of substance in most television programming. Television is directed at the lowest common denominator of public tastes and the excesses in advertising on the little screen are in keeping.

It would hardly be fair to blame television for all of the idiocy that finds its way into printed advertising, but it is a fact that most of the nonsense began with the great latitude that TV allows. The sequential nature of television action from the beginning of a commercial to the end allows it to proceed either according to an orderly plan or in a series of abrupt scenes whose purpose becomes clear only at the conclusion. Printed advertising obviously must work much faster, and when the attempt is made to translate it from television, the result is usually disastrous: too much is either untranslatable because of the static quality of print or impossible to accommodate within the normal limitations of space.

The aberrations that result from trying to apply television techniques to the printed page result in some of advertising's most puzzling inanities. They have the effect of advertising in limbo.

When any advertising at all fails to make clear the answers to Fred Ludekens's original three questions (What is it trying to say? What is it trying to sell? What is the proposition?) and answer these clearly, practically and very personally, it isn't worth either the time it takes to say it or the paper or film that it is printed on.

Fred Ludekens gave up freelancing, except for his work for the magazines, and joined Lord & Thomas, in San Francisco, as head art director in 1933. He continued to illustrate most of our travel advertising. Although color photographs were being used more and more, the colors were still harsh and unreal. In black and white, photography had a documentary quality that was much to be desired, but when it came to color we found drawings much more satisfactory.

For one thing, everyone allows the artist a reasonable amount of latitude for his imagination. Ludekens accepted this and never exceeded it. Also, he had a knack for making the viewer not merely an observer, but a part of the scene. Present-day photographers can do this, too. But in 1933, camera techniques for advertising left much to be desired. Alfred Stieglitz and Edward Weston and Ansel Adams were making great strides. The trouble was, none of them had any interest in advertising. Thus we depended almost solely on Ludekens.

How the two of us drifted apart and later came together again will be told in due course. The drift, I am glad to say, was entirely geographic. Our rigid belief in substance in advertising has never changed.

Getchell

WHEN I returned from the Orient, and the unfortunate two weeks in Hawaii that had cost us a trip around the world, I discovered that I had a new image.

I had been discovered by the advertising trade press. Previously, most advertising made west of the Hudson was considered foreign and inferior — except that Chicago advertising was considered domestic and inferior. In my absence there had appeared in the monthly magazine *Advertising & Selling* an article by Harford Powell, a genial critic of the business, that dealt extravagantly with the series that I was writing, and Fred Ludekens was illustrating, for San Francisco and northern and central California.

As seems always the case with advertising in New York, the game of follow-the-leader began at once and my mail took on astonishing proportions. After Harford Powell wrote his piece, and sent me a beautiful basket of fruit, jams, jellies, chutney and other delicacies from Fortnum & Mason on Madison Avenue, I received a dozen or more letters from advertising agencies, and almost every publisher that I knew had some particular New York agent to make a bid for. It appeared that the advertising elite of the world could hardly wait to make me a member.

There was one difficulty. I had just spent five months as a guest of the Dollar Steamship Lines. Lord & Thomas had paid all my expenses and my wife's, and these had to be repaid. I couldn't leave San Francisco until I had made the slate clean.

Nor did I. Late in the summer of 1934, I used my vacation to go to New York to talk to the most insistent of the agencies that had written me. This was J. Stirling Getchell, Inc., whose initial advertising for Chrysler's new Plymouth automobile, several years before, had created a sensation in both automobile and advertising worlds.

Previous to a stint at J. Walter Thompson Company, where he worked principally on Eastman Kodak advertising, Stirling Getchell had written copy for Albert Lasker at Lord & Thomas in Chicago, on Studebaker, and he had developed some original ideas about the automakers' approach to the public. He thought this should be as far removed from the high-flown prose that so many had attempted to adopt from Ned Jordan and his Playboy as the salesmen themselves, and get down to cases. Getchell was convinced that *cases* here meant salesmanship-in-print, not poetry, and his famous invitation to *Look at All Three* in behalf of Plymouth was the argument of a salesman in a showroom put into automobile advertising for the first time. As an advertising proposition it brazenly made the new car a direct competitor of Ford and Chevrolet, the two traditional front-runners, and it made the designation stick.

The Plymouth had been an overnight success, and when Stirling Getchell sat me down to lunch at the Cloud Club, high among the gargoyles that decorate the Chrysler Building on Lexington Avenue, he was looking for an advertising blockbuster for Chrysler's De Soto, a car that had been launched two years before with indifferent results. Now it was being radically redesigned.

Stirling Getchell was a man whose boundless enthusiasm danced in his eyes, and he painted a glowing picture. He was not a large man, and he had a thin face, but he was made to dominate.

I have an idea that had I tried to insert myself into the picture he was painting, I would have failed. But the salesmanship was all his. Since I didn't want to leave San Francisco, I was sincere in demurring. Stirling Getchell had insisted on my talking to him. He had offered to pay my way to New York, but I hadn't let him. I was determined only to be polite. He had flattered me and I thought I owed him that.

But the intense, impulsive Getchell insisted that I owed myself something more. He warmed to the argument. "It's too easy, the life you're carving out," he said. "Writing about places. Writing descriptions of the same things over and over again. Changing them slightly. Competing with yourself. Writing purple advertising prose. It's a wonderful life you say you have. But what kind of living is it? Certainly not like in New York. Where is the challenge? Where is it going to take you?"

I didn't know and I didn't care. I only wanted to get away from this man who wanted to change a life that I was perfectly content with. But he went on. His tone was deadly serious; he became more and more urgent.

Then he became generous. "If you don't want to work for Getchell," he said, "there are two hundred other agencies in New York. Go see them." He was really excited now, relishing his generosity; completely unaware of its irrelevance.

"I'll give you a letter to the ten biggest agencies in town," he said. "Go see Stanley Resor at J. Walter Thompson. Bruce Barton. Raymond Rubicam. Tom Ryan at Pedlar & Ryan, Harry McCann at McCann-Erickson. See which one you like best."

Here was my chance to shut off the attack. All I had to do was accept the unexpected offer, and quietly disappear into the sunset. Instead, I said, "I wouldn't like any of them best." He had got me on the defensive.

"Then what are we waiting for?" he asked, smiling. The thunder had subsided.

I had no answer. As a matter of fact, I never did answer.

Stirling Getchell put out his right hand, across the small lunch table, and I shook it. The deal was made. A few minutes later, down on the Chrysler Building's thirtieth floor, Walter Bornhoft, the agency general manager, told me what my salary was to be (Getchell had not mentioned money). Then I left for San Francisco to inform my wife and pack up our belongings.

I had been in New York less than six hours and had turned my life around.

On the way West this took another twist. Stopping in Chicago to change trains, which you had to do in that long trip of three nights and three days, I spent the hours between at the Century of Progress Exhibition on the lakefront; and in the middle of the afternoon I became deathly ill. I staggered to the railroad station and after that day I was sick most of the time for seven years.

According to my promise, I arrived in New York in October and settled down to work as best I could.

A month earlier I had had my tonsils removed. That was the medical fad of the year, but the operation had no effect. I continued to feel rather more dead than alive in long stretches.

Despite this, I wrote the advertising plan for the introduction of the 1936 Plymouth. Lead time being what it is in the automobile business, this was two years off. Getchell was pleased. But I had no success at all trying to make the teardrop design of the De Soto Airflow models more important than what the public was convinced were its hideously ugly lines.

This was before the German Volkswagen with its similar body design and its superb advertising burst upon the scene. Aerodynamics had no appeal at all to the auto buyer of the mid-1930's.

The De Soto Airflow was the most conspicuous failure in the automobile manufacturing business until the Tucker fell straight off the drawing boards into oblivion in 1951, and Ford's Edsel descended to the depths of unacceptability ten years later for much the same reason that the De Soto came a cropper. The European automobile buyer may accept or even seek out radical new designs and mechanical innovations, but the typical American (which is almost all Americans) has always picked his car for the romantic picture he sees of himself at the wheel. Among his inconsistencies, he refuses to be original.

Stirling Getchell was a kind and generous employer as well as a crack advertising man. When he saw that I was sick he immediately put me in the hands of his own eminent physician who discovered that I was in the throes of a kind of undulating case of jaundice. This appeared and disappeared according to no discernible pattern. When it came I was almost entirely incapacitated; when it went away I seemed as good as new.

Unfortunately, this was not true. The recurrences became chronic. No treatment effected any lasting relief; and in the bitter cold of January, 1935, I decided to leave New York and return to California. There, at least, I could look forward to being sick in the sun.

Getchell, who was a practicing hypochondriac and a specialist in dealing with the exotic ailments of professional men, had what he thought was a much better idea.

"Take a long ocean cruise," he said. "Or go for six months to France. The south of France. Or to Portugal." The only place he didn't want me to go was back to California. That was a battle he had already won and he didn't want to fight it again. "It is perfectly clear," Getchell insisted, "that all you need is a change from me." And he offered to pay all the costs — for me and my wife and our new baby.* No man could have been more solicitous or more openhanded.

But everything I tried was worse than the thing before. I had deserted Getchell's doctor and got myself into the web of a spidery Vien-

---

* Mary Mastick Cone had been born in November at the Sloane Hospital for Women in the Presbyterian Medical Center at the northern end of Manhattan Island, while I languished in the New York Polyclinic Hospital, down toward the island's southern tip.

nese who forbade me to eat anything but meat. "Fruit and vegetables," he insisted, "are garbitch." I was slowly starving. Also the offices in the Chrysler building had become filled with foreboding.

My friend Faulkner, with whom I had sailed on the *Haxtum* and who had been editor of the *Daily Californian* when we both were at Berkeley, had preceded me to the Getchell company and we worked together. That is, until the Sunday morning in December when one of the other copywriters telephoned to tell that there had been an accident in the office.

"Jerry Faulkner," he said, "just jumped out the window." The window was thirty floors above 43rd Street.

There was a note rolled into Jerry's typewriter, dated that morning. But it made no more sense than did his jumping, which could never be explained. Jerry Faulkner was able and normal and popular with his associates. He was healthy (he was an exceptional swimmer). He had recently been married.

I couldn't get the mystery out of my mind.

Getchell kept after me to pack up my family and take the long trip. He even had his secretary working for me; she rounded up a collection of travel folders and brochures that would have done credit to an American Express agent. But I was determined not to take anything more from this man.

Lord & Thomas had never ceased to urge me to return to San Francisco; and late in February I did.

The only thing that I was sorry to leave behind in New York was Getchell himself. I had done poorly for him. While we had numerous exchanges and various contacts in later years when I helped him to hire a number of people, I have a haunting memory of his unsuccessful attempt to make me productive.

I can see him sitting on the floor of my office pulling crumpled yellow sheets from my green metal wastebasket.

"Whatever are you doing?" I asked him.

"I'm looking," he replied, "to see if you've thrown away anything we can use. I'm not sure you would recognize it."

The truth is, I mightn't have, at that. I was much too sick to learn anything from Stirling Getchell except a long-lasting lesson in generosity. Like all the good advertising men I have known, Getchell's greatest talent was in maintaining a person-to-person relationship in his copy. It was never pompous, never graceless. It was always direct, thoroughly understandable, and warmhearted—because he was, too.

Getchell would never have fathomed today's offbeat advertising that depends upon insult, invective and innuendo, in about equal parts, to build up to shock. He would have applauded the unequaled advertising of Volkswagen. The strained efforts of Volvo and Renault would have left him icy cold. "Look at all three" was what he would have said to a friend. And that is what he said in advertising.

At the same time that the editors of *Time* and *Fortune* were experimenting secretly with a picture magazine, Getchell was experimenting with his picture magazine. He had introduced large candid photographs into automobile advertising for the first time, and he foresaw the possibilities of photojournalism in documentary terms while the editors of most magazines were still using photographs to illustrate their words.

Stirling Getchell died shortly after the *Time* editors produced and distributed the first issue of *Life*. They had both been right. The documentary picture magazine was soon to kill off one of the then two largest weekly magazines and mortally wound the other. *Collier's* went down screaming that the Madison Avenue advertising people had done it in; and the *Saturday Evening Post* tried without avail to argue that its words were much more important than *Life*'s pictures. Getchell instinctively knew better. He knew the power that is in pictures to communicate instantly and fully.

Life was in tune with the times and the *Post* was not. There was a great deal of whistling in the dark by a succession of *Post* editors who followed Ben Hibbs (a staunch Norman Rockwell character) who had followed George Horace Lorimer. Pictures, they insisted could never take the place of words. But they forgot that the tuned-in, turned-on editors of *Life* were perhaps the best word people in the publishing business; that pictures were only part of *Life*'s appeal.

Even so, had television never been perfected, I have no doubt that the *Post* would have survived. In the dozen years prior to its death in the spring of 1969, it showed a good deal of editorial vigor. It published some splendid candid articles. But these are the forte of *Esquire* and the smaller magazines: the *Atlantic*, *Harper's*, the *Saturday Review*; and two very large ones, *Life* and *Look*. The *Post* made it to the top with entertainment, and it was this that television took over.

One of my chief regrets about Stirling Getchell is that he didn't live to see television. Much of it would have distressed him; he was not an entertainer. The unexploited possibilities in this new medium to instruct would have been his greatest challenge.

Two Getchell men that I was to see more of were Carleton Healy, who was known as Tim, and Harry Berk.

Underneath the fierceness of thick, shaggy eyebrows, Tim Healy was a polished gallant who deserved his designation as a scholar and a gentleman. He had been Stirling Getchell's client at the Kodak company, and I think it tickled Getchell to contemplate Tim's quiet demeanor in the charged atmosphere of an auto advertising agency where the crises succeeded each other with each tick of the clock.

Every automobile dealer in America wants something special in advertising to meet some situation that he deems to be unique in his territory every week, and we were out to give this to the Plymouth and De Soto dealers without fail. We worked seven days a week and six nights — except for Tim Healy. He worked five and a half days and no nights, and he refused to be hurried.

He couldn't have been more out of place. But he was one of the anachronisms that Stirling Getchell loved. Besides, when other men in the office complained of the pressure, Getchell could point to the unruffled existence of Tim Healy.

However, this didn't last. Healy moved quietly on; and eight years later, soon after my own advertising company was formed, I heard from him quite out of the blue.

"Is it possible," he asked over the telephone, "is it possible that you could talk interestingly to our management for, let us say, a half-hour about your agency?"

"I think I could," I replied. "But first I would like to know who your management are."

"They are the principal officers of the Canadian distilling firm of Hiram Walker-Gooderham & Worts, Ltd., and I have suggested that they look at your agency for the advertising of one of our brands."

Tim Healy always talked like a conversation in a book. He had become vice president of Hiram Walker, in charge of advertising and public relations, and he fitted as appropriately, I think, as any man could into the ivy-covered red brick headquarters at Walkerville, outside Windsor, Ontario, where he was the soul of decorum and sobriety in the monastic atmosphere of the distillery.

The result of that brief telephone conversation, in which I agreed to come to Walkerville to try to be interesting, was the assignment of what proved to be one of Walker's larger brands, to which others have been added from time to time in an association that is now in its twenty-fifth year.

I owe a great deal to Tim Healy, and I shall have more to say about the Walker business.

An equally great favorite of Stirling Getchell's was an implausible redheaded former newspaper man named Harry Berk.

Berk had been a front-page by-line reporter on the San Francisco

Examiner when I was in the classified advertising department. At about the time I joined Lord & Thomas, Harry became a public relations and publicity man. It was in that role that Getchell discovered him and took him to New York.

His name was originally Bercovich. He was well known by that name, too; but one day, in a rare idle moment, he toyed with the idea that it was, or might be, too long. Characteristically, he dispatched a ballot to twenty-five friends requesting their opinion. Should he remain Bercovich or should he become Berk?

It was my opinion that he was so widely and favorably known by the original name that it would be ridiculous to change it. I added a lengthy comment to my negative ballot and felt sure that I could convince my impulsive friend. But my letter crossed another from him in the mail which enclosed an engraved announcement that Harry Bercovich would now and forever be known as Harry *Berk*. Some of his Jewish friends were offended. They thought this was in deference to the anti-Semitic prejudices that were abroad in the world at the time, but I am sure this had no effect or importance for Berk. Anyway, anti-Semitism played a small part in the advertising business. Some of the finest creative people in the industry have always been Jews.

Harry Berk's only difficulties have been of his own making. Several years after I had returned to San Francisco from New York a young man came to see me about a job, and gave as a reference Walter Bornhoft, whom I have mentioned as Stirling Getchell's general manager.

"If you worked for Getchell," I said, probing, "surely you know Harry Berk?"

"I'll say I know him," he said. "I know him much too well. He used to make me wear his shoes downstairs every morning to get them shined in the barbershop in the Chrysler Building basement!"

The young man said this bitterly, and I suppose it had been humiliating. But this would have never occurred to Harry Berk; and I said so.

"Yes," the young man said. "But his damn feet were two sizes smaller than mine. That any fool could have seen."

Harry Berk was as impetuous and impatient as Tim Healy was quiet and collected. He was also always ready with a large idea. When I asked him, casually, one day to think about a spectacular event that we might stage to inaugurate the San Francisco exposition that was planned to celebrate the opening of the bridges across the Bay of San Francisco and the Golden Gate, Harry didn't keep me waiting a minute.

"When does the exposition open?" he asked.

"In May," I said.

"Mother's Day is in May," he said. "Invite Eleanor Roosevelt, Queen Mary and Mrs. Dionne to San Francisco and make it the greatest Mother's Day in history. That'll open your exposition like none was ever opened before. Every radio station in the world will broadcast what those three mothers have to say."

He was probably right. But even had such an event been possible to arrange, the thought of inviting the Democratic President's wife would have been anathema to the Republican Establishment in San Francisco, and the tempting idea was never officially considered.

Harry Berk spent the last two years of World War II in London as an intelligence officer in the United States Army, and there he got a large idea of an entirely different kind. He had developed an affection for England and the English people, and he wanted to live there. How better to do this, he thought, than to open a London office for an American advertising agency? And what better agency than ours?

Berk was a man of striking ingenuity who made his own rules. Once when he was complimented by his guests after a delicious meal in a small, exclusive London supper club, during a period of strict rationing and austerity, he modestly presented the chef. It was Mrs. Berk, to whom he had assigned the kitchen and the delicacies flown in from the Continent by friendly airline pilots. Colonel Harry Berk has never done anything in a small way. Today, although he claims to be retired, he is painting expansive landscapes on a large Vermont farm.

Copywriter into Businessman

DURING the years between 1934 and 1939, more than half of my life was spent in bed. The trouble that began in New York continued in San Francisco. The only difference was that now I knew what the matter was: I had the opposite of diabetes. An overactive pancreas was bringing me close to insulin shock every few hours, and the effect was devastating.

When a proper treatment was discovered I literally became well overnight. But this was a long while later. For the better part of four years I was able to be up and about in stretches of no more than four or five hours; it was something like the watches on the *Haxtum*: four hours on, eight hours off. I worked mornings in the Lord & Thomas office in the Russ Building, then taxied four blocks to call on John Cuddy and Hugh Mackenzie. After that I went home and to bed until evening. Then I put in another shift at my bedside table.

Gradually the idea took hold of me that my intermittent schedule of lost hours tinged with dread could only be the result of a psychosis, and I decided that what I needed was a psychiatrist. This was a popular thing at the time. Stirling Getchell had been analyzed, and advertising people were supposed to live under just the kind of pressure that results in mental breakdown.

The only reason I can give for this is that the decisions that affect them most are almost never made in their presence. Agency people are continuously perched on the edge of anxiety. Will their recommendations be accepted or rejected out of hand? If they are rejected will the agency be given another chance, or will the advertiser turn to an eager competing agency? Representatives face the same uncertainties. Will *Ladies Home Journal* get the schedule or will it be *McCall's?* Will television take over from printed advertising? Or which television or radio stations will get the schedule? These are some of the questions.

As I say, the decisions are nearly always made *in camera.* The advertising agency man and the media salesmen live much of the time on a tight wire that stretches thinly between hope and despair.

Of course one gets used to the exercise. The rewards for success in advertising, in many of its phases, are considerably greater than in businesses that look more skeptically at change. The search is always on for something new, and anything that is radically new is a gamble. This is why research has become so important in advertising.

My own research in 1936 took me to a number of doctors to see if I could get one to suggest psychoanalysis. The decision was one I didn't quite want to make on my own. Fortunately, I didn't.

After listening patiently to my story, Garnett Cheney, an internist at Stanford University Hospital, who was a friend of Fred Ludekens and Walter Doty, made a pronouncement that settled the matter once and for all.

"I can't tell you how to get at the source of your trouble," he said. "This is something we're just going to have to put up with for a while. On the other hand, I *can* tell you something about your principal worry. There is nothing at all the matter with your mind. And there won't be. The insulin that is burning up the sugar in your system, and making you weak, is the surest cure for psychosis."

I have always loved Garnett Cheney, for what he didn't say as well as what he did.* Anyway, I accepted the staggered hours that had become my way of life; in two shifts, after breakfast in the office and after dinner in my bedroom I managed to do as much work as I ever had before. Indeed, I did somewhat more.

With my return to San Francisco, Walter Doty moved away from the transportation and travel accounts, and while I continued with the steamship company advertising and the advertising for San Francisco as my chief responsibility, I began to look over Doty's shoulder at some of the product accounts.

At the time, Lord & Thomas in San Francisco produced the advertising for M.J.B. coffee and tea, Skippy peanut butter, Rainier beer and Associated (subsequently Tidewater) gasoline and motor oil, and the California prune growers' association and the local dairymen's league.

The main thing that was different about these commodity ac-

---

* What Garnett Cheney didn't say was that some doctors thought I must have cancer of the pancreas.

counts, aside from their more competitive muscle, was the fact that they all used radio, which was something travel advertisers consistently ignored. The travel people didn't think radio was selective enough; and it wasn't. Prospects for the steamship company required ample time, a much scarcer commodity than money. In 1936 we were still working ourselves out of the great depression, and if there was anything the businessmen in San Francisco were afraid of it was that their advertising for tourists might increase the influx of ragged refugees from Arkansas and Oklahoma. John Steinbeck had yet to write *The Grapes of Wrath*, but emigrés from the Dust Bowl already were flooding the valleys of the Sacramento and the San Joaquin. Advertisers on radio, the city fathers thought, would surely increase the flow.

Elsewhere radio was entering its heyday. Albert Lasker had recognized its potential at the outset and there was a period in the middle 1920's when Lord & Thomas placed almost half of all national advertising on the twin Red and Blue Networks of the National Broadcasting Company. (The Columbia Broadcasting System was not formed until 1927.)

Remarkable as it may seem in the ceaseless jangle of commercial messages on radio in later years, advertising in the beginning was limited to naming the company through whose "courtesy" any given program was broadcast. This, plainly, was not enough for Albert Lasker, and in no time at all the radio commercial as we know it now was on the air. Salesmanship-in-print had become also salesmanship out of the sky.

It was this striking new dimension in advertising and selling that Mr. Lasker wished most to exploit, but he was an impresario at heart, and the programs that carried commercial messages for Lord & Thomas clients were among the most successful in attracting and holding large audiences. One, *Amos 'n' Andy*, brought to the air a pair of blackface comedians played by Freeman Gosden and Charles Correll five nights a week between 7 P.M. and 7:15; and the program became a national habit. Telephone calls throughout the country dropped fifty per cent and water pressure increased by the same amount during the fifteen-minute time period, and movie theaters were forced to stop their projection machines while they piped in the radio show.

Tall-talking Andy was a dreamer of fantastic dreams and a designer of eccentric schemes, none of which got him into anything but trouble. Gentle Amos had to bail him out. Most of the dialogue took place in the office of the Fresh Air Taxicab Company in which Amos and Andy were partners. Correll and Gosden (who later became one of President Eisenhower's favorite golf and bridge partners), played the leads and all the supporting parts. Doubtless they could have gone on for many years in radio, where every listener saw them his own way in his mind's eye. Translated into television they became finite and their magic was gone. They simply didn't fit the mind pictures.

Nevertheless, *Amos 'n' Andy* wrote a chapter in the history of entertainment that is unlikely ever to be duplicated. (For one thing, the NAACP would never stand for even such genteel caricatures.)

For better or worse, and certainly the point is moot, Lord & Thomas also engineered the first successful radio serial of the type that came to be known as soap opera. This first of a kind was the simpering *Story of Mary Marlowe*. It was written by Frank Hummert for Albert Lasker for the advertising of Kleenex tissues and it was widely copied. Hummert and his wife were the masters of the long-drawn-out, lugubrious cliffhangers; at one time, after Hummert left Lord & Thomas to found his own advertising agency with Hill Blackett and Glen Sample, the Hummerts had a dozen soap operas running simultaneously. Such was the pace of these daily fifteen-minute programs that a conversation in an apartment-house elevator between floors could be stretched over three fifteen-minute broadcasts.

It was the job of the agencies in those days to put most of the programs together, and no one did this better than Lord & Thomas. When Albert Lasker decided that *Amos 'n' Andy* had sold Pepsodent to everyone they were ever likely to, his son, Edward Lasker, shrewdly chose an unknown named Bob Hope to take their place, and Hope became radio's brightest and most durable luminary, and one of the few who would increase his popularity in the movies and television.

Walter Doty was the first of our group in San Francisco who foresaw the possibilities in radio. By 1937 the Associated Oil Company was broadcasting Pacific Coast League professional baseball games and Pacific Coast Conference collegiate football games; the M.J.B. people were sponsoring a singing group called the Rhythm Boys which featured a youngster from Gonzaga University named Harry Lillis Crosby, who later would become known as the incomparable Bing.

In New York and Chicago, the comedians held the top spots. Besides Bob Hope for Pepsodent, Jack Benny held sway for Jell-O, and the homely team of Fibber McGee and Molly made the microphone a joy for Johnson's self-polishing Glo-Coat floor wax. Altogether the comedians had the whole nation listening, and repeating their best gags, and laughing again each morning after their nighttime programs.

Radio in the years preceding America's entry into World War II was

Bing Crosby, fresh out of Gonzaga University, was one of the
three Rhythm Boys who sang
tunefully for M.J.B. Coffee.

Hedda Hopper reported on
Hollywood, first for Sunkist
oranges and lemons, later for
Armour canned meats.

no more serious than television is today. But somehow it managed to follow somewhat less of a pattern. To be sure, it was comedy that drew the largest audiences, with popular music and drama following in that order, but the attempt was made seriously to keep the comedy fresh. Radio didn't cost as much as television. The temptation to play safe with carbon copies of successful programs was not so fearfully embraced. Radio was a new communication form (or so a lot of people thought); television in its present condition is purely a device for making money.

Radio represented the youthful, wide-eyed, hopeful phase of broadcasting, when everybody in it was trying to make a mark. Insofar as advertising was concerned, a radio commercial was relatively easy to produce; you wrote it and you got a cast to act it out, in shirtsleeves or sweaters. Television requires a complete theatrical or motion picture production. It may take dozens of people, not counting the cast or getting the actors ready, simply to record a single minute's action in a simple outdoor scene.

The cost is fantastic. A one-minute commercial in color may easily cost $30,000 to make, and as much as $70,000 to broadcast over a network a single time. But all television costs are incredible, and the profits are even more so for the networks and the stations. It is an unlucky network station in a major market that doesn't net an amount equal to the owners' original investment every year!

The broadcasters learned a bitter lesson when they let radio programming get away from them, into the hands of advertisers and their agencies, and they have been careful that no such calamity should befall them again. It would be foolish to deny that in its last days as the principal means of broadcasting, radio had deteriorated. It never did approach its potential in any area save popular entertainment. Television, on the contrary, has shown signs of limitless possibility in every field where it is applicable, from documentary news reporting to grand opera, and at every subdivision in between.

The possibilities are ignored by the broadcasters. They are in business for profit. Their rare attempts at program improvement are aimed solely at beating the competition at whatever it is doing successfully to attract audience. Since this is inevitably at the lowest artistic and intellectual level, we find television today a huge disappointment as a cultural medium.

The broadcasters who took programming away from the advertisers and the agents, as they most surely should have done, have proved to be capricious and irresponsible. Any use of the airwaves should be a public trust. Instead, all too often, the networks and the stations have exploited their privilege entirely in their own interest.

In my long hours in bed, which Garnett Cheney insisted on even when I couldn't sleep, I began to think about advertising not so much from the standpoint of a copywriter with clients to please and deadlines to meet, as in the complete sense of the business and its obligation to produce results.

There was another factor. With manuscripts pouring in from the *Post* and other periodicals, Fred Ludekens had no time for the smaller advertising jobs. He designed and illustrated the color pages for Californians, Inc., and for the Dollar Lines. But I began to make a good many of my own layouts for the black-and-white advertisements, and I planned and ordered the illustrations and the typography.

This was different from the days at the *Examiner* and at the Waldron agency. There I was illustrating someone else's ideas. Now I was planning the whole advertisement. I was seeing it totally and applying the rules that Ludekens and Doty and I had worked out to the complete presentation; and I was putting all the parts together.

Despite Getchell's admonition about the softness of travel advertising, I began to apply to ours a single hard measurement. This was the number of requests for literature that each advertisement returned, and where these came from and how many resulted in sales. It was no good to get batches of requests from a single neighborhood in Peoria, Illinois, or Bronxville, New York, or Lexington, Kentucky, for example, because these only meant that some hard-pressed teacher had suggested as a project pasting up a picture book with scenes cut from our brochures. But we had become expert in our suspicions and the respondents who were suspect got small, inexpensive folders.

Moreover, we checked the names on the likeliest-looking coupons through retail credit associations and determined whether the senders could reasonably be classed as prospects. When they could, the names were sent to local travel agents throughout the country for follow-up. The results of this told us pretty specifically which advertisements worked best, and these were either repeated or carefully adapted in what we conceived to be their most important aspects.

Of course, if Dollar Lines advertising produced the sale of a single stateroom that would otherwise have gone unoccupied, say to Manila, it would have paid to spend right up to the cost of food to sell it. And I suspect there were times when we approached this limit. However, our total advertising cost was something less than five per cent of U.S. passenger revenues. In every case, we followed up our inquiries as carefully as we could, and tried to build our advertising accordingly.

One thing our Californians, Inc., coupons told us was what appealed most to people who wanted to visit San Francisco and central and northern California. Whenever we ran a good-sized picture of the Wawona tree in Yosemite National Park we hit the jackpot.* Pictures of the giant redwood trees along the Coast also did well. Yosemite Falls did well. Lake Tahoe produced more than an average number of coupons. But the Wawona tree, with the road running through its massive trunk and the automobiles emerging from this unique tunnel topped every other attraction. San Francisco's cable cars were next. Then came the Spanish missions.

When you think about these things, the reasons are fairly obvious. People react to variations of things they know, to new dimensions and new shapes and colors that relate clearly to past experience. They do not react favorably as a rule to new things, and they are apt to be ill at ease with new aspects.

Everybody knows what a tree is like. But the Wawona tree was big enough to drive a car through. Almost everybody (in 1937) had ridden in trolley cars on flat streets; in San Francisco there were cars that climbed impossible hills, pulled by cables in a slot in the street. Churches are churches the world over, but the California missions were the relics of a foreign influence in our history that had been broken less than a hundred years ago.

In 1938, when the San Francisco–Oakland Bay Bridge was nearing completion, panoramic pictures of this world's longest span brought inquiries to Californians, Inc., at the lowest cost in our experience. A bridge was something anyone could understand, and it was clear that everyone in America wanted to see this one.

A year later when the much more dramatic Golden Gate Bridge was about to be completed, we undertook to make an unusual presentation of it by looking down from the bridge deck, along one of the giant red towers to the pier below and the deck of a passing ship. This was not the way people look at epic bridges and our coupon return was dismal; the cost was about ten times what we had expected. Variety may be the spice of life, but advertising works best in familiar terms.

1939 was not only the year when the long Bay Bridge was complete, and the white ferryboats began to disappear. It was also the year when I was made manager of Lord & Thomas in San Francisco.

My days in the office had lengthened almost to the conventional

* On May 2, 1969, the United Press reported the discovery by a road-clearing crew that the mammoth tree had toppled during the winter. The tunnel chopped after a fire in the tree's base in 1881, measured 8 feet wide, 9 feet high, and 26 feet long. The tree itself stood 234 feet tall and was estimated to be two thousand years old.

pattern. I now went to bed immediately after dinner each evening, and stayed in bed all of Saturdays and Sundays. I was slowly recovering more strength, but the daily ebb in my energy persisted. I had moments of fears and hours of depression because I never knew when the fatigue would become overpowering. Fortunately, no one among my business associates knew that it still existed; I had learned to cover up.

Even so, my elevation to manager was not so much any doing of mine as it was Walter Doty's. Had he not decamped to *Sunset* magazine, where he became editor, in the fall of 1938, he would surely have been named manager of Lord & Thomas when there occurred a series of shifts throughout the company that left the San Francisco office without a head. Don Francisco, the Pacific Coast manager, who lived in Los Angeles, became president of Lord & Thomas and was moved to New York. John Whedon, the San Francisco manager, was put in charge in Chicago. Fred Ludekens was recruited by Don Francisco to become chief art director in New York.

Had I had any inkling of the impending change, I selfishly would have urged Walter Doty not to accept the proffered editorship; I would have tried to keep him in the agency where he had contributed so much. Still, I doubt if I could have succeeded. Doty's is a pioneer spirit. He has little interest in repeating experiences, however satisfactory they may have been. At about the time when I began to feel at home with our product accounts, and in radio, Doty had had enough of both.

A series of poster stamps that he had conceived for the Associated Oil Company had been a spectacular success. These were distributed throughout the eleven Western states in the 144 scenic and historical areas they depicted, and collecting and trading them became a source of pleasure for thousands of Western motorists. The stamps fitted into folders that carefully described the scenes and placed each one in historic perspective.* The illustrations were by Fred Ludekens, but the concept had been Walter Doty's and he carried it with him to *Sunset*, where the authentic interpretation of Western living in its pages soon came to have encyclopedic authority.

The new editor made his writers write the way he had tried to teach me to write; to forget everything but the message; to be sure that this was accurate, and to make it clear and complete. Before long several hundred thousand subscribers to *Sunset* were using the magazine as an inspired homemaking guide. The national home service magazines had failed to discover that living on the Pacific Coast is

---

* How much better than the money giveaway games the oil companies are playing today! They used to show more sense.

different from living anywhere east of the Rocky Mountains. *House & Garden, House Beautiful,* and *Better Homes & Gardens* were studied for their beautiful pictures of unlikely interiors and exteriors alike and Walter Doty capitalized on the need in the West for more useful material.

The success of *Sunset* has been exceeded in regional magazine publishing only by the *New Yorker.*

The appointment of Don Francisco as president of Lord & Thomas was one of the saddest mistakes in our business and it gave me a lesson in human relations. Don Francisco was a man of marked ability. As manager of Lord & Thomas in Los Angeles he had led a successful fight against a discriminatory tax that would have put all of California's chain stores out of business. Such was the appreciation of some millions of aroused housewives, who liked the savings the chain stores brought them, that I believe he could easily have been elected governor.

He would have made a good one too. Don Francisco looked every inch a governor. He was tall and broad-shouldered, with a tanned handsome face, almost a movie actor's profile, and a warm, ingratiating smile. His Spanish-sounding name was pure chance; he had been born in Michigan of English parents; but the name had a special appeal to Californians with their Spanish heritage, nevertheless. More important, Don Francisco had a gift for organization and cooperation that was outstanding. Everyone who knew him both liked and respected him.

Unhappily, it was a disorganized and noncooperative advertising agency that he went to New York to head. He stood between the giant personalities of Albert Lasker and George Washington Hill, who, as president of the American Tobacco Company, was Mr. Lasker's most important client. They inevitably agreed with each other at the expense of the man in the middle. To do otherwise would seem to be to follow him, and this neither was willing to do. It was a matter of honor. And ego. Don Francisco, like a number of men both before him and after him, was the victim.

He resigned from the uneasy presidency of Lord & Thomas to join Nelson Rockefeller in his Office for Latin American Affairs, and served there with distinction until he returned to the advertising agency business as a principal in J. Walter Thompson Company, the largest agency in the world (then and now), at the end of World War II.

Fred Ludekens was more fortunate at the outset than Don Francisco. As art director in the New York office he quickly ran afoul of George Hill because he, too, was inserted into the continuing contest between the two principals. So far as Mr. Hill was concerned, Albert

Lasker insisted upon being his own art director, just as he insisted upon being his own copy director. He wouldn't let Ludekens see Hill, and Ludekens was given full credit for anything and everything Hill didn't understand or didn't like.

Later I learned that Mr. Lasker was almost always right, and almost never wrong. He sincerely believed that the right ideas and designs were either his or inspired by him; the ones that proved wrong or unacceptable were always someone else's. Here the wrong ideas were charged to Ludekens. When I came to know George Hill, I realized that he and Fred Ludekens would have enjoyed working together. Both admired ability in other people. But it was too late then. Ludekens had all the orders for illustrations that he could fill, and he left Lord & Thomas to become one of the most successful illustrators of our time.

The departure of Walter Doty and Fred Ludekens from San Francisco meant that I became manager of Lord & Thomas without either of its strongest talents.

Garnett Cheney had rescued me from what a number of other doctors had concluded was a fatal illness. His insistence upon rest had given me long hours to think about my business, to dissect advertising and study its anatomy as few advertising men have probably ever had time to do. I had become so sure that I knew both what I wanted to say in advertising and how I wanted to say it, for each of our clients, that I set my typewriter to the required column measure and wrote out the requisite number of lines time and time again without recourse to an eraser. Moreover, I saw to it that if I was writing an advertisement that was to be set in type in two or three columns, I made every bottom paragraph cross a column — to avoid an easy place to stop reading.

The truth is that I had learned the basic principles of advertising from Doty and Ludekens, both of whom insisted upon the obligation of the advertiser to return something of interest and something of importance in exchange for the reader's or listener's time. John Cuddy had taught me a great deal about writing; he did this by questioning my use of words, making me hunt for precisely the right one to say exactly what I meant; and to know that I meant it.

But none of this would have had any meaning without Garnett Cheney's faith that over a period of time he could arrest the progress of my debilitating condition and return me to a normal existence. That he died before my rehabilitation was complete was a tragedy. He was only a few years older than I, three at the most, and his health gave every evidence of being perfect while mine could hardly have been more wretched.

He died of the cancer that I was supposed to have had.

With Tears in His Voice

On my first day as manager of Lord & Thomas in San Francisco, I was summoned by the president of the coffee company that was the second largest client of our office, and fired. There had been no warning, no word of dissatisfaction, and I was aghast.

The M.J.B. Company was a family concern. Originally M.J.B. had stood for M. J. Brandenstein. The German name had been altered during World War I to the more neutral Bransten. I had never met Edward Bransten, the patriarch of the family and the company president. I had dealt only with his nephew, Joseph, a patron of the arts, and their advertising manager, Paul Beutas. This was my first visit to their offices.

"I am sorry, Mr. Cone," Mr. Edward Bransten said, and I believe there were tears in his eyes. "I am sorry that I can no longer be associated with Lord & Thomas."

What possibly could I have done, I asked myself; or what had I not done, in less than four hours in my new job, to alienate the Branstens? But Mr. Edward went on. "I have nothing but respect for you, Mr. Cone," he said. "I have nothing but respect for Mr. Lasker. But Mr. Lasker has not the same respect for me."

"That is impossible," I said, interrupting; I thought it was.

"Wait," Mr. Edward said. "Wait. If Mr. Albert Lasker had respect for Edward Bransten, he would not have notified me this morning by Western Union telegram that Lord & Thomas in Chicago now will make advertising for the coffee of Folger's."

"But — ," I tried to interrupt again, for I knew that Folger's and M.J.B. were marketed in different regions of the country. They were no way competitive. Furthermore, advertising for the two brands would be made in different offices by different people.

"But not a single word," the sad-eyed, bald little man continued. He shook his head mournfully, and with the tears now in his voice he repeated, "Mr. Lasker has not the respect for me to tell me first that he is going in bed with Folger's, to let me hear this in a Western Union telegram when the arrangement is completed. No, no, no," he said. "We must find a respecting advertising agency."

And they did. Four months after the abrupt notification of our dismissal, the New York advertising agency of Batten, Barton, Durstine & Osborn, under a guarantee from the Branstens that they would not lose money, opened a San Francisco branch that became in a few years the largest of all the national agencies operating in California.

If only Albert Lasker had taken time to telephone Edward Bransten before the acquisition of the Folger account was announced, it is doubtful if Edward Bransten would have raised the slightest objection. He would have had no reason to. However, the kindly old gentleman found it impossible to accept what he considered an affront to his dignity.

There are so many reasons to call upon to fire an advertising agency that no one has ever listed them all. For one thing, terminating an advertising agency relationship is one of the easiest things in business to do.

As an agent, this has rarely been my prerogative. Once when it was, as we shall see, I made my biggest mistake. Otherwise, I have been on the receiving end of a dismissal a number of times, and for various reasons; some good and some not so good. Once our company was dismissed because one of its office managers mailed some harsh political judgments to a hostile California newspaper editor in an agency-labeled envelope. It was felt that he was trying to influence the press, and that he was I have no doubt. Later on we were terminated by the client who had inspired the ill-considered mailing. Apparently we hadn't done anything foolish for him lately.

Another client walked us unceremoniously off the plank because one of our managers wouldn't quit his job and team up with the client in an advertising agency of their own. This was a client that we stood to lose either way.

Sometimes the timing of a dismissal is almost unbelievable. Several years ago we were discharged by a large advertiser only a few weeks after his company had dramatically done away with its entire advertising department and delegated its authority as well as its duties to the agency. No reason was ever given for the termination, which was handed to me by a junior officer of the company while the man who was responsible hid in his office. We were generously paid off; so generously that it seemed to represent a feeling of disturbed conscience. Still, there was no explanation for the company's abrupt action.

About half the time agencies and their clients who come to a parting of the ways do so because of a gradual deterioration in their regard for each other. It is something like a marriage when the bonds become dry and brittle. On the other hand, management changes lead almost as a matter of course to agency terminations in many cases. New managements that result from dissatisfaction with old management tend to look askance at continuing with the same agency; others seem to feel that inheriting an agency impinges upon their personal prerogatives. I think we have lost more accounts for this reason than any other.

Still, there are others. One account, a large one, was lost by us because a sales manager blamed the agency for a costly mistake that was really his own. Several years later this man was expelled from a country club for fabricating his golf score in a tournament. What exactly this had to do with our reappointment by his company, I do not know, but he was discharged by his employer and we were reappointed shortly after the incident on the golf course.

Terminating an advertising agency is a little bit like changing a doctor. One rarely tells the old doctor why one has left him. Maybe the patient doesn't really know. Maybe he has heard something about a new man who has developed an interesting theory of medication or diet or exercise that he thinks might successfully be applied to himself; maybe he has just caught up with the theory in that bane of all doctor's existence, the Medicine section of *Time* magazine. Whatever the reason, the patient goes off to the new man, avoiding the old doctor on the street and at parties, and easing his conscience by saying what a wonderful fellow he is — "a little old-fashioned, perhaps, but terribly good just the same."

This is the way people talk about advertising agencies, too; after they secretly call in, or let in, a new group. The only thing wrong with this is the hypocrisy that it involves. The reluctance with which most advertisers admit to their agencies that changes are impending, even when these are completely planned and dated, can only be accounted for on the assumption that the reasons for the change were not very good ones. Somebody had been sold something.*

---

* As part of the very great attention being paid currently to the youth market, there has developed a cult in advertising that is represented by a group of small

But let me come back to the analogy with the doctor-patient relationship. Let us say that the agency in question hasn't been doing a thoroughly satisfactory job; something is wrong, somewhere, somehow. The easiest thing in the world is to fire the agency. The trouble is that this may have the worst possible result. The new agency may take months and all kinds of risk to acquire the knowledge and experience that was discarded in the change. A friend of mine had an unsuccessful operation for the removal of a cataract; in fact, it was a total failure. But when it came to a second operation, he went resolutely back to the doctor who had failed him. "Who knows more about my case?" he reasoned. "Who else could know so well why the first operation did not succeed? Who has so much at stake in success this time?"

The answers to these questions were the same. The operation was performed by the original surgeon, and it was a complete success.

If more businessmen took the same sensible attitude toward their advertising agencies, and worked out their problems with them instead of transferring those problems, this would be a more productive and satisfactory business for everyone concerned. The longtime relationships between such highly successful consumer goods companies as Procter & Gamble, General Foods, General Motors, Kodak, Kimberly-Clark, Armour and Company, Hallmark Cards — and most other industry leaders — and their agencies is easily overlooked by executives recruited from law and public accounting firms who view advertising through the narrow apertures of their own prejudices.

It is one of the ironic axioms of the business that everyone is an advertising expert, for it is the self-appointed and self-anointed experts who are responsible for most advertising failures.

All this, however, has nothing to do with the Branstens. Their feelings had been hurt. They had the best of reasons for dismissing the agency, and I have been good friends with Joe Bransten ever since the eventful day.

How does it feel to be fired?

The answer is *awful*, and the initial reaction is usually a combination of pain and resentment and a wild wish somehow to retaliate; all this without regard to the circumstances.

---

advertising agencies devoted fanatically to the offbeat. Some of this is undoubtedly an attempt to capitalize on the irreverent copy that Doyle Dane Bernbach created for Volkswagen and Avis, but in following a "hippie" concept Bernbach's effective realism in advertising is lost.

The Bransten case was an exception. The agency was clearly to blame and I could only be sorry for what had happened.

Usually, as I have indicated, the break in advertiser-agency relations results from a series of dissatisfactions or a growing gulf between the two parties that may be philosophical or more often, representative of nothing more specific than a difference in personalities on the two sides of the advertising manager's desk.

The final decisive action is almost always the advertiser's. It is the agent whose feelings are usually hurt; and the hurt is no way lessened by the fact that he has usually anticipated the fateful action. He has done everything he could to heal the breach, and as his attempts have failed, his resentment has grown. He begins to think that he should have resigned the account at the first sign of trouble; or at least gone over the head of the client's advertising people to the general management to present his case. It is the advertising department people who should have been discharged, he thinks, and he writes out all the reasons he can think of to present in rebuttal.

The truth is, though, that there is no rebuttal. The advertiser must back up his people or discharge them, and it is a rare circumstance when he knows enough about the inner workings of his advertising department or brand managers with the agency even to question them seriously in such matters. When things go according to plan, there is no reason to dig into them; when they do not, the first place to look for trouble is in the agency operation. The fact that agency plans and agency production must always be approved by the advertiser's own people (except when an unusual Hugh Mackenzie waives this right) and that they have been approved all during the troubled period is usually overlooked. Anyway, most problems in advertiser-agency relationships are problems of temperament and these tend to become mutual.

As a consequence of feeling himself badly dealt with, the discharged agent is filled immediately with thoughts of revenge. He tells himself that he will solicit his ex-client's chief competitor and if he is successful he will bring the ex-client figuratively to his knees. That this rarely happens is well known, and the dream of retribution soon is dissolved.

The only solace in the unhappy affair is that if the advertiser was truly at fault the people involved will eventually be found out and discharged in turn. This has no effect on the employees the agency was obliged to let go when the account was terminated, but this is the way it is. Most terminations give ninety days' notice, and such is the continuing growth in the advertising business that this is usually sufficient time for most of the displaced to be reassigned within the agency or to arrange new employment.

Nothing, however, compensates for the awful feeling that comes to every advertising agency person when the announcement is made that an account is leaving. It comes like a hard blow in the pit of the stomach. You can't do anything about it except wait to get your breath back.

Woefully, that is all you are likely to get back. A bad advertising agency decision is something most advertisers like to forget. Not very long ago our company was discharged by a manufacturer for whom we had done a job that had to be rated excellent on the basis of sales results that could only be attributed to advertising. Nevertheless, when the president of the company was replaced, for reasons having nothing to do with sales, and a new sales manager was subsequently appointed, the agency was at once put on notice.

"I want everything new, everything different," the man announced with the jut-jawed finesse of a Marine drill sergeant. In our initial confrontation he refused to discuss any of the strategy of the successful past. After two more bitterly unpleasant meetings where the man's attitude reached its high point of rudeness when he turned his back on the presentation of new television commercials, the agency was discharged.

Three months later, both the belligerent sales manager and the foolish president who had hired him met the same fate. One agency change was enough for the company's chairman; I am sure he ordered no more. But that hardly righted a patent wrong.

The tragedy of unemployment that results to advertising agency people as the result of account losses is apt to be overdramatized. Advertising agency salaries are adjusted to the vagaries of the business. They are set with the expectation that relatively few will grow old in agency service. This is mostly because the reciprocal advertiser organizations are in constant flux, with younger men moving to the top. These young men inevitably want their own counterparts, and they get them.

However, this rarely spells disaster for the older agency man. He has been extremely well paid. He has usually accumulated a considerable estate; and, above all, he has acquired a competence that very often makes it possible for him to become a valued principal in some burgeoning manufacturing or distributing business that lacks just what he has to offer by way of this experience.

If this sounds like too pleasant a generalization (particularly in view of the rash of sordid novels about business politics and intrigue,

and the dispirited army of losers), let me say that I do not know
of a competent advertising agency man who has retired into
penury.* One reason, of course, is that advertising people are in the
business of establishing and explaining values; they are aware of the
uncertainties of the business and they fortify themselves accordingly.

* The only indigent former advertising man of my acquaintance is an incompetent
who was fired out of my company twenty-six years ago.

The Colonel's Lady

DESPITE the loss of the coffee account, Lord & Thomas in San Francisco prospered.

The Sun-Maid raisin growers returned to the agency after a hiatus of several years. We received a number of assignments for food and laundry products from Safeway Stores. Lingan Warren, the impulsive, somewhat quixotic president of this dominant chain, was determined to beat the nationwide brands at their own game, which was advertising, and the accounts for Safeway's private brands, which we shared with J. Walter Thompson Company and McCann-Erickson, were very desirable. In addition, we were appointed for the advertising of California's leading brand of olives, Lindsay; California's largest-selling wine, Roma; the account of a small but ambitious fruit and vegetable packer, Sunnyvale; and two important retail chains, Roos Bros., which was, and is, the West's leading men's clothing company, and Safeway again, this time for institutional advertising.

The next to last was in many ways most exciting and most rewarding.

The half-dozen Roos Bros. stores, in San Francisco and the San Francisco Bay area (now grown to thirty-one after a successful merger) were characterized even then by a policy of innovation that approached audacity. The Roos stores were the first in the country to advertise "wardrobes" rather than "suits" for men. These were based on the combinations that were possible with matching coat and trousers and complementary and contrasting sports jackets and slacks. Just so, Roos Bros. discovered a gold mine that unlike most of the diggings in California has been an unfailing producer every year since.

Colonel Robert Roos was a brilliant, irascible potentate who moodily ran his satrapy from a black-walled, white-carpeted throne room whose doors were electrically opened and closed, and at whose bar the very simplest agreements were generally sealed only after long and often tempestuous arguments, but in rare old scotch or bourbon.

I very nearly was not invited to sample either one.

It was strictly a hunch on the part of the Colonel's advertising manager that brought me to the inner sanctum at all. The hunch belonged to an extraordinary woman. Her name is Eleanor Lyons. She never, to my knowledge, has had an advertising idea that wasn't practical and worthwhile, because that is the way her mind works. You could almost watch it under her nicely coiffed, prematurely gray hair. She knew precisely what she wanted and she outlined it in broad terms. Then she let you work out the details.

What she wanted from us was advertising that would give the Roos stores some of the aura of authority that Kenneth Collins had built into the advertising for Macy's in New York.

"There must be something better, something more important, than merely another retail clothier shouting low prices," Eleanor Lyons insisted. "There must be a way to establish an important character, a unique personality, to be an institution, like Macy's. Or, if you won't laugh, like Tiffany."

I said I thought there was. And I told Eleanor Lyons that I thought I knew how to do this.

But when I was let into the Colonel's black office, through the electric doors, I wasn't so sure that I wasn't out of my depth. Wanting not to seem cocky (which I certainly didn't feel) I ventured the opinion that Roos Bros. was doing a mighty good advertising job as things stood.

"You couldn't be more right," the Colonel boomed. "One hundred thousand dollars a month right. Twelve hundred thousand dollars a year right. It is a crazy idea of this dear girl that some advertising agency can do something for us that we ourselves can't do much better. Tell me what it is that we should expect from some advertising agency that has never sold a necktie or a suit.

"Nothing," the Colonel said, answering his own question. "Nothing. Absolutely nothing."

The answer in the man's mind appeared to be clear; as far as he was concerned the matter was settled.* But the distaste with which the Colonel had spit out the words "advertising agency," and on

* It should be mentioned here that retailers pay a lower rate in newspapers than either manufacturers or wholesale distributors. No agency commission is allowed. And Colonel Roos was obviously not intrigued with the idea of adding an agency fee to his bill for space.

"some" advertising agency that was obviously Lord & Thomas, made it necessary for me to make him eat those words if I could.

By trying to be polite, I had let Eleanor Lyons down badly. I hadn't been adroit enough to follow the lead she had given me, and the Colonel had pounced on my pleasantry and turned it against both of us. He was a hard man to sell, and I hadn't helped his lady at all.

It was midday on a Friday when Colonel Roos coldly pressed a button in a panel on his desk and opened the way out of his office. I wished that I might never have to see him again; but Eleanor Lyons had told me that the man knew Albert Lasker very well, and I knew that I would have to make another try, disagreeable as this might be.

On Monday I telephoned him to say that I wanted to see him.

"I want to show you a newspaper advertisement," I said. "It will show you how to do everything Eleanor Lyons was trying to tell you and all she wants to do in advertising, and it will do everything you're already doing well better than you've ever done it."

I didn't sound like me even to myself. But the Colonel's unwillingness to listen to me after my soft opening three days before had made me furious. Also, there was the possible involvement of Albert Lasker in the affair. I was a new, insecure young manager, and I couldn't have his friend casting doubts about me.

"All right," the Colonel said, with what seemed a great effort. "I'll see what you've got, but I haven't much time." And off I started with my exhibits.

The idea that had come to me in Eleanor Lyons's office had grown on me on Friday night, in bed, which is where I have always done my best work, particularly under pressure, and most particularly when angry. I had written the full-page newspaper advertisement on Saturday, and had it laid out and illustrated on Sunday by a puzzled young art director named Harry Fletcher who couldn't understand why he should give up a picnic with his girl for a cranky non-client.

In the beginning, I was only working to square myself with Eleanor Lyons and to build up my case if I had to use it for Albert Lasker; but by the time I got the Colonel on the telephone on Monday morning I had no doubt that I would accomplish both my objectives at Colonel Roos's expense. What I planned to do was show the man the advertisement I had made, get his acknowledgment that the idea was good for a long series, then make him an elaborate gift of it and depart on my high horse.

When I showed him the advertisement he stared at it for several minutes, saying nothing. Then he got up from behind his enormous black desk and standing between the two silk flags that flanked it at the rear, the stars and stripes of the United States and the flag of

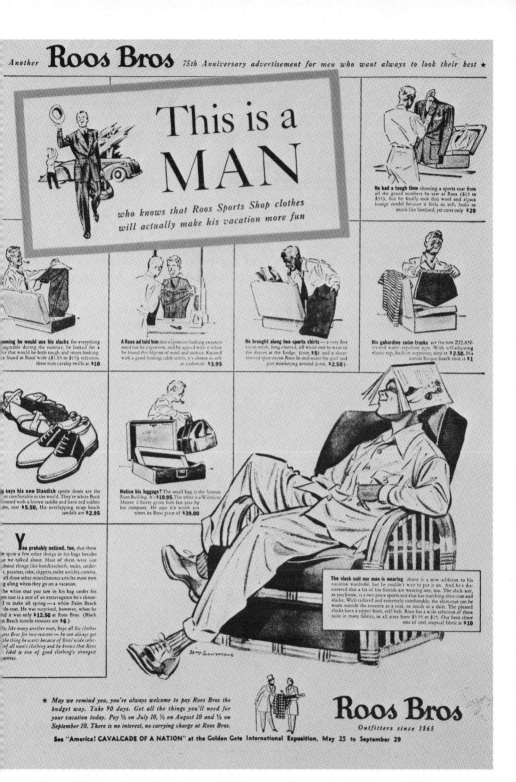

One of a series of large-scale newspaper advertisements that sold whole wardrobes instead of merely suits.

his own California National Guard regiment, the Colonel cleared his throat and said, with full military dignity, "I knew you would come through."

I had hoped to win the day. But I only tied it. Colonel Roos had known very well that I would react to his taunts; for despite his dislike of agencies (and their fees, in this case) he wanted Eleanor Lyons to have her way.

The advertisement, which was framed at top and bottom with an institutional promise from Roos Bros., and which told the story of the featured merchandise in specific terms of design and manufacture instead of the generalities and tired expletives that were the rule in retail men's clothing advertising, became the pattern for a series that ran unchanged in format for almost ten years.

So proud of it did the Colonel become that he sent me to New York to present the story of the Roos advertising to Bernard Gimbel with the idea that Gimbel's would jump at the chance to get something like it from Lord & Thomas in New York. Mr. Gimbel, whose daughter had recently married Mr. Lasker's son, knew all about Colonel Roos's advertising and he was unimpressed. In his view, the only advertising worth copying by any New York store was Macy's.

One of the things Colonel Roos pretended not to understand was our use of radio. His wife turned it on, he said, and it was a confounded nuisance. You couldn't show merchandise on it. No one could make a sensible comparison of what was offered. "Besides," he maintained, "no one listens to radio anyway. Only Mrs. Roos."

But the Colonel was a chronic grumbler.

Once we had established our newspaper advertising, which he understood thoroughly, he let us play with radio and we had a hilarious time. We already had Hoagy Carmichael on the air for Safeway, but he had been Ling Warren's selection and he was Ling Warren's personal property. The Roos Bros. show was entirely our own. Audience participation programs were just beginning to be popular in 1939 and 1940, and we built one in which the listening audience could play detective. The name of our program was *Whodunit?* The plots were devised, the dramas written, and the leading parts played by a one-time burlesque comedian named Louis X. Lansworth, who was another longtime friend of Fred Ludekens; and if the plots were something less than original, the parts Lou Lansworth wrote for himself ran the whole gamut of stock burlesque dialects from German to Jewish to Irish to Chinese, and they were full of fun.

The big programs in those years were *The Chase & Sanborn Hour*, with Edgar Bergen and the ventriloquist's saucy dummy, Charlie

McCarthy; *Maxwell House Showboat*; *Lux Radio Theater*; *The Jack Benny Show*; and *The Fred Allen Show*. Benny was the favorite performer. Allen was the most brilliant and the dialogue that he wrote was unfailingly witty and frequently inspired. Still, none of these people and none of the shows pleased us as much as *Whodunit?* with its murders always pinned on the unlikeliest prospects.

The series performed well for Roos Bros. Items advertised on the show sold well. However, I am afraid that our greatest pleasure in *Whodunit?* was in naming the characters after various of our friends. On the chance that they would be featured in incredible roles they were our most avid listeners. The program ended when Lansworth married our leading lady and they emigrated south to the greener pastures of Hollywood. Somewhat later Lansworth wrote a novel with the strange title of *Over the River, Charlie* that was as complicated as some of his radio scripts, and I never could finish reading it.

The last time I saw Colonel Roos was after I had moved to Chicago and he came there to investigate the murder of his sister-in-law, who was killed in her room in the Drake Hotel by an assailant who has never been identified — although one of the Chicago newspapers is supposed still to have a reporter assigned to the case.

Eleanor Lyons I see whenever I can. She is constantly engaged with new ideas and she always shares them. Her latest is the conviction that advertising is the most dynamic force in any retail operation, everything else being fixed once the shelves and the racks are stocked and the selling personnel assembled. Roos-Atkins, which is the company that resulted from a merger, is making this theory pay off via the largest advertising schedule of any men's stores in America.*

Our second venture into the retail field, triggered by our success with Roos Bros., proved to be more educational than lucrative. This was with the Safeway stores which, traditionally, had run large newspaper advertisements that were really no more than price listings (the private label product accounts being handled independently and apart from the shopper pages).

The shopper advertisements were almost repulsively ugly, and a little research indicated to us that most housewives paid a minimum of attention to the listings except to scan the lines of heavy black type for real bargains. Where there were no deeply cut prices the advertisements, even in full facing pages, apparently had no tangible effect. They merely kept the stores' name before the public.

* Most famous of Eleanor Lyons's graduates in advertising is William A. Hewitt, chairman of Deere & Company.

No one who was a passionate follower of Albert Lasker could believe that this was truly advertising. Or that the prodigious space that was involved couldn't be made more productive.

Again we set to work, as we had with the sterile Roos Bros. advertisements, to transform the Safeway newspaper pages into something that rewarded readers for their attention. By designing the pages in orderly columns and reducing the extra bold type, we made space for menu suggestions, recipes, party hints, even diets; and facts about Safeway's procurement of all the items of fresh produce, meat and dairy products that were available at Safeway stores on an exclusive basis.

It didn't matter, we reasoned, where one bought Wheaties or Bisquick or Carnation milk or Jell-O; wherever these well-known products were purchased they were the same. Moreover, Safeway's private labels and usually lower prices on similar packaged groceries had a long way to go to prove superiority. On the other hand, it was possible to show persuasive and memorable reasons why meat and produce at Safeway were fresher and more select because of Safeway's tremendous buying ability and its massive private transportation system that hurried food to market. We reasoned that if we attracted customers for these good reasons, they would buy the nonexclusive groceries at the same time.

We asked people to take note of the Safeway trucks they passed on the highways at night, bringing huge quantities of fresh fruit and vegetables and meat and milk to market. And we mentioned the courtesy of the road that the drivers of those trucks exhibited.

What we undertook was a kind of public relations advertising. We tried to make friends by being friendly, rather than by continuously assaulting the newspaper readers with fat black type in a cascade of prices that tumbled together dry groceries, laundry products, candy, disinfectants, small hardware, shoe polish, cheese, etc., in an inebriate jumble.

But if the Safeway management thought well of our efforts, the store managers had very different ideas. Years later, as a director of Montgomery Ward & Company, I encountered the same lack of interest in public relations advertising. The conclusion I drew was that most store managers are like most salesmen. They are usually so price-conscious, so demoralized by lower price competition whenever it raises its little pointed head, so demanding of a price advantage that they think of little else. This is one of the reasons that most salesmen try not to buy anything at retail. They have friends who are salesmen for everything from bicycles to ornamental beads, and they exchange wholesale privileges. If they can't, they wish they could and think they ought to; and this, for the state of their minds, is just as bad.

Our noble experiment with Roos Bros. was a notable failure at Safeway. There was no Eleanor Lyons who was dissatisfied with the advertising situation the way she had been, there was no Colonel Roos to back her up, however testily. Not until a dozen years later, when Franklin J. Lunding and George Clements of the Jewel Tea Company initiated similar advertising in Chicago was the idea vindicated. Fresh, informative advertising gave the Jewel stores an inviting character that was followed up by alert, carefully trained managers and department heads, and Jewel became the dominant food distributor in the area.

Our frustrations at Safeway were matched by a major disappointment with our advertiser of canned goods. One of his principal products was Rancho soup, which he was able to sell at retail at five cents per can. This was about half the price of Campbell's, which had to include a heavy freight charge for transportation from Camden, New Jersey, or from Chicago, to the Pacific Coast.

Rancho soups were excellent products. The vegetable soup, which, like the rest of the line, was made from the cuttings and trimmings of vegetables that were packed individually and had to be uniform in size, was full-bodied and tasty (though lacking Campbell's base of good beef stock); and the cream of asparagus was almost as thick as custard.

The difficulty with Rancho soup was that advertising couldn't sell it. It was *too* cheap. Campbell's soup, at ten or eleven cents a can, had established itself long before as one of the food wonders of the world. The consensus was that Campbell's could not be equaled at *its* price, and certainly it couldn't be equaled for less. So strong was this conviction that Rancho soup was never seriously considered by most shoppers. The few brave souls who tried it liked it, but they weren't enough to build a business, and the Campbell Soup Company (for whom I was later to work) remained unchallenged, as it is today.

One of the facts to be remembered about advertising and selling is that it isn't enough to be right, it is necessary also to *seem* right. To be successful, an advertising promise must never seem too good to be true. There are undoubtedly some people who are moved by large promises, but the bulk of the public is wary of them. It cannot be repeated too often that the average American housewife has no peer as a purchasing agent.

Rancho soup might have been a bargain, but California housewives were completely satisfied with Campbell's.

Man with a Suitcase

It was on a sunny morning in the spring of 1940, while we were wrestling with Rancho, that a shiny, well-scrubbed little man (my life in advertising seems to have been filled with well-scrubbed little men) came into our office in the Russ Building and introduced himself as a onetime member of the staff of Lord & Thomas in New York.

"I want to show you something," he said, opening a fat leather suitcase. "I want to show you something that is going to revolutionize the soap industry."

"This I would love to see," I said. I was thinking how Rancho had failed to revolutionize the soup business. Large talk was out of place from such a little man. But I was bound to be polite.

"If I could have a little hot water in this pitcher," the man said. "I've an aluminum pan here. And this plate, which I am going to rub thickly with this cube of butter. Then I'm going to show you a miracle."

When my astonished secretary brought the hot water, the little man poured some white powder into his pan, then added water until the pan was filled to the brim with thick, iridescent suds.

"Now," he said, "I want you to see what happens to this greasy plate when I merely pass it through the suds."

What happened was that the dish reappeared as clean as if it had been rinsed and scrubbed and rinsed again in clear water. There wasn't a particle of grease on it. We had watched our first demonstration of a synthetic detergent.

The small magician was named Raymond Soat. He had been a business solicitor for Lord & Thomas. One of his subjects for solicitation was Allied Chemical Company, and there he had come across the miraculous soap substitute that was made (as so many other new things were soon to be made) from petroleum.

Soat had persuaded the Allied people to let him work out an arrangement with Safeway Stores to test market the new product which he called Swerl. What he wanted from us was advertising to show Safeway what he had in mind to get the new product into consumer hands before the big soap companies became aware of what was happening. Raymond Soat, with suspicious glances over his shoulder, was playing for big stakes. I didn't know it then, but it was the biggest game I had ever sat in (or watched), and I soon learned what happens when you haven't a sufficient stack of chips.

The demonstration in my office, on my desk, was repeated for the Safeway management, and as a result, since they were as excited as we were by what we all saw, we went to work for them immediately to tell the world about the wonder product.

What we didn't know — and Raymond Soat didn't tell us, perhaps because he didn't know either — was that far away in Cincinnati the Procter & Gamble chemists were perfecting a synthetic detergent which they called Dreft. The only difference between the two products was that Dreft was made by one of the world's most knowledgeable consumer goods companies and Swerl was being made by an industrial products manufacturer whose experience and whose interest in retail distribution was nil. All he had was a new, unexplored product, fortified by Raymond Soat's enthusiasm.

These were not enough.

Although our initial tests were more than satisfactory, Safeway backed away when Procter & Gamble's Dreft appeared in the market; even so powerful a retailer had no wish to compete with the giant soaper. Later on I was to do just this, with considerable success, for a client who was first in the market. But Soat had no such luck. He tried valiantly but in vain to get Allied to finance a fighting operation. He then worked with a number of contract packagers and built up a small business. But Procter & Gamble had stepped out in front with a whole series of synthetics for various household uses, and its heavy-duty detergent, Tide, became the largest-selling laundry product ever known. Tide entered the market, close on the heels of Dreft, with an advertising campaign in test markets that was projected to a national level of $18 million per year. Dreft's was about half that. Swerl's never got up to $1 million. But, the most important thing was that Dreft and Tide were excellent products, demonstrably better than soap.

After Soat left Allied, Swerl was distributed by the H. J. Heinz Company for a short while, then discontinued. To the end, it appeared in the pale lemon-yellow package with the large white swirl on the face that Ray Bethers designed for it in our San Francisco office, and that we were sure would be more effective than the Dreft package.

During all this time that we hopefully engaged in new activities, our old standbys, the railroad, steamship and community accounts, and the food and petroleum accounts were going along at increased tempo. The war in Europe had stimulated domestic travel and tourists were flocking to California; also the number of substantial people who had come first as visitors, then returned as residents, created new population that may have made the old-timers shudder, but it also helped make our clients' businesses satisfactory and their advertising increasingly profitable.

We also added the S&W account. Originally called Sussman & Wormser, and later shortened to S&W, this was (and remains) the distributor of California's finest line of canned fruits and vegetables. S&W packs nothing in its own plants beyond some marmalades and jellies and a collection of glacé fruits. The rest of the long line is purchased from various sources according to the most stringent specifications in the trade. The only complaint I have ever heard against S&W is their inability sometimes to supply what is wanted; if S&W buyers don't like the Bing cherries one year, or the celery hearts another, the company doesn't buy any. Adrian Falk was the president and he had only one standard. He also didn't have anyone to please but himself and his customers.

Altogether, we were working for good people. Even Colonel Roos was proving tractable; and despite the loss of the coffee account of M.J.B. the volume of the office had increased and the new manager received several complimentary letters from Albert Lasker, whom he had yet to meet.

Then, in the fall of 1940, we stumbled into our greatest opportunity.

A Question of Priorities

WHEN three gentlemen from Seattle came into our fifteenth-floor Russ Building office one afternoon in October, I listened to them at first with mixed emotions.

They wanted, they said, to talk about the advertising of the Albers Milling Company, a subsidiary of the Carnation Milk Company, and an important and growing factor in the cereal business which included not only ready-to-eat breakfast cereals and pancake flour, but also a new dry dog food called Friskies. It was a beautiful account, but I found its representatives cold and calculating, and I quickly wished they would go away.

They were as ill-assorted in appearance as one could imagine. The skeletal tall man was so pale that his features all but disappeared into the whiteness of his face. Looking at him I could only think of Edwin Arlington Robinson's Richard Cory, who "one calm summer night, went home and put a bullet through his head." The tall man looked just that unhappy. His contribution to the meeting was total silence.

The second of the trio was another of my well-scrubbed small men. He was no more than about two-thirds the tall man's height, and twice as ill at ease. His eyes darted behind silver-rimmed glasses, and it was obvious that he would have preferred to be somewhere else—almost anywhere else.

The third member of the group was a large man uncomfortably compressed by his clothes and bursting out all over. The front of his vest met only at the buttons; and then barely. His neck overflowed his collar. His voice was gruff. He was in charge, and he clearly relished his role.

"We don't want any canned presentation of your agency," he began without any of the amenities beyond introducing the small man as Mr. Herold, Albers's general manager, and the tall man as Mr. Izzard, Albers's advertising manager.

"We've been all through your list of clients," he said. "We don't see any conflict. But we're a very particular company. Very damned particular. There is one thing we insist upon. We are the largest customer of the can company that makes our containers. We are the largest customer of the lithographer who prints the labels for those containers. We are the largest customer of the trucking companies that bring in the milk to our processing plants. We are one of the largest customers of the National Broadcasting Company.

"For these excellent reasons," he concluded, "we demand preferred treatment. We demand top priority from all the people we do business with. We demand it for the Carnation company and we demand it for the Albers company, too. If that is understood you can tell us what you think your agency has to offer that is different from any other. But remember the priority."

All this was fairly belted out. And I am afraid that my voice, unlike that of Stanley Roberts, for that was the loud man's name, was thin and high and reedy. I was fairly shaking. I had never been more angry.

"Mr. Roberts," I said, "I can only tell you that no matter what you get from anybody else, you'll never get priority from Lord & Thomas."

I didn't wait for a reply. I was aware that Izzard had coughed into his handkerchief and that Herold had his handkerchief out, too, polishing his glasses, waiting for Roberts to reject my response. But I went on. I had closed the door and I wanted to nail it shut.

"If we had any priorities," I said, "the first would be allocated to the Southern Pacific Company, which was the first client of this office. The second would be to the American President Lines, which used to be the Dollar Lines, which was the second client of this office. And the third would be the Associated Oil Company, which was our third client in this office." When I had gone through the entire list of our San Francisco clients, I said, "If we had priorities you would come after all those."

That, I thought, ought to take care of my visitors, and apparently it did.

"Gentlemen," Stanley Roberts said, scowling at his companions, "I think we have been here long enough." It was plain that Herold and Izzard were relieved. The unpleasant meeting had become an angry one; and the three stamped out.

When they were gone I gathered the office staff and told the men who had been waiting eagerly to hear the outcome of the promising meeting that I had failed utterly. A desirable advertiser had come to our office, in an unprecedented visitation, and I had become irate and jumped down his throat—simply because this advertiser wanted all that he could get for his money.

There must have been a way, I said, to accommodate him, and I had failed even to look for it. Instead of a solicitation, I had given the men a lecture. As director of advertising for the Carnation company, Stanley Roberts was responsible for one of the country's largest advertising appropriations. He dealt with one of its largest advertising agencies. He presided over one of the most notable radio programs, the *Carnation Hour* of classical and semiclassical music. I had not even been polite to him. I had been rude, and I had been stupid.

I have no idea how long my mortification might have lasted, or with what total effect, had I not received an unexpected second call from the gentlemen from Seattle in the middle of the following afternoon.

"May we come over?" Stanley Roberts asked on the telephone. The throaty voice was almost dulcet.

"What in God's name do you want to see me for?" I wanted to ask. But I had been chastened by a long night and a morning of dreary reflection, so I said, "Of course."

When the three arrived they looked like the Three Wise Men. Izzard seemed to have his color back. Herold's gaze had ceased to be shy and uncomfortable. Roberts was the affable stout man.

Their smiles were wide and warm.

"You were pretty mad at us when we left here yesterday," Roberts said, beaming, while he patted his stomach. "You were pretty damned mad, and we didn't blame you. What you didn't know, what you couldn't know, was that we came here with a trick question. We asked the identical question of three agency principals — one before we came here yesterday; one this morning. You were the only one who answered it correctly."

"You mean —" I said. Could it be that I had come up against another Colonel Roos?

"Yes," Roberts said, and Izzard and Herold came as close to grinning as they could. "The one about priorities. One of the other agency fellows promised without any hesitation to make us his first consideration; the other thought he could surely work things out to our satisfaction. You were the only one who said, 'Nothing doing,' and for the best of reasons. You said you couldn't promise anything that any other client of Lord & Thomas wasn't getting. Only the same things.

"You didn't know it, but we'd talked to some of your clients. We had a pretty good idea what they are getting. Furthermore, we like your point of view, even to getting mad at us.

"Under all these circumstances, we'd like to have you take over Albers advertising on January first."

My relief at Stanley Roberts's words was almost greater than my pleasure. But I am sure I stammered out something appropriate, for a few weeks later we were deep in the Albers business.

My association with Roberts lasted as long as he lived. He loved to tell the story of the angry outbreak that he provoked. He would go through the complete list of our accounts that I said would have to have priority over Albers if there were going to be priorities. With each one his voice rose (as he insisted mine had), and when he concluded with the name of a small olive company, he said it was that that resulted in his immediate decision to appoint Lord & Thomas.

NBC broke Stanley Roberts's heart when they refused to renew the *Carnation Hour*, under the direction of Percy Faith, in the fall of 1943. The network said the stations were complaining that the audience was too small. The great race was on between NBC and the Columbia Broadcasting System, and CBS was pulling ahead with comedy and comedy-drama and popular music. Stanley argued but he couldn't win. When he died the following year there was no program of classical or semiclassical music left in radio.

Albert D. Lasker

It was in March of 1941 that I met Mr. Lasker for the first time. He had been my employer for twelve years. But until that spring day when I was summoned to the La Quinta Hotel at Palm Springs, my principal contact with the proprietor of Lord & Thomas had been in the abstract shape of mimeographed letters, accompanying several year-end bonus checks, which informed me that I was not to take such largesse for granted. It had to be earned every year, the notice said; and even so it might or might not be forthcoming, depending upon unnamed contingencies.

Albert Lasker was cautious about future commitments. He had a lifelong habit of consulting his fears when business and profit were concerned. This meant that he preferred to face the future when he got there. For one thing, this was much safer; for another, it was possible that it would be more economical.

One year when Bob Hope was setting the pace (for Pepsodent) in the radio audience race, Hope's scrappy personal manager, Jimmy Saphier, told Mr. Lasker that he was sure Bob would be unhappy with a proposed increase of only five thousand dollars for the next season's broadcasts.

"How would he feel about a ten-thousand increase?" Mr. Lasker asked quietly.

"Bob would still be unhappy," Saphier replied.

"Then," snapped Lasker, "let him be unhappy for five thousand and we'll save an equal amount."

As it turned out, the contract was drawn for a substantially larger figure. Everyone wanted Hope to be happy. In the meantime, Jimmy Saphier had learned that playing a money game with the master of Lord & Thomas was playing in a very fast league.

I never tried it. To tell the truth, I have never tried it with anyone. The idea that my services were something of a bargain seemed to me to guarantee that I would be well paid. I wasn't necessarily brighter than anyone else, but I worked harder than most with the result that my productivity was greater. I had no other hobby than work. To be sure, I read a great deal, on the theory that you have to replenish what you take out of your head, but my physical situation was such that I partook of neither daytime sports nor late night life. My status as a bargain was accepted. Like Bob Hope, though hardly in the same magnitude, I was kept happy, too. Nevertheless, the invitation to meet Albert Lasker at Palm Springs came as a surprise.

His appearance was as startling as his invitation. Although his height was no more than average, Albert Lasker seemed taller than most men. His carriage was erect. His strong face, with its aristocratic, aquiline nose was framed in soft, gray-white hair combed to rise and billow like a short mane toward the back. His eyes were dark and very bright. His blue suit jacket was cut and pressed so that the lapels dipped narrowly to the lowermost button, accentuating the vertical; and I learned that all his clothes were made this way. His shirt was plain white and his necktie plain blue. He wore exquisite shoes; exquisite because his feet were very small. When Albert Lasker appeared at the door of his suite I knew that I was in a presence.

My visit was short and cordial but with no small talk. It began and ended at lunch with only Albert Lasker, Don Belding, who was manager of Lord & Thomas in Los Angeles, and myself in the flower-filled living room. I have never known anyone else who was so consistently surrounded by flowers as Albert Lasker; if there was no other place for them they were put in vases on the floor.

Mr. Lasker addressed me first. "Mr. Cone," he said, immediately upon sitting down, before even picking up a napkin, and looking straight at me, "I know all about your experience in New York. Had you been with me it would have been different. But you weren't. D'you? D'you see?"

I was to learn that Albert Lasker punctuated most of his sentences either with *D'you see?* or simply *D'you?* These occurred in place of periods, commas, colons, semicolons and real question marks. Sometimes they were complete disconcerting sentences. Albert Lasker's mind raced and his speech came in torrents. *D'you* gave his listeners a chance to catch up.

Albert Lasker was as dynamic in appearance as he was in conversation, and he suited his actions to his words to become the richest of all advertising men.

In this initial encounter, I couldn't have been more confused. Could it be that he wanted me to join Francisco and Ludekens in New York?

"But no," he said. "New York is not for you. D'you see?"

This I knew better than he. New York to me was a nightmare filled with doctors and hospitals, and looking through a dark bedroom window into a gray light well. New York was something I wanted no part of. As if he were reading my mind, Mr. Lasker said, "I know just how you feel. Mr. Francisco would like to have you. D'you? But I will not let him."

It seemed that he had brought me a long way, all the way from San Francisco, to tell me this; but I didn't know Albert Lasker. I didn't realize until much later that I had been chosen for a typical Lasker assault. This first brief phase was to assure me of his clear understanding of my prejudice against New York, and to establish that he was on my side against it. The next would be to make me forget both. Mr. Lasker wanted me in New York and he had mapped out a comprehensive plan for my transfer. Don Francisco had told him, I am sure, that I couldn't be moved, and he had made up his mind at that moment to move me.

It wasn't long after my excursion to Palm Springs that I received the first of a long series of personal and often handwritten notes from Mr. Lasker; and here I should mention that I never called him anything but that. Only his closest friends outside the business addressed him as Albert; and they referred to him as A.D. He never called me anything but Mr. Cone. Notwithstanding the formality between us, his letters were cordial, and I think he spent some time on them.

He had found out who some of my favorite writers and spokesmen were, and he sent me reviews of their new books and clippings of their daily and weekly columns from the New York newspapers. He received proofs of all the advertisements prepared in the San Francisco office and he commented on these frequently and favorably.

In July I was invited to visit the New York office for a week or two "to see some interesting things we are doing here." My wife was invited, too; and I was more than a little concerned. But Albert Lasker again relieved me of my fears. "It must be clear, perfectly clear, that Mr. Francisco and I would like to have you here, d'you?"

"I do." I said. "But ——"

"But it is also something I could not bring myself to do, to ask you to move," he went on. "The war in Europe. D'you see? The United

States will be in it within a year. You will be in it. D'you? I couldn't be responsible for your wife, your little girl, in a strange city. This is why I couldn't let you come, d'you see?"

I hoped I did. I realized that somehow the idea that I should move to New York had now become *mine*. But this seemed safe enough, what with Albert Lasker's evident understanding and his patience.

It wasn't until he invited me to come to New York in October for the World Series, that I began to feel thoroughly uneasy. It was clear now that it was only Mr. Lasker's reluctance to upset my family life that was keeping me from moving. I began to feel ashamed; I began to feel selfish and ungrateful.

Then one rainy day in Chicago, where I had stopped off on my way to New York to the baseball games, Albert Lasker sprang the soft trap he had been preparing. He was in Chicago for just a few hours (he himself had moved to New York the year before) and I stepped into his office in the Palmolive Building as a matter of courtesy.

"I'm glad to see you," Albert Lasker said. "I've been thinking about you. D'you? Thinking how glad I am I didn't let you move to New York. Thinking that if you got down on your knees out there in the rain and begged me to let you come now I would have to say no. D'you?"

For the twentieth time I said, "I understand."

"That," said Albert Lasker, "is where you are wrong. For if you understood, you would know that if you don't join me right now in what I am planning in New York, then my whole plan blows up! D'you? D'you see? If you don't take charge of our copy department and our art department, d'you? If you don't take charge then I'll have to start planning all over again." Now he was pleading, and he pled as if he were bleeding.

One of my weaknesses of character is a sense of responsibility that is easily exaggerated out of all proportion by the exigencies of a given situation. This one had been exaggerated already by Mr. Lasker, but I couldn't let well enough alone. I had to make a grand gesture.

Standing up, looking down at him for the only time in my life, I said, "Mr. Lasker, when do you want me to come?"

"If you will wait a moment," he said, raising his hand, palm out, like a traffic policeman. "If you will kindly wait one moment," and then to his secretary, over the telephone, "If you will get me Mr. Hill, at the tobacco company, d'you?"

Many people have said that Albert Lasker could have been anything he chose: a lawyer; a judge; a senator; a diplomat; a doctor; and actor;

a banker; a professional gambler.* The facts of his life were that he played at being all these things and his success in each one, in and out of advertising, came out of his colossal assurance that, given the same circumstances, nothing that he was doing could be done better. Nor could it, in most cases.

The role he now assumed, waiting to speak to George Hill on the telephone, was that of a deserving man against whom cruel fate had been unavailing; the happy warrior who became victor through his adherence to right against wrong.

"George," he said, when the telephone buzzer sounded and he picked up the instrument. "George. D'you? A wonderful thing has happened." He grinned widely at me.

"George, you know how we have talked about Mr. Cone. But how we couldn't ask him to leave San Francisco. D'you? The war. D'you see? Now, what do you think? Mr. Cone is here in my office at this minute. He just came in, d'you? And he said before I could say anything more than 'good morning,' he said, 'Mr. Lasker, when do you want me to be in New York?' That is what he said, George, d'you?"

The amazing thing is, I believe Albert Lasker could have sworn that that was exactly what had occurred. Anyway, the pact was made, and I arranged to move to New York with no further discussion. I had lost the decision, and I was determined to be cheerful about it. After the baseball series I took off for San Francisco to pack our belongings once again, just as Albert Lasker had known I would.

Our turnaround was accomplished in less than two months and we arrived in Manhattan for my second tour of duty there on December 5, 1941. Two days later the Japanese attacked Pearl Harbor. Albert Lasker had been right about the war, too.

---

* Mr. Lasker gave up large bets at golf when he lost $40,000 one afternoon to the San Francisco banker Herbert Fleishhacker. When the 20-by-8-inch check which he had had especially made was returned, canceled, he had it framed and hung on an office wall to remind him of his folly; he never gambled for high stakes again.

With Men
Who Know Tobacco Best

IF Mr. Lasker had a grand plan for the New York office, I never found
out what it was. I only knew that he wanted to change its tone.

In time I came to understand how Albert Lasker viewed the advertising business. First of all, he refused to dignify it by calling it a profession. His idea of a profession was the strict one that called for
specialized knowledge and extensive academic preparation, followed
by the degree of Ph.D. or its equivalent. Advertising at its best began
only with apprenticeship and there were no degrees. This last was as it
should be, he thought, for he saw advertising as a business. And he felt
that as it was practiced on Madison Avenue and its environs it lacked
most of the elements of salesmanship that he believed vital to success.

The psychological possibilities in advertising that were being ex-
amined by Ernest Dichter and Alfred Politz, emigrés from Vienna
and Berlin respectively, left him cold. He had been psychoanalyzed.
He was deeply interested in medical and biological research, and he
supported it generously. The Lasker Foundation awards for medical
research stand high among the world's honors for scientists. This,
thought Mr. Lasker, is where honors belong. It was enough for advertising to finance the facilities with which they are won.

It is not surprising, I think, that while Raymond Rubicam, William
Benton, Chester Bowles, Bruce Barton, Stirling Getchell, Ernest Elmo
Calkins and others were winning kudos in advertising circles for
technical innovations, Albert Lasker was unimpressed. He had no interest whatever in advertising for itself. If it had any artistic overtones at all, they were only to help make the basic promise of the advertising more personal and more compelling. Despite the fact that

in 1941 he was beginning to acquire a magnificent collection of paintings, he couldn't find any enthusiasm for art in advertising.

In his business Albert Lasker was *all* business. His success was not equaled by anyone else in what he called the trade. He was a millionaire when millionaires were few; and he gave away money in large amounts before most of the rich men of his time had stopped collecting it. He wanted his money to work against world problems. This was a man who had no small thoughts. He was as impatient of them as he was of small talk. He was what is called a direct-actionist. He was also something of an exhibitionist.

The story was told of one day in Chicago when a group of his men returned to the Palmolive Building after a discouraging meeting with a prospective client. The man remained adamant against their strongest arguments. All the hundred or so advertising successes of Lord & Thomas that were paraded before him made no impression.

"I think I will go see that man," Mr. Lasker said.

In a few days he did. When he returned it was with a signed contract, and the master of Lord & Thomas waved it in front of the men who had failed. What, they demanded to know, had Albert Lasker promised that they hadn't thought of.

"I told the gentleman," he said, "that I would make him rich."

There was all the authority of forty or fifty million dollars behind that promise.* No one with very much less could have made it. No one with still less could have turned it down. It has been my conviction in business and in advertising that a promise is only as good as its promiser. *The world's best pie* lettered on the greasy window of a run-down restaurant is not an attractive proposition nor one that is likely to be made good. Mr. Lasker was very careful what he promised and how he promised it.

It was in February of 1942, when the nightly blackout made New York extremely nervous and rumors of squadrons of approaching German planes floated through each day, that I was bound up in one of those promises. It was made to George Washington Hill, just before Albert Lasker departed for his annual winter vacation in Arizona and California.

"Mr. Cone," Mr. Lasker said, "I have arranged it that you are to call on Mr. Hill each day while I am away. D'you?"

---

* How much money Albert Lasker made in advertising and through advertising was subject to his mood when referring to it. Once when he was losing an argument I heard him say to his opponent, "You are right. I am wrong. I am so wrong that I have only made $60 million in this business!" At other times the amount was somewhat less. Perhaps the difference had to do with money made directly in the agency, and additional money made elsewhere.

The fact was that I didn't see at all, either why I should want to call on George Hill every day or that he conceivably would let me, and I said so. "Also," I added, "Emerson Foote is in charge of the account." Emerson Foote was manager of the New York office.

"You do not understand," Mr. Lasker said with asperity. "Mr. Foote represents the agency. You will represent me. D'you?"

I couldn't see how a recruit from San Francisco, a man who had been in New York less than two months, a man who had never laid eyes on George Washington Hill and who was prepared to flinch at the sight of him, could represent one of the world's most formidable advertising men who was also Hill's longtime associate and intellectual sparring partner.

"How could Mr. Hill possibly want to see me every day?" I repeated.

"Because I have positioned you," Mr. Lasker said. "D'you?"

"Positioned me how?" I asked him.

Smiling archly, Mr. Lasker said, "I reminded Mr. Hill that once I had Hopkins and once I had Hummert. He agreed. Now, I told him, you are about to see a man who will become the equal of either of them."*

"You couldn't have," I said.

"Do not be quixotic," Mr. Lasker said. "I know Mr. Hill and I have arranged the meetings. D'you?"

Suddenly I remembered the telephone conversation, when Albert Lasker told George Hill from Chicago that I had asked him to let me come to New York.

George Washington Hill was accused of devouring advertising people, especially savoring the better ones. What bothered me most was that George Hill's American Tobacco Company was one of the country's largest and most successful radio advertisers, while the most important program I had ever had anything to do with had been a small-time audience-participation show on a single San Francisco station. *Kay Kyser's Kollege of Musical Knowledge* and *Your Hit Parade* were radio's two top musical programs, and they were Mr. Hill's pride and joy. He was devoted to music and I was tone-deaf; "Yankee Doodle" was the only tune in the world that I could be sure of when I heard it. This was worse than being color-blind. But at least it was an affliction that I shared with Albert Lasker. It seemed that he couldn't tell "Yankee Doodle" from "Dardanella."

---

* Claude Hopkins was the father of "reason-why" advertising, and his theories became the backbone of the business. Frank Hummert, the most successful of all the radio writers, had left Lord & Thomas some years before to found his own prosperous agency, Blackett, Sample, Hummert.

Just then he didn't have to. American's Lucky Strike was the largest-selling brand of cigarettes in the United States, and while I wasn't the agency executive in charge of the Lucky Strike account — that was Mr. Foote — I would surely be held responsible for anything that went wrong with it in Mr. Lasker's absence. Much too soon the hour came when I could no longer put off calling Mr. Hill for an appointment. I had never seen the man, and I would gladly have postponed our meeting forever. Failing that, I wanted Emerson Foote to go with me; but he had his orders from Albert Lasker. This was something Mr. Lasker had arranged. Mr. Foote would have no part of it; nor could I really blame him. To stay out of such a fiasco as this promised to be was surely in the firm's best interest.

"I have something I would like to show you," I said to Mr. Hill on the telephone. He replied that of course he would be glad to see it, and I only wished that he hadn't said "of course." This was in deference to Albert Lasker. He had to be full of doubt about me.

Nevertheless, I did have something that I thought would improve the printed advertising of Lucky Strike cigarettes to a considerable degree. I had just returned from a trip through the tobacco company that was mandatory of everyone who worked on the account. I had watched the fast-moving, noisy auctions at Greensboro and High Point, North Carolina, and at Valdosta, Georgia, and I believed that to picture the action in these primary tobacco markets was all that was required to make the Lucky Strike promise.

The fact was that American Tobacco Company buyers bought the choicest baskets of tobacco at auction after auction. They bid for it primarily against the R. J. Reynolds Company buyers, and the two divided the spoils of the spirited bidding.

Moreover, one of the earlier visitors from Lord & Thomas to the auctions, a keen observer named Cyrus Nathan, had made an astonishing discovery. Approximately three out of every four crushed cigarette packages on the auction floors were green Lucky Strike packages with their bright red bull's-eye. And to capitalize on this fact an advertising campaign was born. It was typical of Mr. Hill that before it began he trimmed the preference figures from three-to-one to two-to-one.

George Hill had been accused of exaggerated advertising, but this had to do more with figures of speech than with claims. "I know the great preference for Lucky Strike is a fact," he had said. "But the public won't believe it. Anyway, two-to-one has a better ring to it. 'Two-to-one' is one of the great, confident expressions in our language. It is rarely argued with."

"Scouting the crop before auctions open." Painted from life on a Southern farm by Georges Schreiber

So Round, So Firm, So Fully Packed — So Free and Easy On The Draw

No one ever expected George Hill to go for easel painters. But he did, and the advertisements they illustrated helped keep Lucky Strike on top. This was by Georges Schreiber.

LUCKY STRIKE
"IT'S TOASTED"

It was my conviction that the statement *With men who know to-bacco best — with independent auctioneers, buyers and warehouse-men — it's Luckies two-to-one* — as the crushed packages showed — should stand alone in print. It required no formal text to make it do everything it could. In radio there was time and a place to re-create the auction, ending each scene with the chant of the tobacco auc-tioneers and the words *sold — American,* and quoting the price paid above the average for a given market. But too much of this was making the printed advertisements much less dramatic than I thought they could be. It reduced the size of the illustrations; and the long text be-came an argument. It reduced the stark authentic quality of the pic-tures by Thomas Hart Benton, Aaron Bohrod, Arnold Blanch, Paul Sample, Peter Hurd and the Associated American Artists stable of painters that was making its first appearance in advertising.

The pictures were first-rate. They made their point. There was something rich and romantic in the soft tones of the tobacco country. The figures were solid and soiled and real, no way glamorized. Neither needed the adman's touch; I thought it was spoiling each scene. Many more advertisements are poor because of things they contain than what they may leave out. And it was this that I wanted to change. I wanted to eliminate all but the preference story, in its shortest form.

When I took my sample advertisement to Mr. Hill, I saw that cer-tain of his idiosyncrasies had not been overdrawn.

George Washington Hill was short and round-faced and deeply tanned, and he was wearing his hat pulled low over his eyes as he sat at his black mahogany desk, just as I had been told he would. The hat was a soft-brown Knox crusher, a sportsman's hat, dented with three large dimples like a gandy dancer's, and the band was decorated with a dozen or so trout flies. His suit was of brown gabar-dine; and the jacket had four pleated military pockets and two in-congruous suede patches at the elbows.*

It wasn't hard to believe that this man pasted packages of Lucky Strikes in the windows of his Rolls-Royce limousine; he couldn't think of a better display place. Or that he refused to meet the performers he hired at fabulous prices for his radio programs, where he insisted that whatever the music be, it be played loud and fast; he knew they didn't like him and he didn't care. He both looked and sounded like a man playing Nero.

What didn't show was a devotion to his business that was his

---

* Later I learned that the patches were a patriotic overstatement; Mr. Hill was encouraging his employees not to buy new clothes during what he thought promised to be a long war.

greatest characteristic. His was the first of the tobacco companies to install modern research facilities. He chose and blended the tobacco for Lucky Strike cigarettes as well as he knew how, which was very well indeed, and he advertised Luckies with drama and substance.

"Let me see," he said (craftily, I thought, because I didn't know him), "What you have to show me."

"First I would like to tell you something," I said. I was trying to hold off the attack that I felt sure was to come.

"Mr. Cone," Mr. Hill said firmly, as if to settle the matter at the outset, "you don't have to *tell* me anything. If what you have is advertising, and I can't think of anything else that you would be bringing me, it needs no explanation and I will ask you to reserve any comment. You can't stand behind even a single listener to the radio in his living room or in his car, or lie down in bed beside a single reader of a newspaper or magazine late at night and tell that person what you were *trying* to say to him in an advertisement. Nor can I," he added with finality.

I was astonished. Here was the great George Washington Hill, one of the titans of the advertising business, talking like Bailey, Doty, Ludekens; talking the advertising language I had learned. But what I had wanted to say had nothing to do with the advertisement in my brown Lord & Thomas envelope. And I blurted it out.

"Mr. Hill," I said, "what I want to tell you is about Mr. Lasker. He talked much too big about me. He told me what he said. He said that he had positioned me alongside Claude Hopkins and Frank Hummert. And I want you to know that I know better. I appreciate Mr. Lasker's enthusiasm," I said. "But I know much more about me than he does. On the record, I think I am a pretty good advertising man. But the record is not a very long one."

It was exactly at this point that Mr. Hill and I became friends. In a way I had put something over on Albert Lasker. I hadn't succumbed to his extravagance, and I think Mr. Hill enjoyed this almost as much as if he had punctured the balloon himself.

"You and I are going to get along," he said. Removing the soft Knox hat from his head, he rose behind his desk and held out his hand to shake mine. Then we got down to the paste-up that showed how I thought the Lucky Strike magazine advertisements could be simplified and strengthened.

That single page was all I ever had to show George Hill. He grasped immediately that the endorsement of Lucky Strike cigarettes by tobacco men themselves, as proven by the two-to-one preference margin, actually lost conviction when it was tied up to standard phrases in praise of the brand. Moreover, strong graphics, which ours were, had no need of such verbal support.

All this Mr. Hill took in without a word from me. How *far* he took it in soon was evident all through the advertising for Lucky Strikes. It had been part of the radio strategy in presenting "the men who know tobacco best" to reproduce sounds of the auction, and out of this there now evolved the proposition that *Lucky Strike means fine tobacco*, and Mr. Hill went to work on this with a will.

It was only a few days after my first visit with him that I went into his high-ceilinged office to find him sitting alone under his hat, tap-tapping on the glass top of the mahogany desk with a small gold pencil shaped like a piece of bamboo.

"Listen," he said. "What does this sound like?"

"Like a telegrapher in a railway station," I said.

"Right," said Mr. Hill. "Morse code. That is what it is. And do you know what it is saying? Listen."

He repeated the rhythmic tapping.

"It is sounding out L-S-M-F-T," he said. "Lucky Strike means fine tobacco, L-S-M-F-T."

It was one of Mr. Hill's remarkable faculties for advertising to find dramatic expressions for very ordinary statements. *Nature in the raw is seldom mild* had led into the story of toasting tobacco to rid it of harshness. *Nature in the raw* was something only he could have conceived. And *Reach for a Lucky instead of a sweet* changed a mild suggestion that smoking was not fattening into a challenge to every sweet-eater in the land to abstain and smoke a Lucky Strike instead.

LS/MFT, as it came to be printed on each Lucky Strike package, began as the telegraphic device on the Lucky Strike radio programs, with the tapping out of the letters followed by the full statement. But George Washington Hill was no man for half-measures. Soon everything that was superfluous in Lucky Strike advertising had to go. James Chapin's painting of a gaunt tobacco farmer in an old straw hat and blue shirt, holding up a large brown leaf to the sun, appeared on five consecutive days in full pages in every daily newspaper in the United States, with only the letters LS/MFT to speak for the cigarettes in the Lucky Strike package that was superimposed. Soon it was repeated on five more days.

Such was his genius that until Mr. Hill's death, when his successors undertook to put their own imprint on Lucky Strike advertising, the brand continued in first place. In fact it was only with the trite proposition to *Be Happy, Go Lucky* that Lucky Strike sales began to slip. This was a bromidic set of words that had been submitted by mail dozens of times during Mr. Hill's tenure; so many times that it was surely in the public domain. But Mr. Hill insisted that it had no meaning. It was only a trite application of a catch phrase.

While it was established immediately with Mr. Hill that I should not put in an appearance at 111 Fifth Avenue, which held the American Tobacco Company offices, unless I had good reason to, both Mr. Hill and I kept up the fiction for Mr. Lasker that I was following to the letter his order for a daily visitation.

But I did see a good deal of Mr. Hill. His son, George Hill, Jr., who had held the title of advertising manager, and who was being carefully tutored by his father to be his successor, had left for Army duty. So had a number of others on the staff. Mr. Hill, fearing that all the young men would go, began to replace the departing men with women. The acting advertising manager was a resourceful and vivacious young lady from Lord & Thomas named Polly Polzine. She had been Emerson Foote's secretary.

Despite the influx of ladies, and despite his gallantry where they were concerned, Mr. Hill preferred the society of men, and we had lunch together regularly. I was Mr. Hill's guest. He insisted that these were business lunches and that he was taking up my leisure time. We lunched always at the Vanderbilt Hotel, on Park Avenue, where Mr. Hill had a table reserved every day under cover of a forest of potted palms.

Once, upon finishing a large portion of eggs Benedict, which we had both ordered, and thinking to thank my host fittingly, I said, "Eggs Benedict are one thing in this world that I have never had enough of."

"Neither have I," Mr. Hill replied. Grinning, and signaling the waiter, he ordered a full second helping for each of us. Together, that noon, we ate eight large eggs and a quantity of ham.

This was the man who looked more than a little like Charles Laughton, who was pictured usually in Laughton's unloveliest roles and never in his happier ones, who would turn up in a novel and a movie called *The Hucksters* as a demonic tycoon in straw hat and galluses who accomplished the destruction of integrity in everyone who came within his grasp.

George Washington Hill deserved better from the author of *The Hucksters* and he could have answered any charge against him. But he was a shy man. He refused to talk to reporters under any circumstance. He had felt the sting of scandal when a federal judge was bribed by an attorney for the American Tobacco Company, and while he was never connected with the case, an unfriendly press had made him a target for abuse. Perhaps he was more the victim of his eccentricities than anything else. No matter what the tobacco men did in their offices in the tobacco country, businessmen in New York's Fifth Avenue didn't wear their hats in their countinghouses. That was Mr. Hill's trademark and the height of his impropriety.

Also, of course, he was author of the Cremo cigar advertising that had begun: *Spit is a nasty word, but it is worse on the end of your cigar.* While this undoubtedly influenced many smokers against handmade and tongue-sealed cigars, in favor of Mr. Hill's more antiseptic machine-made panatellas, it was hardly a sentence to win over his critics.

George Hill was a remarkable individual. He looked upon business as a form of warfare, but his warfare was an exciting game and he played it with glee, and never with malice.

One of his admonitions to advertising people was not to underestimate the public's intelligence but not to overestimate its knowledge. It was Mr. Hill's conviction that advertising should challenge what was known about the subject at issue and add to that knowledge with new facts or make a proposition that any reasonable person would understand and accept. When this was done with swinging rhythm, then, Mr. Hill thought, it became irresistible.

The man who was tagged as the model for Evan Evans, the satanic soap king of *The Hucksters*, was one of the most imaginative advertising men of all time. But he was one of the poorest at public relations. I have mentioned that he refused to meet the performers on his radio programs, and I should add that he often chose the music against their better judgment. This wasn't so bad when Kay Kyser and his orchestra broadcast from army camps and naval stations to throngs of service men and women, but it infuriated the professional listeners, the critics, and they damned George Hill's *Hit Parade* and claimed that he chose that music, too.* Then there was a long-running feud with Dan Golenpaul, the owner of one of the greatest of all radio programs, *Information Please*, who kept upping the price for the services of his famous panel of experts.

John Kieran, Franklin P. Adams, Oscar Levant and Clifton Fadiman were regular members of the cast, and the wide assortment of guests ranged all the way from Eddie Arcaro, the world's winningest jockey, to Wendell Willkie, who, partly as a result of his very favorable ap-

---

* Numbers to be played on *Your Hit Parade* were selected entirely on the basis of sheet music and record sales and juke box popularity across the country.

pearance on the panel, had become the Republican presidential candidate in 1940. The hitch was that *Information Please* did not attract a large audience. Kieran's equal agility with questions on Shakespeare and sports, and Levant's uncanny ability to solve musical conundrums, along with Adams's searing wit and Fadiman's urbanity and the erudition of the guests failed to excite the mass audience. But this was of no importance to Golenpaul, who took his fight to *Variety*, the theatrical weekly, and the newspapers, where Hill was pictured as a spoiler who was unwilling to pay for services rendered.

Frank Sinatra and Jack Benny could have testified otherwise, for he paid them top prices. Also, he paid all expenses for Kay Kyser's long tour of the service centers that lasted throughout World War II. But when it came to the show-business critics, George Hill could do nothing right. They objected to the squealing youngsters who greeted Frank Sinatra and almost drowned him out (twenty years before the Beatles touched off similar pandemonium). They objected violently to the fast dance music on the *Hit Parade*. They sided with Golenpaul. And, most of all, they objected to the Lucky Strike commercials.

Had there been fewer of these they would probably not have minded. But one couldn't escape the loud, rhythmic chant of the tobacco auctioneers, and the critics made it the symbol of all they disliked in advertising.

Nothing like Frank Sinatra had happened before to America's teenagers. Their reaction to his singing was hysterical.

The most successful of radio entertainers, Bob Hope alone was to make it big in all three forms: radio, the movies, and TV.

The Third Transplant

ALBERT LASKER returned to New York from Arizona and California early in April, and at once called me into his oak-paneled office that looked down on the hundreds of flags that flew in Park Avenue in defiance, as it were, of the Germans and the Japanese. I didn't know it then, but the entrance of America into the war had had a profound effect upon Mr. Lasker; and it was to have an effect upon my life that no one could have foreseen.

First, though, he had another surprise in store for me. "How would you like it," he said, "to live in Chicago? Before you answer, let me tell you. Mr. Faryon is leaving Lord & Thomas for Quaker Oats. You would take his place in charge of the Pepsodent account. D'you see? My largest client in Chicago. An opportunity. D'you? I want you to take care of Pepsodent for me."

It was one of Albert Lasker's favorite gambits to suggest that whatever he wanted you to do, no matter how it changed your life, was vital to both your interests. Also, nothing that had gone before bore any relation to the new proposition.

That I had been moved from San Francisco to New York to head the creative departments there was entirely forgotten within a matter of weeks when I was assigned to devote myself to Mr. Hill. Now, within another few weeks, that assignment was rescinded, and I was to move to Chicago.

"Mr. Hill," Mr. Lasker said, "understands completely."

Months later I discovered that when he stopped in Chicago on his return from the far West, Mr. Lasker had been informed by Charles Luckman, president of Pepsodent, that the proposed replacement for the departing Mr. Faryon was unacceptable. This was largely a matter of principle; advertisers are invariably opposed to agency personnel changes unless they themselves initiate the changes; they think someone is getting the best of them.

Pepsodent was the largest-selling toothpaste in the world. It had an excellent formula; and thanks to the fast-growing popularity of the Bob Hope radio program, the public was exposed to more advertising for Pepsodent than for any other dentifrice. It was unthinkable that this client should long be unhappy with the agency. Furthermore, if they were right about the unsuitability of the suggested replacement, this could have serious personal consequences for Albert Lasker. He was a major stockholder in the Pepsodent Company.

There was no time to lose. And none was lost in arguing with me. I had proved myself amenable to sudden change before.

"I cannot think of a greater opportunity. D'you?" said Albert Lasker. The last was not really a question.

In a matter of days the uprootable Cones, the Japanese maid they had brought from San Francisco, and the tiny black poodle that had been given their daughter in New York, were on their way to Chicago; a city they had only seen before between trains, a grim and murky place where they knew but four living souls (two of these aged ten and twelve).

Our second adventure in New York had lasted no longer than the first. But where our initial experience had been ugly and frustrating, this time we had found the city good. The war, despite the nightly blackouts and the recurring rumors of approaching German planes, was still far away and unreal.

To be sure, the draft card in my pocket was real enough, and the streets were beginning to be filled with men and women in uniform, but New York was bravely ignoring the conflict, living largely as usual. There were several midtown apartment houses where windows had been crisscrossed with wide ribbons of adhesive tape as a precaution against shattering. The windows of the Metropolitan Museum were boarded. Here and there in hallways one saw buckets of sand. The burned hulk of the sabotaged French liner *Normandie*, which was to have become a troop transport, lay on its side, shutting off the New Jersey skyline across the Hudson River at 49th Street. New York restaurants were not serving butter.

The *Times* broadcast war bulletins every hour on the hour. But these were always favorable in those first months. Outwardly life was going on the same as before the disaster at Pearl Harbor. That too, shocking as it was, had occurred far away. A mishap. It was generally agreed that nothing like it could happen again.

I wrote Jane Sullivan, my longtime secretary in San Francisco, that this time we didn't want to leave New York at all. It was easy to rhapsodize. I said we would miss the soft spring days that we had waited for through a cold and snowy winter. We would miss the trees budding and leafing in crosstown streets and in Central Park; and the warm smell of the restaurants at night. New York, like San Francisco, is a city of superb restaurants and we felt at home in them.

Our apartment in East 73rd Street, a few steps away from Fifth Avenue and Central Park, had been carved out of the dining room of Joseph Pulitzer's sandstone mansion. Our friend Harry Berk had an apartment in the next street that had been constructed within the walls of Clarence Mackey's indoor tennis court. But a whole, large apartment inside a dining room was something I had never expected to see; our 20-by-30-foot living room had a ceiling that was 18 feet high!

The actress Luise Rainer lived across the street, and we saw her coming and going, and drying her long dark hair in the sun on her balcony.

And there were other things that we would miss.

We would miss the dogs of Manhattan. The little dogs and the big dogs; the clipped poodles and Irish terriers and the shaggy, puzzled sheepdogs and apologetic Bedlingtons; all the thousands of dogs, well-behaved and ill-behaved, straining on the sidewalks and waiting at each street crossing, underfoot in stores and markets and restaurants. The beautiful, ugly, fashionable dogs of New York.

We would miss the small private army of uniformed doormen who decorated the entry to almost every building on the route of our neighborhood walks; and particularly the corps that guarded our own iron-grilled entrance — two in short black apprentice aprons, two in the long, brass-buttoned coats of the concierge. All of them spoke to our daughter and our dog.

We would miss the shiny Rolls-Royces, with their smartly uniformed chauffeurs and footmen; and the block of private garages on East 69th Street, where we peeked in at polished Minervas and Isottas and Mercedes, all kept shyly indoors because gasoline was being rationed and they were voracious (and because Hitler himself rode in a snarling Mercedes-Benz).

We would miss the theater. This was the winter of *Arsenic and Old Lace, Watch on the Rhine,* and *Lady in the Dark,* with Gertrude Lawrence; and the musical *Panama Hattie* with Ethel Merman was in its second rousing year.

We would miss the art galleries on East 57th Street and upper Madison Avenue. (We hadn't yet been in the Metropolitan or the

Museum of Natural History.) We would miss the rollicking double-decked buses; and the carriages that stood at the edge of Central Park hitched to livery stable nags; and the large Belgian draft horses that inexplicably drew small bread wagons marked *FINK* through an otherwise motorized city.

All these were things for which we were sure Chicago had no substitutes.

Still, it was the people we knew that we would miss most. Some, like the Ludekenses, we had known for many years. Some of the publishing and broadcasting people we had met and entertained as part of my job and my life in San Francisco. Through them in return we were meeting the top layer of New York's advertising and professional people.

Since I do not wish to be accused of name-dropping, let me only say that through Ludekens and Albert Dorne, who was an artist I had first met years before when he was making illustrations for De Soto automobile advertising for Getchell, and who was president of the Society of Illustrators, I quickly had come to know many of the leading artists in advertising and several in the finer arts. I met them at the Artists & Writers Club and the Society of Illustrators, where I had become a member; and at luncheons of the Dutch Treat Club, in the Park Lane Hotel, where I was a guest.

The publishers, editors and writers whose host and guide I had been in San Francisco now were showing my wife and me their city and introducing us to their friends.

In the broadcasting field I had not got below the top. Lord & Thomas was the agency for the NBC radio networks and also bought a good deal of time on CBS, and I soon got to know the biggest wigs. My experience with performers would come later.

Altogether, our days had been filled with energetic and entertaining people, not the least of whom worked in the offices of Lord & Thomas at 247 Park Avenue. Mr. Lasker had surrounded himself with an all-star cast. Sheldon Coons, who had taken Don Francisco's place as president of the company, had come from Macy's. Leonard Massius had been recalled from a conspicuous success in London to be manager in New York for the duration. Emerson Foote had been lured from the Getchell agency. Walter Weir, one of advertising's most prolific writers, was head of the copy department. Edward Lasker, who had discovered Bob Hope for Pepsodent, was in charge of broadcasting. Victor Ratner, from the Columbia Broadcasting System, where he had learned about research from Frank Stanton, was in charge of that activity — although Albert Lasker looked upon research with a decidedly unkindly eye; he thought his own instincts were sufficient, and often they were. Anyway, he was much more interested in a young man named Alan Jay Lerner, who was turning out Lucky Strike radio commercials. This was the Lerner who would one day collaborate with Frederick Loewe and write the unforgettable lyrics for *My Fair Lady*. Jimmy Cannon was in the publicity department. And there were others. I would particularly miss the picture of five Irish misses — Hannigan, Horrigan, Kerrigan, Finnegan and Mulrooney, sitting in a row outside the offices of the firm's five Jewish chief executives.

Most of all, of course, I expected to miss Albert Lasker and George Washington Hill. But it soon would be evident that Mr. Hill's "understanding" of my removal to Chicago was an understanding also that I should continue to be interested in the advertising for Lucky Strikes, and available on any notice. And I was.

When we entrained for Chicago on the afternoon of April 19, on the Twentieth Century Limited of the New York Central railroad, this proved to be only the first of more than seven hundred trips that I was to make back and forth on that train. Outside of the train crew, I was its most constant rider. When I didn't go to New York to see Mr. Hill, I went to see Mr. Lasker; and when the time came that they both were gone, I had other interests there.

On the dark morning of our arrival in the steamy, smoky old La Salle Street station, Chicago was epitomized in our first view of it. The narrow, lumpy asphalt aisles between the railroad tracks were crowded with mail and baggage trucks and strewn with rubbish. The posts and the latticework of girders that held up the shed roofs were rusted and flaking away. Policemen with paunches, and cigarettes cupped in their hands, were taking tips for handing passengers into dilapidated Yellow and Checker taxicabs. Chicago was dirty, ugly and corrupt.

A noisome political machine had the city in its grip. Chicago in 1942 was still marked by the depression of the decade before, and bound by it. There hadn't been a new building of any consequence erected since 1929. The city's business leaders lived out of the city in Kenilworth, Winnetka, Highland Park and Lake Forest on the North Shore of Lake Michigan, and in the western suburbs of Oak Park, Hinsdale, Wheaton. They were Chicagoans only from nine until five each weekday. The city belonged to the Kelly-Nash politicians, and they divided the spoils with the lords of the underworld.

Altogether the prospect was dismal. It was perfectly clear why Reg Faryon had wanted to get out of Chicago, and this had nothing to do with Lord & Thomas.

The agency had been established here by D. M. Lord and Ambrose

L. Thomas, as brokers of space in magazines in 1873. Albert Lasker joined the firm in 1898 as a salesman; fourteen years later, when he became its sole owner, the company had advanced from a space brokerage operation to a full-fledged advertising agency, much as we know one today.

Albert Lasker had been fascinated by the possibilities that he felt in advertising for developing sales, but he wasn't sure how these were to be realized until, dramatically, one afternoon the total concept was opened to him by a onetime Royal Canadian Mounted Policeman, sitting in a Chicago saloon. A few minutes before, a card had been handed to Mr. Lasker in his office, and on it he read "I am in the saloon downstairs, and I can tell you what advertising is. I know that you don't know. It will mean much to me to have you know what it is and it will mean much to you. If you wish to know what advertising is, send the word 'Yes' down by messenger." The message was signed John E. Kennedy.

It was a name Albert Lasker had never heard. But he was intrigued and sent for Kennedy, who then appeared in his office. According to his own story, after an hour they went down to the saloon together, and emerged at midnight. From that time on, Albert Lasker knew what advertising was. First Kennedy asked him what his own ideas were, and the advertising man mentioned news.

"No," said Kennedy. "News is a technique of presentation. Advertising is a very different thing. I can give it to you in three words."

Lasker said, "I am hungry. What are those three words?"

Kennedy said, "Salesmanship-in-print."

And these three words have defined advertising ever since, although "print" now includes radio and television.

As for John E. Kennedy, he was immediately hired by Lord & Thomas, and two years later the agency, which had never before paid a copywriter more than thirty dollars a week, gladly contracted for Kennedy's services at seventy-five thousand dollars per year. This in 1906!

The successes of Albert Lasker in advertising are legendary. Claude Hopkins followed Kennedy in Lord & Thomas, and his insistence on the reason-why became the focal point of salesmanship-in-print in such memorable campaigns as those which described the sterilization of Schlitz beer bottles by scouring with *live steam,* the *school girl complexion* that Palmolive soap promised to maintain, Quaker puffed cereals as *food shot from guns,* Pepsodent as the *film-removing toothpaste,* New York Central's *water level route* between Chicago and New York, Goodyear — the *all-weather tire.*

Today we are used to such argumentation. But in the 1920's and 1930's advertising was just emerging from its complete absorption with keeping one's name before the public by means that had nothing to do with the reasoning process. Together, Albert Lasker and Claude Hopkins led a revolution, and advertising ceased to be merely publicity.

As this is written, the advertising industry is painfully undecided as to whether its first requirement is to attract attention to itself or to present the product or service that is involved as clearly, directly and as forcefully as possible to its most logical prospects.

The latter has always been the Lord & Thomas way, and I found it in full sway in Chicago in 1942.

As seemed often to happen, my new assignment in the agency turned out not to be at all what I expected. Instead of replacing Mr. Faryon, I was assigned at the outset to the Frigidaire appliance account, and I never did work on Pepsodent until after Mr. Lasker had retired and taken the name of Lord & Thomas with him.

Albert Lasker had won the Frigidaire business a few years earlier because he had talked about selling problems and selling practices and selling propositions rather than the kind of beautiful advertising which had been the fashion in appliance promotion ever since the advent of the mechanical refrigerator. The business philosophy that Mr. Lasker expounded appealed to E. G. Biechler, the General Manager of General Motors's Frigidaire division, and he appointed Lord & Thomas, in New York, over the choice of the Frigidaire advertising manager, who had recommended the J. Walter Thompson Company.

L. A. Clark, the Frigidaire advertising manager, was a friend of mine from San Francisco days and when it was announced that I was being moved to Chicago, he was able to persuade Mr. Biechler that the account would be better off there — for a number of reasons that had nothing to do with me. The truth of the matter was that Albert Lasker and Elmer Biechler were running the advertising as an adjunct to some other aspects of the business in which the two men were deeply engaged, and Lee Clark and Philip M. Bratten, who was the general sales manager, wanted to get the advertising back in their own hands where they were sure it belonged.

I was simply the medium through which this was accomplished. Thus it was Frigidaire on which I worked, and not Reginald Faryon's accounts, until October, when suddenly my job was changed again. I was made manager of Lord & Thomas in Chicago.

History had repeated itself. Just as Walter Doty would surely have become manager in San Francisco had he not moved to *Sunset* magazine, Reginald Faryon would undoubtedly have been made manager in Chicago had he not transferred to Quaker Oats in Canada.

I think I should repeat that in Faryon's case it wasn't at all Lord & Thomas that he wanted to leave, it was Chicago; and Chicago was destined to change more radically and more dynamically in the next twenty-five years than any other American city. This was an undisclosed dividend that I was to receive.

Part III

Part III

Advertising
with No Goods to Sell

It was a little while before it dawned on me that the events that led to my appointment as manager in Chicago had not been exactly as they seemed. The appointment, which came in a surprise telephone call that reached me late one afternoon at the Frigidaire plant in Dayton, Ohio, had actually been planned when I left New York six months before.

As long as Faryon had been in charge of the Pepsodent account, Charles Luckman, Pepsodent's president, had no concern about the quality of the work, but when Faryon departed he insisted that the incumbent manager, who was a topflight personal salesman, be replaced by a more creative advertising man. I was the nominee, and when the appropriate time came, I would be named manager. This was a job to which I did not aspire and Mr. Lasker knew it. Accordingly he nominated me to be Faryon's replacement, in a capacity that I could not reject.

Sometimes Albert Lasker won his points with pure, direct argument; at other times he played cat-and-mouse. He would appear to abandon his point, or even not to have one, but then he would close in, and rare was the decision he failed to win. When Don Francisco at first refused Mr. Lasker's invitation to move from Los Angeles to New York, the proprietor of Lord & Thomas was hard put to change his mind. Francisco was adamant. His wife was adamant. But Albert Lasker was not to be denied. John Gunther tells the story in his book *Taken at the Flood: The Story of Albert D. Lasker.*

"Don," a stern-faced Lasker said, "I have just made a will. I have designated you to succeed me as head of this business. This means, of course, that you will have to move to New York when the time comes. D'you?"

"Yes," said Francisco.

"You accept to do this for me?"

"I do."

"You will do it for me dead?"

"I will," Francisco repeated.

"Then why not do it for me alive?" Mr. Lasker asked calmly, and Don Francisco could only capitulate. He telephoned his wife and told her to pack.

It was almost the same kind of inverse argument that had got me to New York. ("I couldn't let you come. . . . But if you don't join me right now . . . my whole plan blows up!") The move to Chicago, however, was accomplished by stratagem. I was sent to do a job that I would be happy in in order to position me for one I would have turned down had I been faced with it directly. I had no desire to manage anything.

Advertising in the United States was at a crossroads in 1942. Goods of every kind were becoming short as factory after factory was recruited for war production or essential materials were requisitioned. There was no need for advertising in most industries, and there was a question as to whether advertising for those goods that were available only in limited supply was not unpatriotic. There was also the fact that newsprint and magazine paper were scarce and growing scarcer.

On the other hand, it was known to everyone in the government that (then as now) newspapers and magazines could not continue to publish without advertising because advertising paid more than half of their cost.* Thus if these vital lines of communication with the public were to be kept open for the government, there would have to be advertising. Perhaps there would be some curtailment, perhaps some rationing of space, but there would be advertising.

Naturally, manufacturers whose products or whose facilities had been commandeered were anxious to be remembered against the day when they would again be making and marketing products for civilian consumption, and some of the most dreadful advertising in advertising history was perpetrated in this endeavor at the start. Most of it took the form of advertising of nonexistent goods, ending with the promise that they would be back someday. These were superseded by self-conscious accounts of many an advertiser's war efforts, and advertising might well have continued in this boastful and unrealistic

---

* It is estimated, for example, that a single copy of *Life* without advertising would have to sell for $1.50 on the newsstands today.

pattern had it not been for a misstep on the part of the usually astute George Washington Hill.

For a considerable period of time Mr. Hill had been contemplating a change in the traditional green Lucky Strike package with its gold-rimmed red bull's-eye as the center of attraction. Albert Lasker had convinced him (based on some occult research of his own) that a white package would be far more attractive to the growing army of women smokers, and Raymond Loewy had been commissioned to develop an appropriate design. Still, the tobacco man resisted; he hated to tempt fate, he said, by changing something so well established in so many minds.

There the matter lagged and lapsed until one summer day when someone in the government decided that the war effort required the full production of a chemical element that was the base of the green ink that colored the Lucky Strike package. This was all George Hill needed to announce to the world that *Lucky Strike Green has gone to war!* If this hadn't been put in large type in newspapers and magazines and blasted over the air as often as the tobacco company could arrange to buy space or time for it, the "sacrifice" might have passed as just another rather silly attempt by an advertiser to capitalize on the war. Instead, it became a cause célèbre in the smoldering dissatisfaction with advertising excesses in a time of trouble.

Newspapers screamed about it in editorials. Pastors preached about it from their pulpits. People talked about it everywhere. George Washington Hill was pictured as an ogre whose crime against the public was exploitation by advertising to a degree not reached before by anyone; and advertising itself shared the blame. As it turned out, the furor lasted for months. No other advertising had ever been attacked so bitterly, and while Mr. Hill was overwhelmed by the commotion he had set off, I am inclined to think he enjoyed all the noise, just as he had the violent opposition to his *Reach for a Lucky instead of a sweet.*

Not so the more sober-sided advertisers. They became acutely aware of the backfire that could come from attaching oneself too importantly to the war effort, and although Lucky Strike sales were not adversely affected by the contretemps of the green package, advertising, as a result of the uproar, took a sharp turn. Boasting was confined largely to publicizing awards for war-product excellence and war-production efficiency that were made by the government in the form of E-flags (E for excellence) without which there came to be no respectable manufacturer's head office flagpole. Sometimes one flew several of the proud white banners, floating beneath the American flag. The trouble with

What U. S. Sailors eat on board ship

Whether on a Destroyer, Carrier, or Cruiser, Navy dinner plates are heaped with well-balanced, sustaining food! These are good examples.

Soup and Crackers
Breaded Beef Steak   Brown Gravy
Mashed Potatoes
Buttered Carrots and Peas
Bread and Butter   Combination Salad
Coconut Cream Pie, Coffee

Soup and Crackers
Pot Roast of Beef   Vegetable Gravy
Baked Brown Potatoes
Buttered Cauliflower
Bread and Butter
Ice Cream   Coffee

Grilled Pork Chops
Cream Gravy   Mashed Potatoes
Buttered Corn   Bread and Butter
Lettuce Salad   Thousand Island Dressing
Apple Sauce
Cake   Coffee

Even after months at sea, Navy commissary officers make sure every man on every ship gets his full quota of fresh meat.

A man eats hearty in Uncle Sam's Navy. For every fighting ship clears port with its food lockers bulging with fine, nourishing foods . . . plenty of vegetables and fruits, and plenty of fresh meat.

Meat is the main item in Navy meals. For meat builds stamina and strength. Meat stays by a man, and helps keep him in fighting trim.

That's why U. S. Navy Commissary officers see that choice meats like Star Beef and Veal, Star Ham and Bacon, Cloverbloom Poultry, are aboard ship in abundance. Enough to last for weeks or even

months at sea. Our Navy . . . and the other services too . . . need and get millions of pounds of meat daily from Armour and Company and other packers. Obviously, to help us supply this vast and vitally necessary amount of meat to the armed forces, you on the home front must share the meat that remains. When you ration yourself to your weekly quota of meat, you perform a patriotic duty. For you help us see that every sailor will eat hearty in Uncle Sam's Navy... that every soldier and marine will get the sustaining, stamina-building meat he needs.

Armour and Company

For finest quality and flavor ask for Armour's Branded Products

Star Ham and Bacon   Star Beef, Veal, Lamb   Star Sausage
Star Canned Meats   Cloverbloom Poultry and Dairy Products

This was one of the first purely service advertisements published during World War II. Here Armour told who was getting the meat the public couldn't buy.

the E-flags was that they lacked exclusivity. Every plant had them, and the advertisements that announced the awards could only look very much alike.

Then came an entirely new development. The advertisers' own businesses were forgotten for the time being and their advertising pages were devoted to exploring and explaining various aspects of the war effort as a truly unselfish public service.

One of the first advertisements with this new thrust was prepared in the Chicago office of Lord & Thomas for Armour and Company. It told *Why the average soldier gains 7 pounds during his first month in the Army* and proved its thesis with a typical seven-day menu provided by the Quartermaster Corps; a menu far superior to that obtainable in most homes.

A. J. Bremner, who wrote the entire series of Armour advertisements of which this was the opener, explained, "I wanted to make the mothers feel good. Instead of apologizing for civilian meat shortages, or reporting pridefully on Armour's war output, which was large and important, we used this advertising to assure the mothers and fathers and wives of our servicemen that they would be well taken care of."

The Armour series was conceived at a time when Washington was debating the need for any advertising at all in a wartime economy. Advertising had almost disappeared from the British press. The *Kiplinger Letter* said the U.S. government was planning to eliminate boastful advertising by firms who were "helping to win" the war. The Armour campaign helped to turn both the tide at Washington and the objective of advertisers everywhere — to use their advertising to *aid* the war effort.

Urged by Robert Koretz, a particularly thoughtful member of our staff, International Cellucotton Products Company, the sales agency for Kimberly-Clark Corporation, the makers of Kleenex and Kotex, both of which were strictly rationed to the public, substituted a full schedule of advertising for nurse recruitment that is said to have helped significantly to increase the number of enlistments.

Ours was one of the first advertising agencies to go all out in this direction. When Albert Lasker telephoned me in Dayton, to tell me that he had appointed me manager of the agency's Chicago office, I was working with Lee Clark to put the finishing touches on a series of advertisements for Frigidaire dealing with food conservation and "making do" with plain and plentiful foods in unusual combinations. These had been worked out for us by home economists at *McCall's* magazine and at the Good Housekeeping Institute. They were authentic and authoritative and invaluable. The authenticity was supplied by accepted homemaking authorities writing in conjunction with the world's leading designer and manufacturer of food-keeping and food-preparing appliances — that is to say, refrigerators and ranges.

The value to readers of the advertisements was quickly established and Frigidaire received widespread recognition and thanks for its help.

To make friends by being friends became an avowed function of American business for the first time in advertising. The principle of being right was an old one. But now it was demonstrated once again that to be right is not sufficient; it is necessary in our competitive economy, to appear right, too. Rightness of attitude is something that is difficult to explain, something that is impossible to argue. It must be demonstrated. This was a lesson that many of us learned from wartime advertising and never forgot.

Another result of the diversion of so much advertising in 1942 was the formation of the War Advertising Council to solicit space and time from national advertisers and newspapers, magazines, broadcasters and outdoor and transportation plant operators, to make a pool of these facilities for various campaigns in the public service. The Council was immediately and lastingly successful, for it has been continued to this day. All U.S. Savings Bonds advertising has come out of this pool. All National Safety Council advertising has come out of this pool. All Red Cross advertising for help in disasters has come out of this pool. So has the advertising of Smokey the Bear, whose admonition to help prevent forest fires has been credited by the U.S. Forest Service with saving millions of acres of irreplaceable timber land.

Smokey the Bear and the advertising for the National Safety Council were our initial contributions to the continuing effort. But these came later.

In October of 1942 we were concerned with the war.

Nothing could have astonished me more than Albert Lasker's surprise call to me in Dayton. Things, so far as I knew, were going fairly well in Lord & Thomas in Chicago.

There had been only one hitch. After a stormy few months, in which it became impossible for us to satisfy the sales management of the Pabst Brewing Company, we had been discharged — this time for a reason that was not included above in discussing the traditional excuses that are encountered for agency terminations. Our manager had gone over the heads of the sales and advertising executives and taken some advertising, which they had turned down, to the president of Pabst. This was a fatal mistake, as it usually is. Advertising decisions that are made by the staff are upheld by chief executives nine times out of ten.

This was something that Mr. Lasker could not understand. His dealings with his agency's clients had always been carried on in the top echelons and usually with the president or chairman of the board, whichever was the chief operating officer. He could not bring himself to the level of the new young executives who were taking over the management of advertising in the increasing complexity of business organizations.

Today, except in a very few instances, the whole advertising operation, including the advertiser-agency relationship, is in the hands of professional marketing men, many of whom are the product of the graduate schools of business administrations in our leading universities. They are conservative by training and by necessity. They are not principals; they operate with someone else's funds; and taking chances of any kind is unthinkable to them. It is also impossible if they are to fulfill their function.

The Pabst termination gave Albert Lasker a clear view of what was to come in the changing pattern of agency-client relationships. And he didn't like what he saw. He had already come to a parting of the ways with General David Sarnoff for much the same reason; he was denied access to the General, who had decided that it was time for the advertising of his Radio Corporation of America to be handled by his marketing people.

RCA was an old Lord & Thomas client. General Sarnoff was an old Lasker friend. When it came to doing business according to the dictates of the General's subordinates, Albert Lasker resigned the RCA account. Had he been in Chicago instead of New York when the Pabst situation became acute he might have resigned Pabst, too, and been satisfied. As it was, he was distressed by the termination, and the fate of the Lord & Thomas Chicago manager was settled. I was put in his place only a little sooner than planned.

The End of Lord & Thomas

WHAT none of us knew was that the change in managers in Chicago was a small incident in a large discontent that was growing in Albert Lasker's mind.

Lord & Thomas had been bigger and Mr. Lasker had been richer than many of the firm's clients. The relationships had been cemented at the top. When their structure began to change, when he became a supplier instead of a valued consultant, Mr. Lasker lost interest in the business. He saw that the day of the individual owner or the lasting partnership of two or three men in any large undertaking was gone. Business had become too big for that. And it was going to be bigger. But it was not for him. There was too little action in it for a man whose driving passion was impatience.

On December 18, almost two months to the day after I had succeeded to the front office in the Palmolive Building, I was summoned to New York to be told by Mr. Lasker that he was going to shut down Lord & Thomas on December 31, and retire from advertising forever. Were it not for the fact that Mrs. Lasker sat beside her husband when he made his announcement to Emerson Foote and me, I would have doubted that he was doing anything more than setting us up for some further declaration, some even more startling proposition. And, in a way, he was. But, not any way that anyone in Lord & Thomas could have conceived.

First, he said, he wanted Mr. Foote and me to know exactly what the reasons were for his decision. "To begin with," he said, "I am tired. I can't seem to get enough rest. D'you?"

Here I shall not try to reproduce Mr. Lasker's unique verbal punctuation because it would seem to mock him in his fairly long speech, and I have no wish to do that.

"I go to bed tired, and when I wake up I wake up more tired than when I went to sleep. The reason is that I am bored. The reason why I am bored is because, except for Mr. Hill and Mr. Luckman at Pepsodent, and Mr. Kimberly and Mr. Mahler at Kimberly-Clark, I find myself overridden and overcome by juniors.

"These are young men who have no wish to meet challenges with boldness, but only hope that somehow they may be able to escape from those challenges. This is a breed I cannot understand. They bore me beyond belief. I owe it to myself to be rid of them; boredom is a disease and it is fatal, and I have resolved to live.

"About the war. I feel only that we are doing less well than we want the world to know. I have some ideas about this, and I would like to help. I am haunted by the specter of a German victory.

"I want now to devote my life to new interests. I have used up the old ones.

"Also, and finally, I have no obligation outstanding. There were many years when I looked forward to turning over this business to my son, but Edward has informed me that when he returns from the Navy it will be to something other than advertising. I think he accepts my view of the changed status of the agency that makes its principals employees instead of partners with their clients in their undertakings together.

"Anyway, Lord & Thomas will come to an end on the last day of this year, and I have it in mind that you, Mr. Foote, in New York, and you, Mr. Cone, in Chicago, and Mr. Belding, in California, may figure out ways and means to carry on the separate parts of the business independently, and in this way serve my clients and make a place for my longtime employees.

"I want you to think about this, and meet with me here again tomorrow, with Mr. Belding, whom I have sent for."

Thus we were informed that Lord & Thomas, at least as we had known it, would be no more. When I left Mr. Lasker's house in Beekman Place, I left in a daze; I couldn't quite believe what my ears had heard. That anyone who had spent such a colorful life in business and arrived at such conspicuous success could suddenly abandon it was beyond my comprehension.

Then I began to think.

After the death of his first wife in 1926, Albert Lasker had lived adrift and unhappy most of the time until his meeting, twelve years later, with an extraordinary woman named Mary Woodard Reinhardt.

After their marriage in 1940 her broad interests became his interests, too, and he was supercharged. The things about the advertising business that had distressed him because he couldn't conform to the new concepts, now were eliminated from his concern. In their place he found himself absorbed in a new world of science and the arts to which Mary Lasker had introduced him.

He had turned full circle from hectic business to a calm and consoling life filled with endless unexpected wonders, and he was using his large fortune to seed a growing list of projects in the public interest. He had traded what he saw as a life of repetition for one of new exploration and discovery, and he wanted to make the closing of the first so complete and so unequivocal that it could never impinge upon the second.

Albert Lasker had decided that to be an adman, or any other kind of businessman for that matter, was only important and only satisfactory if success there could be capitalized for some greater good. Mr. Lasker had been a generous contributor to many causes. Now he became an active participant in the affairs of a number of others to which Mrs. Lasker directed his attention.

He felt that the advertising agency business below the top layer of such firms as Lord & Thomas, J. Walter Thompson, N. W. Ayer, Young & Rubicam, Benton & Bowles and a few others was superficial, unstable, irresponsible and slightly immoral. This was one of the reasons for Albert Lasker's defection. He felt that the business had been sullied; and it had, by glib operators and such medicine men as two nondescript brothers named Townsend who had patented twenty-six checkpoints for guaranteed advertising success, and the gurus from abroad who wanted to make it a mystery.

Sometime during the hours between Mr. Lasker's first intimation of his intentions and the meeting next morning with Mr. Foote, and Mr. Belding and me, together with Mrs. Lasker and Albert Hopkins, the Chicago lawyer who was the Lord & Thomas attorney, the original proposition to replace the old agency with three independent companies was changed. And although it took a number of meetings between Mr. Lasker and Mr. Hopkins and Arthur Andersen, the famed certified public accountant, to arrange for the liquidation of Lord & Thomas, the terms by which the business was to be carried on were agreed to at once, and these were never altered. Instead of the three separate companies suggested the day before, Mr. Lasker now proposed that Mr. Belding, Mr. Foote and I form a partnership to take over whatever we could of the domestic business of Lord & Thomas and operate this just as it had been operated in the past.

"I will recommend it to every one of my clients," Mr. Lasker said. "And I believe most of them will go along with you.

"As for money, you will need very little of your own. If you can raise a hundred thousand dollars, I am sure that I can arrange a loan for a similar amount from a private banking house, and Mr. Andersen assures me that there will be no trouble in securing continuing bank financing as soon as the new firm opens for business."

Albert Lasker had thought it all out.

It sounded simple, and it proved to be just that. All but two of the Lord & Thomas clients, two of the smaller ones in California, agreed to transfer their accounts to the new agency.

Foote, Cone and Belding quickly raised thirty-two thousand dollars each, and William R. Sachse, longtime treasurer of Lord & Thomas, who was to occupy the same position in the new company brought the total of employee financing to the agreed hundred thousand dollars.

At Mr. Lasker's urging and presumably on his guarantee, for surely they had never heard of either Foote, Cone or Belding, the private banking house of A. G. Becker Company in Chicago loaned the triumvirate a similar amount.

Arthur Andersen convinced the Bankers Trust Company, in New York, that the new firm was in effect backed by twenty of the most soundly financed companies in America. These ranged from the American Tobacco Company and Armour and Company at the beginning of the alphabet of corporations, through General Motors (Frigidaire), Kimberly-Clark and Pepsodent to the Sunkist growers and the Union Oil Company of California at the end, and the names in between were no less distinguished.

It was only our own names that anyone could question. At the beginning of the negotiation we had taken it for granted that as "successors" to the business of Lord & Thomas we would also succeed to the name, but this was not to be. "When I retire," said Albert Lasker, "the name Lord & Thomas, which is synonymous with my own, retires too. That you cannot have." When we asked Mr. Lasker to reconsider, he stood firm; and we began to understand that all that Lord & Thomas now meant to him was wrapped up in the name. When he left, it was all that he could take with him.

The total of our payment for the firm's going business, which was at the rate of $20 million per year,* and the firm's great goodwill, was $168,000, which was the depreciated value of the furniture and

---

* The figure represents the advertisers' bill. Publishers, broadcasters and other media allow the agency a commission of 15 per cent. Thus our gross income would be $3 million. Our net would be a hoped-for 10 per cent of that.

fixtures in the several offices, and two engraving and typographic plants — one in New York, one in Chicago.

Any question about a name for the new firm was settled once and for all by Mr. Lasker himself. "The full name," he said, "should be Foote, Cone & Belding and in that order, going across the country from New York to Chicago to California, in westward sequence. D'you?"

Later, as his last suggestion before the final papers were signed in Mr. Hopkins's office in Chicago on December 29, Mr. Lasker pointed to Emerson Foote, and said, "Mr. Foote, you should be the president of the new company, because Mr. Hill would want to deal with the head man." Turning to Don Belding, he said, "You, Mr. Belding, should be chairman of the board, because you are the oldest."

Then he scratched his head. But only for a second.

"You, Mr. Cone," he said, "should be chairman of the Executive Committee, which should be made up of you three and Mr. Sachse."

So it turned out that on the afternoon before New Year's Day in 1943, as Albert Lasker and I left the Lord & Thomas executive offices in the eighteenth floor of the Palmolive Building, a workman in white overalls waved us through the door where he was scraping off the time-honored name.

After the holiday it would be replaced with the new one.

On that same biting cold day the liquidation of Lord & Thomas was reported in newspapers from California to New York, and *Time*, the weekly newsmagazine, in its issue dated January 4 (which presented Joseph Stalin on the cover as *Time*'s Man of the Year) took an icy look at the advertising news from Chicago and decided that it wasn't very good. What bothered *Time* most was the passing of a famous name.

"To the advertising world," the item concluded, "it was almost as if Tiffany had announced that from now on it would be known as Jones, Smith & Johnson."

It is entirely possible that *Time*'s dim view resulted from Mr. Lasker's failure to consult his friend Henry Luce, *Time*'s editor, about the changes he proposed. But in this instance he kept his own counsel and he kept his own secret — with but one exception.

One of the clients of Lord & Thomas was most important of all. George Hill could have cast serious doubts on the competence of the new agency merely by withholding his decision for a few weeks. But he didn't. He pledged his account to Foote, Cone & Belding as soon as Albert Lasker informed him of his impending retirement and before he had told Mr. Foote and me.

"Mr. Lasker has advised us of his decision to dissolve the firm of

George Washington Hill, benign in this picture, was a master of explosive advertising. He wanted his advertisements talked about, and they were.

Lord & Thomas," Mr. Hill told *Advertising Age*. "Of course we are sorry. I have always looked upon Mr. Lasker as outstanding in his profession — a genius in fact. He and I have been continuously associated for 19 years. During all that time his firm has handled the advertising of the American Tobacco Company with a success that has made advertising history. We will continue to place our advertising with the young men Mr. Lasker trained and who will now be on their own."

It was with this acquiescence that Albert Lasker had unfolded his plan to us. The next to hear it were the Pepsodent and Frigidaire and Kimberly-Clark people. The rest were informed within the week. None let the word escape.

I suspect they were as startled as we were. But the war was on everyone's mind and this was no time to question a mere advertising decision. That Foote, Cone & Belding was destined to handle some *billions* of dollars worth of advertising, both within the United States and abroad, was beyond anyone's dream.

Foote, Cone and Belding

HAD anyone told me that we would enjoy Chicago I would have thought he was crazy. I had seen all of Chicago that I needed to between trains, riding from the drafty old Chicago and North Western station to the sooty old La Salle Street station under the grinding elevated; and I had got deathly sick at the Century of Progress Exposition on the hot, humid lakeshore. I had also drunk beer during Prohibition in a West Side speakeasy that shared a building with a firehouse and a police station.

Chicago was something I had wanted no part of. I was sentenced to it; and I only hoped that my indefinite term would be a short one.

Now it is twenty-six years later and my devotion to the city is complete. That Chicago emerged so slowly as a great city (as opposed to merely a large city) resulted, I believe, from the fact that its cocoon was a thick shell of indifference. It had been easy to brand the belligerent stronghold of Medill and McCormick and the swashbuckling Armours as uncouth and unpleasant. "Hog butcher to the world" was part of a poem by Carl Sandburg, but Chicagoans were open to suggestion, and Sandburg's further suggestion that the beautiful shore of Lake Michigan lay in the city's front yard like "lace on a pair of dirty drawers" was true enough to make the citizenry self-conscious.

There was also the buffoon mayor, William Hale Thompson, who campaigned not on civic issues, but against King George V of England whom he threatened to punch in the nose, should the English ever try to invade Chicago. After "Big Bill" Thompson came the gangsters; and it was typical of the city that its attitude toward the mob that seemed to be concerned mostly with itself should be one of indifference. Indifference to any and all criticism was a necessary defense; and it was easy to practice for people who only worked in Chicago and spent their evenings and their weekends on the heavily wooded North Shore and in the western suburbs, serenely detached from the bustle and the blight that marked the naked city.

It would be more than ten years before Chicago's climb to its present position would begin, but the city's growing importance as a commercial and industrial center was laying the groundwork. The packinghouse was giving way to the banking house and the steel mill as the city's symbols. Chicago was soon to take Pittsburgh's place as the leader in steel production. It was the center of rail transportation, and it was well on its way to becoming the center for the burgeoning air transport industry. The crossroads of the nation was coming into its own.

The war woke Chicago up, not only to the responsibility which its people could no longer dodge, but also to the possibilities they had so long ignored. It had been, as Carl Sandburg had said, "a sleeping giant." But now it was awake.

Perhaps most important was the flood of newcomers drawn to the city by the obvious advantages of its central location, its unexploited resources of manpower, and its untapped wealth. A tightly closed business and banking community became a wide-open one as longtime owners and operators loosed their hold on commerce and industry, and joined with the newcomers to open up Chicago to the hundreds of new businesses that wartime developments had spawned.

What had not been obvious for the very simple reason that it did not exist was good government. The city's taxes had been held to a minimum, but so had the services that taxes are meant to provide. The police were notoriously corrupt. Badly lit streets made Chicago a dark jungle at night. The antiquated elevated system gave it the poorest mass transportation of any large city; and, save for the spectacular Outer Drive along the lakeshore, there were no expressways either within the city proper, or as approaches from the surrounding suburbs. City water was not fit to drink. The fire department was inadequate. The rat-infested old wooden slums were a health and fire hazard. The schools were too few, and many school buildings were relics of the nineteenth century.

All this began to change with the aid and support of the newcomers who had no binding political or other ties to the city's strangling past, and who gradually enlisted the old selfish interests to join the new order.

Not surprisingly, one area in business where the city had long been alert was in advertising. One reason was the presence of Albert Lasker on the scene for so many years. He had pushed the concept of salesmanship in print and he had successfully extended this to the air when radio was introduced. He had resisted any notion that advertising was anything but a hardworking device for selling, and advertising in Chicago was made in the mold he had fashioned.

This was something that I had ample time to think about.

When I arrived in Chicago to work in the Palmolive Building — where my office looked down on the gray stone mansion of Edith Rockefeller McCormick and, a little beyond on the Gold Coast, Potter Palmer's turreted castle — and to live in Glencoe, twenty miles north on that same lakeshore, advertising was one of the least of the business world's worries. And, as I have suggested, it was one of the least of our clients' concerns.

Restrictions on the use of steel and the facilities for manufacturing consumer durable goods had hit the appliance industry perhaps harder than any other. Moreover, restrictions on the use of meat and grain and sugar for civilian consumption had cut deeply into the production of processed foods. Restrictions on the use of pulp and paper threatened to reduce the size of newspapers and magazines, and curtail packaging. Restrictions on the use of tin eliminated it entirely from consumer goods. Manufacturers of drugs and cosmetics, including such everyday requirements as toothpaste, were hit by rationing; they could make just so much and no more, and a goodly share of what they made was requisitioned for the armed forces. So it was with batteries and tires and gasoline; even heating oils.

Altogether, the principal clients upon whom the new agency must depend for its existence faced a rocky and uncertain future.

Nevertheless, when Albert Lasker was asked at the time of the formation of Foote, Cone & Belding what he thought the future of the new company would be, he chuckled. "If it fails, people will say that it couldn't succeed without me," he said. "If it succeeds, they'll say that I trained my men so well that they couldn't fail." Mr. Lasker was a master not only of the closed-end question but also of the open-end answer.

In this case he might have added that barring the possibility that advertising still might be eliminated from the scene, the situation held certain advantages for the new firm. Competition was practically at a standstill. The agencies were shorthanded, but so were the advertisers. Changes in agency assignments were being made only of necessity. It was pretty clear that there would be a period when our clients would not be vigorously solicited by other agencies, and we would have a chance to make good.

That we did was because Mr. Lasker *had* trained his men well, and there were a sufficient number of these who were at the upper limits of the draft and recruitment age that our staff, at the top, remained largely intact.

Nevertheless, there were questions to be answered.

"When the great advertising agency of Lord & Thomas was dissolved with dramatic suddenness and Albert Lasker, its heart and soul, announced that Emerson Foote, Fairfax M. Cone and Don Belding, executive vice presidents, would organize an entirely new agency under their own names," S. R. Bernstein wrote in *Advertising Age*, "there was sad shaking of the heads." Who, after all, were Messrs. Foote, Cone and Belding?

"Belding, it is true," Bernstein noted, "has achieved a position of some distinction on the West Coast. But Foote, in New York, and Cone, in Chicago — who were they, what did they look like, what accounts did they control?"

The questions were perfectly fair. And the facts were almost painfully clear.

Certainly Don Belding was distinguished in advertising in the West, and he had had a colorful career. An artilleryman in World War I, he had become a Western Union telegrapher in Grant's Pass in his native Oregon, and then publisher of the Klamath Falls *News* when an illness that was a result of the war sent him into a government hospital for more than a year. Upon his release, in 1923, Belding was moved to Los Angeles and enrolled in a training program for veterans; the training consisting of a job as office boy at government expense in the advertising firm of Lord & Thomas.

Before long Belding became a regular employee of the agency — on the agency payroll at sixty-five dollars a month. When Foote, Cone & Belding was formed he had been in the business for almost twenty years, in the media and copy departments and in account management, successively; and finally, from 1938, as manager of the Los Angeles office of Lord & Thomas where the principal clients were a formidable quartet whose trade names were Lockheed, Purex, Sunkist and Union Oil.*

Belding was forty-four, and he had been active in industry and civic affairs. He was one of the founders of the War Advertising Council and was the only advertising man who was a director of the Chamber of Commerce of Los Angeles.

Emerson Foote was thirty-six and I was now thirty-nine and we had no such distinction.

---

* Even Don Belding's secretary was a formidable figure. Her name was Helen Gurley, and later, as Helen Gurley Brown, she wrote *Sex and the Single Girl*. Presently she is editor of *Cosmopolitan* magazine.

Born in Alabama, Foote had been trained as an accountant and statistician. He was well read and well spoken. Also, he was tall and very distinguished-looking. After attempting unsuccessfully to land a job in the research department of Lord & Thomas in Los Angeles, he had entered advertising in the Leon Livingston agency in San Francisco. In 1934 he went into business for himself in the partnership of Yeomans & Foote. Here one of the clients was a local Chrysler and Plymouth automobile dealer and through him Emerson Foote came to the notice of J. Stirling Getchell, whom he joined in New York just a few months after I had made my way West from the Chrysler tower.

It was one of my last assignments for Stirling Getchell to visit with Emerson Foote in San Francisco to see whether I would recommend him. When I did this with enthusiasm I opened a straight path to our own later association.

After Getchell's death in 1938, and the dissolution of the Getchell firm, Foote joined Lord & Thomas in New York as an assistant account executive for Lucky Strike cigarettes. It was in this role that he met George Hill, Jr., and, through the young Hill, his father. Soon thereafter Foote was made vice president of the agency, in charge of the American Tobacco Company business, and subsequently, in 1941, shortly before I arrived there, general manager for Lord & Thomas in New York.

My own story up to this point has been told. I should only add that during my first year in Chicago my health continued to be poor. I barely lasted through each day. I was totally exhausted every night. I stayed in bed all through each weekend. But the challenge had to be met.

As to the control of business, the plain fact was, of course, that neither Foote nor Belding nor I controlled a single account in the sort of tight grip with which Mr. Lasker had held so many.

The only resources we had were our strong convictions. We believed that advertising should be thoughtful and honest with no exceptions, and that no other kind should ever play a part in the affairs of Foote, Cone & Belding. Nor has it. The only Federal Trade Commission citation ever issued against this agency was quickly withdrawn when the facts were made known. An overzealous Commission agent cited us for a claim on the radio that Pepsodent toothpaste would remove stains from any discolored teeth. Obviously this could not be true; even dentists couldn't remove *all* stains. But we had made no such claim. The agent had a faulty set of ears, and when the tapes were played for the Commission the case was dismissed.

Despite spirited speculation in the trade with regard to the compatibility of Foote, Cone and Belding, the only serious disagreement the partners ever had concerned a proposition that was made to us to merge our company with another whose sole owner had died suddenly early in our second year. Foote and I felt that while the combination of the two agencies' clients would nearly double the size of our business, combining our lack of experience in management would increase the hazard for everyone concerned. Mistakenly, we voted against Belding; as things went along in both companies it became apparent that the merger would have been successful.

On advice of his doctor, Emerson Foote left Foote, Cone & Belding in 1952, after a prolonged illness which had necessitated frequent lengthy absences from the business.* Don Belding retired in 1959 on his sixtieth birthday.

If this were the history of a company, both Foote and Belding would loom large in the story of its early years and its continuing character and personality, for both are individuals with extraordinary talent for advertising and firm convictions about its use. But this is not a history. It is only an account of one man's life in a business that is essentially personal, for its primary objective is communication between two people.

Despite the war and the slowdown in advertising, things began to happen very fast in Foote, Cone & Belding in 1943, and they forced me to spend half my time in New York.

On a misty Saturday morning in April, when Emerson Foote and I were contemplating the hazards of our future, gazing out the windows of his office at the wet street lined with limp flags, the telephone rang, and Foote answered it.

"Who?" he asked. It was plain that he asked it incredulously.

"The Campbell Soup Company? I don't believe you," he said.

But the call was in fact from Camden, New Jersey; from Campbell's advertising director, Harry Jones. "I thought," said Mr. Jones, "that some ambitious young men who were good enough for Lucky Strike cigarette advertising might be good enough for Campbell's soup advertising."

Foote assured him that we would like nothing better than an op-

---

* Upon regaining his health Emerson Foote became president of McCann-Erickson, a division of Interpublic, the world's second largest advertising organization; a position he resigned in protest against that agency's handling of cigarette advertising which his American Cancer Society involvement had taught him to deplore.

portunity to try to prove this. A meeting was arranged for three days later in Camden, and on Tuesday afternoon in the reception room of the executive offices at the immaculate Campbell plant we shook hands on an agreement to go to work at once. (I mention the reception room because that is where most of our contact with Campbell was maintained; it was the only place in the building where smoking was allowed.)

Our initial assignment for Campbell was to put that company into radio for the first time. We were producing the popular *Hit Parade* and Kay Kyser's musical quiz show for Lucky Strike cigarettes, the *Bob Hope Show* for Pepsodent, and *Hedda Hopper's Hollywood*, a movietown news and gossip program for Armour; and they were doing well.

Just how well we might have done for Campbell no one will ever know. Our assignment there was different from any other one we had, for it began and ended with the creation and production of a radio program. I should point out that to Campbell the most important thing in radio was the sponsorship of a popular program; the commercials were secondary. We were expected to act as a talent agency rather than an advertising agency and this we found both uncomfortable and unreasonable.

When Harry Jones undertook to change our status, and arranged a meeting in which Foote and I were invited to tell Campbell's president, Arthur Dorrance, something about the total interests and abilities of Foote, Cone & Belding, we thought we had it made. We thought the Campbell Soup people should be pleased with a number of innovations their new agency had undertaken, particularly in the area of advertisement testing, and I was telling the story of its ambitions with gusto, when Dorrance could stand this no longer.

"Gentlemen," he said crushingly, "I couldn't be less interested in the saga of your company." Whereupon he rose from his chair at the head of the table and strode from the room.

Twenty-six months after our starting assignment, the Campbell Soup Company ended our association, and I must say that I was relieved. The radio program we had proposed and produced featured the comedian Jack Carson, and while it hadn't attracted our idea of a satisfactory audience, our client seemed to like it well enough, for Campbell kept it on the air for several years. Anyway, although I enjoyed working with Harry Jones and his bright young assistant, Rex Budd, I could never forget Arthur Dorrance's majestic disinterest.

What I failed to realize was that I should have been talking about his business, not ours. Once I had figured this out, I never made the same mistake again. You have to find just the right moment to talk about yourself. To which I might add: You had better be sure.

In 1943 we turned down two proffered Chicago accounts that together were worth $8 million, which was equal to more than a third of the firm's total annual business at the time. The first of these came from a company whose president had gone through a noisy stockholder controversy. He was an able executive. But he also was thought to be sharp. Thus, we felt that we must decline the account; and although the man we spurned was incensed, Foote and Belding and I stood firm in our conviction that he was not for us.

The second and greater opportunity, from the standpoint of volume, was a little bit trickier. We were offered the account of a rapidly expanding appliance manufacturer whose products were no way competitive to Frigidaire. The president of the company was a man for whom great things were predicted. The company was growing by leaps and bounds through war work and it was agreed that after the war it would be a formidable contender in an important field. We wanted the account very much.

There was only one stumbling block. The company had contracted for a packaged weekly radio program. The president himself had made the purchase of time and talent; the agency would have no talent negotiations or talent responsibility. Just so, there was no sound reason in his mind why we should be paid a commission on talent charges.*

"Only because we have to," I said. "All our other clients pay a commission on talent, and you will have to pay it, too."

"But you won't be doing anything to earn it," he insisted.

"Yes, we will," I said. "If we don't actually earn the commission in connection with the program negotiations, we will earn it some other way. But we have to charge you as we charge everyone else. Not to do this would make us a two-price agency. And this we cannot be."

After several meetings that were friendly enough, but in which I failed to carry my point, our discussions were concluded.

We had failed, to be sure, to get the account, but we had established that Foote, Cone & Belding stuck to its guns.

Incidentally, the same appliance manufacturer approached us again some years later. Presumably this time there would be no stipulations, but I didn't try to find out. A conflicting commitment kept us from any discussion of terms and conditions.

---

* All broadcasters, as indicated before, allow agencies of record the standard 15 per cent commission on time charges. Commission must be added by the agencies themselves on program costs, unless they are a part of the broadcasting package— as most are today.

Nothing that happened at Foote, Cone & Belding in our first year was more dramatic than the manner in which I regained my health overnight.

When I was transferred to Lord & Thomas in Chicago I thought no one knew that I rode home every evening exhausted, hoping that I wouldn't be spoken to on the way, for I had no energy left with which to answer; or that, getting home, I fell promptly into bed, clothes and all.

As it turned out, I was wrong. I had hidden nothing from Albert Lasker. One morning, shortly after the name on the door had been changed, Mr. Lasker came into my office. He had come to Chicago for a Pepsodent company meeting.

"I am going to say two words to you. D'you?" he said. "And if they mean to you what I think they will, I will then tell you something more important than anything I have ever told you before in my life. D'you?"

What, I wondered, could Albert Lasker have to say more important than that we were to succeed to his business. But I wondered for only a second.

"The two words," he said, his eyes flashing, "are *pernicious fatigue.* D'you?"

"I do, I certainly do," I said. "I understand those words as well as I have ever understood any two words. Yet I have never heard them used together before."

"I knew you would understand," Mr. Lasker said. "I knew you would understand just as I did when I first heard them two months ago. For I had been suffering too, for years. All the vacations I took from Lord & Thomas, all the trips, all the times I undertook to retire, were only to try to get away from it. Pernicious fatigue.

"Then I found out that it can be cured. Cured by a man here in Chicago. D'you?"

"Who is this man?" I asked. "Where do I find him?"

"His name is Dr. Sidney Portis, and he is waiting for you in his office on South Michigan Avenue at this minute."

By noon that day I was on my way to being well. Several doctors had known that what caused my incapacity was an overflow of insulin. But they had sought to burn this up by the addition of sugar to my diet. Every time I felt myself growing weak I should eat a candy bar, they said.

"All wrong," said Dr. Portis. "Our job is not to burn the insulin up, but to put out the fire at the source. You have been operating on a vicious cycle. Everything you have done to make yourself feel better could only, possibly, make you feel worse. Deadly fatigue is the result.

Pernicious fatigue. Some time in your life you damaged your liver. The jaundice you had so long ago was the first indication. This is the end result."

Beginning that day I took two small red and white capsules that Portis gave me, after every full meal; and I ate half meals in between. The capsules contained atropine to slow the activity of the pancreas. With the added small amount of food on a regular schedule, they changed my life within twenty-four hours after I met Sidney Portis. Never since the first capsule I swallowed have I experienced the old sinking feeling. Never since have I felt the sickening fear that was part of my life for so long.

Albert Lasker had indeed given me his most important message when he sent me to Sidney Portis.

Some months later, in June 1944, I received my telephone call from Carleton Healy, my old friend from the Getchell agency, from the headquarters of Hiram Walker & Sons, Inc., the distillers, in Walkerville, Ontario, and in a matter of a few days Foote, Cone & Belding was appointed for the advertising of Walker's Imperial whiskey, for which the budget was set at $3 million.

In an industry that is constantly under political and crank attack, Hiram Walker's conduct is both calm and sure. This is one of the best managed companies I have ever observed. Anyone could know this from its annual reports; but they would know it better if they knew its people.

The only possible mistake of which I have ever been aware in their marketing was the underpricing of Imperial. It became the second largest-selling whiskey in America. But at a higher price it might have been supreme. At a lower price than the leader, unsophisticated buyers couldn't believe that Imperial really was the superior product that advertising promised.

Imperial whiskey is a blend. It is made of 35 per cent six-year-old bourbon whiskey and 65 per cent grain neutral spirits. The principal difference between whiskey and neutral spirits is that the spirits that are to become whiskey are colored and matured in charred oak barrels; the spirits, which are to remain spirits are distilled from identical grains, but they are not aged.

When blended, then, the result is a much milder whiskey, since the neutral spirits are free of the heavy bodies of the straight product that are continuously increased in barrel storage. The problem in blending is to make the blend smooth; to make one taste instead of two. And this Hiram Walker had accomplished in Imperial better than any other American distiller. It came about by storing Imperial's neutral spirits in used whiskey barrels for a short time to give them just enough of the true whiskey character to make the blend easy and natural.

The previous advertising agency for Imperial had talked about the brand's velveted spirits. But no one we could find had any idea what this meant; it was an empty phrase. It didn't get across by itself, and you couldn't explain it in print. Neutral spirits are neutral by legal definition. Since they are neutral legally, it is against U.S. law to attribute to them any distinctive characteristics, no matter what may actually have been done to develop these. This is the only instance I know where a law *forbids* advertising to tell the truth!*

How we got around this came out of some simple research. I have said that the grain neutral spirits used in Imperial are stored in used whiskey barrels, and seeing these barrels lying row upon row in Hiram Walker's colony of red brick rack houses in Peoria, Illinois, where Imperial is distilled for American consumption, gave us an idea.

"What," we asked some hundreds of whiskey drinkers in a nation-wide, face-to-face poll, "gives whiskey its character?"

"Aging," they answered, to a man.

"And how is whiskey aged?" we asked.

"In barrels," was the invariable reply.

Next we set out across the country with some pen-and-ink draw-ings of barrels standing on end, singly, and asked some hundreds more men, "What do you suppose is in this barrel?" A few answered, "Nails." A few, mostly in German communities, said, "Beer." Flour came up now and again, and pickles. But overwhelmingly our re-spondents looked at the pictures of the unmarked barrels and said in-stantly that they contained whiskey. When later we showed *racks* of barrels to still other people, there was no doubt at all that these were whiskey barrels. I think the vote was about 90 per cent in favor of whiskey.

Thereupon we commissioned a number of distinguished American artists to go to Peoria and paint what they saw in that world of oak casks. We sent Aaron Bohrod and Joseph Hirsch and Luigi Lucioni, Joe Jones and Thomas Hart Benton, and some of the others we re-membered from the tobacco country pictures they had painted for Lucky Strike cigarettes. And we added the illustrators Fred Ludekens and Albert Dorne.

James Chapin wouldn't go. He thought he had been badly dealt

* Scotch is always labeled as a blend of scotch whiskies. This is by courtesy of the international code. A "scotch" whiskey made in America would have to be labeled a blend of whiskey and grain neutral spirits. This is how light some of the constituents are.

"Whiskey Going to the Rackhouse to Age"—painted at the distillery by the famous artist, Thomas Hart Benton

88 years at fine whiskey-making

makes this whiskey good

IMPERIAL

Hiram Walker's Blended Whiskey

86 proof. The straight whiskies in this product are 4 years or more old. 30% straight whiskey. 70% grain neutral spirits. Hiram Walker & Sons Inc., Peoria, Ill.

Pictures like this, in a long list of magazines, told a story for Imperial that the law wouldn't let us put in words. Thomas Hart Benton was the artist.

with when George Hill ran his blue-shirted genii of the tobacco field in muddy black-and-white newspaper advertisements day after day for most of two weeks, and the thought made him ill. He had been exposed to ridicule by other artists and he was afraid of advertising.

Despite our inability to persuade Mr. Chapin to contribute to the project, the campaign was a conspicuous success. We showed barrels inside the red rack houses and outdoors in the sun and in the pelting rain; barrels being charred and filled and bunged and emptied and tested and weighed; barrels standing, rolling, resting. But barrels always.

Under each painting the advertisements carried a single line of text. The barrels told the reason for Imperial's goodness more clearly than the words we couldn't use.

What happened to the campaign? The same thing that happens sooner or later to most advertising campaigns, however effective they may prove. The salesmen wanted something new. Tim Healy, who might have saved it, had moved out of the immediate picture to become an officer of the parent company, Hiram Walker–Gooderham & Worts, Ltd., and Imperial had a new advertising manager who wanted to be responsible for something of his own.

Our initial advertising for Imperial whiskey had more than a little to do with the appointment of Foote, Cone & Belding by General Foods. Don Belding had become acquainted with Charles G. Mortimer, advertising director of the big food company, when both served on the War Advertising Council, and I believe it was mostly a courtesy to Belding that when General Foods decided in 1945 to add a third agency for its expanded business, Foote and Belding and I were invited to meet with the committee appointed to make a selection.

We were asked to keep our meetings secret. General Foods had invited only four other agencies to make solicitations and they didn't want to see any more. To make sure there was no leak from us, we worked on our presentation alone, except for the assistance of William E. Berchtold, a trusted member of our New York staff, and on Tuesday, May 15, we presented to Mortimer, Ralph Starr Butler, advertising director emeritus of General Foods, Mrs. E. B. Meyers, Mortimer's assistant, and Clarence Eldridge, the head of the cereals division, detailed answers to eighteen questions that we had decided we would ask of an agency if our positions were reversed.

Mostly, of course, the questions had to do with what kind of advertising we were making, and how it was performing; but they also asked how we used research and how deeply we were concerned with the fundamentals of marketing. There were a number of campaigns we could talk about. There was Kotex, whose "Are You in the Know?" series of social tips for teenagers was piling up some of the highest readership figures in the women's magazines. There was Kleenex, for whom we had recently lured Little LuLu, Mrs. Marjorie Buell's pixy cartoon character from the editorial pages of the *Saturday Evening Post*, to sell tissues with a smile. There were Frigidaire and Armour with their award-winning wartime conservation campaigns. There was Sunkist, for whom Lord & Thomas had long before conceived the idea of drinking juice daily (prior to that, an orange had been mostly a treat in a Christmas stocking). There were also the campaigns for Lucky Strike and Pepsodent.

All these we talked about. But it was the barrel campaign for Hiram Walker's Imperial whiskey, the problem of the neutral spirits that were not neutral, and its solution, that proved to be most interesting to the keen-minded Mortimer, Butler and Eldridge, and Mrs. Meyers.

We were invited to return to the discussion on July 11, which we did, at length; and on August 2, almost three months after our first meeting in the hideout in the Biltmore Hotel, General Foods announced that Foote, Cone & Belding had been chosen to become one of the trio of General Foods agencies, with Young & Rubicam and Benton & Bowles. General Foods was the third largest advertiser in the country, after General Motors and Procter & Gamble, and together with Lever Brothers these were the elite. Three of the four were our clients. And Neil McElroy and Howard Morgens at Procter & Gamble had told us to come see them whenever we thought we were ready.*

Best of all, our client companies were managed by people who were aware of the value of advertising to their operations. It is simply a fact that an advertising agency can never be better than its clients. It can only try to be as good. If it lags behind, it is almost sure to be replaced. If it gets very far ahead, it had better change its clients. It can have no existence by itself.

One of the things that is frequently misunderstood about the relationship between agency and advertiser is that there can be no immoral advertising agencies unless there are immoral advertisers. It is impossible to have one without the other, for it should always be remembered that it is the advertiser who pays the bill. No agency that I know of ever ran an advertisement without the advertiser's

---

* That we never were was the result of our association with Armour's Dial soap, which was competitive with several P&G brands.

approval, both of the advertisement and of the projected bill for space or time. (None, that is, except Lord & Thomas in San Francisco, where I was in the unique position of being both advertising agent and advertising consultant for the Dollar Steamship Lines and its successor, American President Lines.)

The estimate is the double check. The advertiser always knows what it is that he will be asked to pay for. Still, it is not uncommon to hear someone say: "What a horrible advertisement. I don't think much of the agency that was responsible. Those people have no taste." Maybe it is true that the agency that was responsible lacks taste. But so must the advertiser, or he never would have approved the offending advertising. In bad advertising, as in many other things, it takes two to make the final, binding mistake. In fact, advertising is an activity in which an offense against decency cannot be committed alone. It has to have connivance.

Actually, the connivance must go beyond the advertiser and his agency. These two can only plan and produce distasteful or dishonest advertising. Before it can affect or offend anyone it must be transmitted, either in print or through the air. The medium thus becomes the third partner in deception or bad taste.

What distinguishes the leading advertisers is that every one of them is in business for as far ahead as he can see. Everyone knows that you can't sell a bad product twice to the same purchaser. It may be possible to sell a badly built house or an unsound horse, or even a shoddy pair of pants, and make a profit. But having once done so, you cannot expect to sell *another* house or horse or pair of pants to the customer who feels cheated.

Most widely advertised products require not only repeat purchases but *frequent* repeat purchases simply to pay out the cost of advertising for the original sale. For example, first-year advertising for Dial soap cost almost four times what Armour and Company received from retailers for each case they bought; today, twelve years later, with ten times as much advertising, and at a lower price to the consumer, Dial is sold at a profit.

This same thing is true of almost every other product that has the benefit of national advertising. It had to be good at the start to get the advertising money back. It has to continue to be good to keep the advertising money coming in, to attract new users, to make the business grow. Sometimes we hear it said, in words and tones of bitter complaint, that this or that product isn't what it used to be. And sometimes it isn't. But usually, I think, the product hasn't changed nearly so much as the complainant's taste or feel or sight or smell.

Competition is much too keen to let any large-selling consumer item decline in quality. When it is changed, the change is for improvement. Almost anything else not only invites a quick demise, it almost guarantees it. The exceptions come usually from the substitution of cheaper materials, made to help meet ever-increasing labor costs.

Likewise, I believe that planned obsolescence is largely a myth. To be sure, goods manufactured to meet price competition may not last as long as goods manufactured without regard to cost. But the value had better be there. America votes for its favorite products every day, in millions of over-the-counter transactions. Advertising only puts their names in nomination.

The Hucksters

NINETEEN forty-six was the year of *The Hucksters*, Frederic Wakeman's sensational novel that was widely accepted as the definitive picture of advertising and advertising people in the United States. Unfortunately, for the truth of the matter, this has never been entirely corrected. What keeps the image alive is its almost continuous exposure on late-night television, where Clark Gable as the advertising agent torn between right and wrong and Sidney Greenstreet as the demonic soap manufacturer who is his client and his nemesis have become symbols of a great tug-of-war between good and bad in industry and advertising. Advertising as it is ordered by the wanton tycoon is nothing but bombast, and he enjoys this most when it is achieved in the worst possible taste.

Clark Gable was the top male star in the movies when *The Hucksters* was screened. Deborah Kerr, who is the object of his affection in the picture, was an exciting foreign importation. But the initial success of the book from which the film was made lay largely in the carefully planted suggestion that the incredible soap man and his servile advertising people were not creatures of Wakeman's imagination at all, but only slightly disguised portraits of George Washington Hill and the agency principals.

It should be repeated that the entertainers didn't like Mr. Hill. He knew what he wanted from them and he insisted upon having it. When the entertainers complained of interference (which was usually a cover-up for demands for more money) the columnists rose in their defense. Now they hinted broadly that the rapacious, impossible soap king of the novel, who wore a straw hat in his office and spat on his glass-topped desk to emphasize a point in an argument was indeed a character drawn from real life; and the life was Hill's.

Hadn't Wakeman been a copywriter at Foote, Cone & Belding? A copywriter on the Lucky Strike account? Didn't Hill wear his hat in his office? Didn't he argue constantly with the producers and the stars of his radio programs, pitting his prejudices against their talents? Hadn't he fought bitterly with Golenpaul over the cost of *Information Please?* Didn't he hire and fire stars indiscriminately? Weren't his Lucky Strike commercials long and loud and endlessly repetitive?

The answer to each of these questions was assumed to be equally affirmative and equally applicable. The man who had sent Lucky Strike green to war for his country as an advertising ploy had been further exposed, and with him the whole nefarious business of advertising which was operated in a jungle of broken promises that were never meant to be kept. Or so *The Hucksters* said, and so the moving picture seemed to document. A whole generation of moviegoers has forgotten that Wakeman was writing popular fiction.

In 1946 the stir was all about the book, and it lasted for many months. In advertising circles — particularly in New York, where Madison Avenue is alive with rumor on even the deadest day — it was freely predicted that Foote, Cone & Belding would shortly be sacked by the tobacco company. It was agreed that Hill would wait only a little while before ridding himself of the painful presence of Wakeman's recent employers. It appeared as if the other agencies had placed the blame for the odious comparisons the novel raised upon Emerson Foote, under whose direction Wakeman had worked on Lucky Strike advertising, and they could hardly wait to hear George Hill pronounce his revenge.

Instead, the American Tobacco Company added to Foote, Cone & Belding's responsibility its second-largest-selling cigarette brand, Pall Mall, and Madison Avenue was dumfounded. The agency that was supposed to be fired out of hand had received a $5 million billing bonus.

However, the effect of *The Hucksters* was only beginning to be realized. With the filming of the story and its repeated showing over a period of almost twenty years, it has undoubtedly had more influence on public opinion than either Upton Sinclair's exposé of the unsavory meat packing industry in *The Jungle* or Ida M. Tarbell's *History of the Standard Oil Company*, which focused the country's attention on the evils of monopoly forty years before. For one thing, there were a great many more people in America to be influenced. For another, there has never been a combination of media to equal moving pictures and television in their power to instruct and convince, for better or worse.

It is doutbtful whether Vance Packard's *The Hidden Persuaders* could have achieved anything like the acceptance it did without the lurid setting of the scene by Fred Wakeman. The public that thrives on the exposure of its own exploitation by big and little swindlers, so that it may be ready to greet the next invasion of fakers, is probably a minuscule public. But *The Hucksters* added to this millions of people who enjoy a lively story. Under the circumstances, Packard's, like Wakeman's, proved to be just that.

Even in 1946 advertising agency practice had gone far beyond the creation of a slogan, which was the principal contribution of Wakeman's hero to the beauty-soap advertising around which the story revolved. *Love that soap* might indeed have been used by one of the soapers, but it would have required support based upon a carefully built and researched selling proposition to back it up, and this was entirely omitted in the novel.

If the omission could be carried into real life, if nothing were required beyond catchy phrases, advertising would be a far simpler business. As it is, the approach to the advertising statement to be made for any product is usually a long road, with a succession of forks to be explored because most products and most services have more than one appeal, and who knows which is most important competitively?

I doubt whether anyone who is not familiar with a modern advertising agency has any idea of the amount of time and money that is spent to find out the real reasons for preference; to find out what is most appealing about new developments, and what are considered of little value. The differences that exist between workers in laboratories and men and women in their homes and gardens and in the aisles of a supermarket are apt to be vast, and they must be thoughtfully explored.

A panel of two hundred housewives given twenty choices of words to express their reaction to a new product they have sampled may be divided evenly among three or four, and so the exercise must be repeated and new tests devised in order finally to arrive at the advertising proposition that is most generally understood and accepted as pertinent. None of this has mostly to do with the product involved. Research and development departments have taken care of that. The problem is one of positioning the product in the market so that millions of potential purchasers who have only advertising to guide them will be guided properly. It is not enough that a product shall be a good product; it is necessary also that it shall be a good product for the particular reason and purpose that it was selected.

The typical agency plans board that concerns itself with such things is the heart of the agency organization. In Foote, Cone & Belding it is made up of members of the senior management group, representatives of the research, media, art and copy departments, and members of the account group involved. Memorandums are issued to the participants in advance so that they may have ample opportunity to study the issues in question. When they convene, their sessions are more like inquisitions than anything else I can think of.

"Are you sure?"

"How do you know?"

"Who says so?"

"What do the figures show?"

That is the gist of the questions. And the answers had better be firm and educated; guesswork is supposed to have been eliminated. In all the thousands of client meetings that I have attended, none has ever approached the savagery of the plans board in digging for facts. I've often been glad that I was not the young account executive or a research assistant making a report on an undecided point.

The free and easy day of the huckster was probably never quite what Fred Wakeman described. But if it was, it is a long-gone day.

Which Twin Has the Toni?

A RECENT graduate of Yale University named R. Neison Harris had opened a beauty shop supply business in St. Paul with his brother Irving. Neison Harris had a vision of millions of women putting permanent waves in their own hair, at home.* And he shared with his brother a belief in advertising that rivaled Albert Lasker's.

The problem was to make it believable in print or over the air that a two-dollar home permanent could rival a beauty shop wave at twice to ten times the price. However, it was a fact. The Toni wave, as it was called, lost nothing in comparison with a professional wave except the user's sense of value. It was the old story of the lower-priced whiskey and the bargain-priced soup: all were too good to be believed. Except by the Harris brothers; they had made many tests and they were convinced that they had only to tell their story convincingly to have a great success.

By chance we had the same attorneys and when they learned of the brothers' dilemma, it was suggested that the Harrises take their problem to Foote, Cone & Belding.

The result was that in the same year of *The Hucksters*, I received a telephone call from Neison Harris in St. Paul.

"I would like," he said, "to talk to you about the advertising of a product of which you possibly never have heard. It is the Toni home permanent wave."

"Ah, but I have heard of it," I said. "I have seen your advertising."

"That," he said, "is exactly what I want to talk to you about."

---

* At Yale, Neison Harris was nicknamed, prophetically, "Wishbone."

WHICH TWIN HAS THE *Toni?*

Lovely Consuelo O'Connor of New York, the Toni twin, says, "My twin sister, Gloria, had a beauty shop permanent— I had a Toni Home Permanent. And none of our friends could tell which had which — can you?" (See answer below.)

You, too, will want your next wave to be a TONI Home Permanent

You'll thank the lucky day you give yourself a Toni Home Permanent. For you'll discover an amazingly easy and inexpensive way to keep your hair always at its loveliest. Beautifully groomed with deep, luxurious waves . . . silky soft and natural looking. Because Toni Creme Lotion waves your hair permanently, but *gently* . . . leaves it frizz-free and easy to manage.

Toni works like a charm on any hair that will take a permanent — even gray, dyed, bleached or baby-fine hair. That's why every hour of the day another 1,000 women use Toni.

No trick at all to giving yourself a Toni . . . just three simple steps.

1. Roll your hair up on curlers, and dab on Toni Creme Lotion.

2. Tie a turban round your head and relax for 2 to 3 hours. (No sitting under a hot dryer.)

3. Saturate each curl with Toni Neutralizer and rinse.

Your Toni Cold Wave is finished . . . it's beautiful . . . and will last as long as a $15 permanent.

Now, while you are thinking about

it, get a Toni Home Permanent Kit. On sale at all leading drug, notion and cosmetic counters.

Consuelo, the twin at the left above, is the one who has the Toni Home Permanent. Could you tell?

Listen to "Give and Take" C B S Network Every Saturday at 2 P.M., E.S.T.

$1 25 *plus tax*

Easy as rolling your hair up in curlers — but the wave stays in

 HOME PERMANENT

THE CREME COLD WAVE

Twins were the subject of a gigantic hunt that soon changed to a deluge of applicants, and which twin had the Toni no one could tell.

"Aren't you the client of another advertising agency?" I asked.

"Yes," he said, "but I am anxious to talk to you."

"I would like to talk to you, too," I said. "But not while you are the client of another agency. I don't like it when our clients discuss our work with other agencies and I don't propose to discuss anyone else's. If you should decide to terminate with your present agency, then I will be glad to talk to you."

Harris, who is a thoughtful man, said he would think about this, and that was the end of our first conversation. A few days later he telephoned again, and again he said that he wanted to discuss Toni's advertising.

"Have you settled the matter with the other agency?" I asked him.

"Yes," he said. "That's why I'm calling you."

Later I learned that while having the same attorneys was not immaterial, Neison Harris had checked us out pretty thoroughly. And there began that afternoon one of the most exciting chapters in beauty product history. The home permanent wave was something millions of women had been waiting for, and the Toni product was practically foolproof.

Moreover, it had exceptionally effective advertising. Harris knew what he wanted to convey in advertising, and we managed in our initial efforts to say it in a dramatically convincing way. I think no one in advertising would deny that our first campaign for Toni, which continued for several years, under the direction of Leo H. Rosenberg (who just happened to have been the first commercial radio announcer) was one of the classic advertising campaigns of modern times.

In print, in magazines and Sunday newspaper supplements, this took the form of a simple but unanswerable question, posed over unretouched photographs of a series of neatly coifed identical twins. The question was *Which Twin Has the Toni?* and it soon was on the lips of almost every teenage and adult female in America.

The thing about it was you *couldn't* tell which twin had the Toni and which had the beauty shop permanent. They were identical in the color photographs and they were identical when live twins were paraded past panels of unmistakably confounded jurors in radio studios in Chicago, Los Angeles, and New York. Nobody could tell which was which: the twin with the two-dollar wave or the twin with the twenty-dollar wave. Toni's success was immediate and deserved. For the Toni home permanent wave kept every promise that was made for it. It made a permanent wave available to countless women who never could afford one before, and it gave a softer, more natural-looking wave than many professionals were achieving.

As with most successful new product introductions, many people benefited from Toni's success. First of all, of course, were the women who were the direct beneficiaries. Then there were Neison and Irving Harris, who eventually would sell their business to the Gillette Safety Razor Company for $20 million, but continue to serve it as overseers. In between, there were the druggists who had a new source of business and the Toni salesmen who called on them and earned bonuses equal to four and five times their annual salaries as Toni sales mounted. Finally, there were the publishers and broadcasters who carried the advertising and the agency people who prepared it.

Understandably, the initial reaction of the beauty shop operator to the home permanent was violent. The makers of Toni were accused of fakery and fraud; and it was whispered in loud stage whispers that a Toni home permanent was the first step toward feminine baldness. Beauticians ran joint advertisements in newspapers and filled their windows with posters attacking the home permanent, even to the point of saying that they would not be responsible for the result of any later treatment of home-waved hair.

The result of the propaganda was nil. The demonstrations carried the day. Toni was the most immediately successful new beauty product ever introduced. Women loved it. Also, ironically, it eventually proved a boon to the bewildered beauty shop operators. Women who waved each other's hair with Toni home permanents spent more money than ever in beauty shops as a means to further enhance their appearance.

Only the manufacturers who followed Toni into the field, trying to capitalize on Toni's success, have failed to do very well. The leader in any new field is rarely dislodged, and Toni never has been.

From my own standpoint the Toni experience was most satisfactory in the contribution it made to the confidence and joy of an immense number of women of all ages whose bane was their straight hair. God knows, no woman *needs* curls, but I love to think how happy it has made so many.

Close on the heels of Neison Harris, with his dream for Toni, came Samuel Goldwyn to appoint Foote, Cone & Belding for the advertising of two great films, *The Best Years of Our Lives* and *The Secret Life of Walter Mitty*; and David O. Selznick, to put $2 million into the promotion of *Duel in the Sun*.

Marshall Field & Company asked us to prepare the first national advertising campaign ever to appear for a department store in a mass magazine, and a series of colorful spreads appeared in *Life*. One of these showed an emerald-and-diamond necklace fancifully draped around the neck of a wide-eyed doll, in a kind of fabulous charade.

To show how advertising can sometimes work beyond anyone's expectation, the display proved so intriguing to a Texas oil millionaire that he instructed Field's by Western Union to mail both the necklace and the doll to him collect. This they did, with a bill for eighty thousand dollars, which just may have been the all-time largest mail order.

Those were exciting days. And none more so than the one when the American Tobacco Company appointed the agency for the advertising of Pall Mall cigarettes, for with this appointment came two more top-ranking radio programs; *The Jack Benny Show* and *The Frank Morgan Program;* and Foote, Cone & Belding stood first among all agencies in the size of the average audience to which its clients' messages were broadcast.

George Washington Hill, who, next only to Albert Lasker, had played the most important part in our joint venture, died of emphysema at his Canadian fishing camp on September 13. (The trout flies in his hatband had not been an affectation.) Since my hasty departure from New York, four years previously, I had seen George Hill on numerous occasions. I continued to be a kind of consultant on tobacco company business and I thoroughly enjoyed my role, even when I was sent for, as I was frequently, on a few hours' notice, to discuss all kinds of things. There was only one subject that was taboo. *The Hucksters* had hurt Mr. Hill deeply; and neither of us ever mentioned either the novel or its author.

The only trouble was the picture Fred Wakeman had drawn of the advertising man, for this continued to rankle in each of us.

Because of its parentage, Foote, Cone & Belding had been admitted to membership in the American Association of Advertising Agencies in January 1943, without the usual period of probation, and three years later I became a director of that fairly enlightened trade group. One of the rewards this involved was an intimate association with the leading men in the industry; and a more forthright group of businessmen would have been hard to find. In a keenly competitive field they competed as hard as they knew how, but fairly; and they shared the knowledge they gained in the marketplace.

Something else they shared was a deep concern for the status of the business and its people that was so tinged with the ugly insinuations of *The Hucksters* and the constant carping of the newspaper columnists who blamed the advertising agencies for masterminding radio

(ABOVE) *We used Arthur God*
frey successfully for both Tor
and Frigidaire, for this onetim
Chicago taxi driver was the
world's best low-pressure sale
man. (LEFT) *Red Skelton*
made the switch from radio te
television for Johnson wax pro
ucts, and he was an instant hi

that we feared for the future of our companies. To study this we secured the services of Elmo Roper, one of the most respected of the public opinion samplers, to conduct a series of confidential interviews with important businessmen to discover their attitudes toward advertising and advertising people considered entirely in the light of their contribution to business requirements.

Roper did a penetrating job. And the things he found out were deplorable. Advertising was viewed from the summit as a kind of genteel racket, or necessary evil, a matter of hit-or-miss that no one could ever be sure of; and its people, with only a few exceptions (usually, but not always the respondent's own agency people) men of limited business knowledge bent solely on profit to themselves.

The Advertising Council

THE advertising business, in 1946, was good, as indicated. But the climate was appalling. To help change it became a primary objective of the 4-A members.

Their work with the War Advertising Council had convinced them that advertising could sell ideas as well as goods; and they foresaw that this could help make advertising and the advertising agency business both respectable and respected. While the earliest attempts at selling ideas had been unsuccessful, they thought they knew why. The magnificent advertisements that Ted Patrick* had so forcefully written and Albert Dorne had so strikingly illustrated for World Peaceways in the years before the war were an example. These advertisements were eloquent in their statement of the rights and wrongs of peace and war, but they failed of necessity to tell the reader of them what he could do about it. They couldn't, as all effective advertising must, demand some kind of action.

All this was clear to James Webb Young, the former University of Chicago professor and J. Walter Thompson Company principal, and Theodore Repplier, president of the War Advertising Council, who had worked beside Ted Patrick at Young & Rubicam, where the Peaceways advertisements were conceived; and they took up the cudgels. They knew that the War Advertising Council with its concrete proposals for action (i.e., to buy War Bonds, give blood, etc.) had been eminently successful; and this would be the peacetime pattern.

Again, the media would provide space and time, the advertisers

---

* He later became the brilliant editor of *Holiday*.

would pay for the operation of the Council and for the materials of advertising, and the agencies would provide the advertising itself — all without cost to whatever charitable, educational or other institution could qualify before a public policy committee made up of distinguished citizens.

The stalwarts of the Advertising Council in the beginning included John Sterling, publisher of *This Week*, the Sunday newspaper supplement, and among other publishers, Edwin S. Friendly of the New York *World-Telegram*, Albert E. (Cap) Winger of Crowell-Collier, Albert L. Cole of *Reader's Digest*, Roy E. Larsen of Time, Inc., and Philip L. Graham of the Washington *Post*, all of whom saw a new role for advertising, and with Jim Young, Ted Repplier and Charles Mortimer made sure that this was not allowed to lapse through any failure to pursue it.

Frank Stanton, the scholarly and persuasive blond president of the Columbia Broadcasting Company, who rationalized the Council's aims and gave generously of his network's time to promote them, did yeoman service; as did Robert Kintner, the Washington newspaper correspondent who had become president of the National Broadcasting Company; and Edgar Kobak, president of Mutual Broadcasting System (and, like myself, a graduate of Lord & Thomas).

All of these, and many more who had been most involved with selling advertising, now, under Ted Repplier's direction and his urging, brought it to bear on an ever-increasing list of public interests.

On the advertiser side, Mortimer; Samuel C. Gale, vice president of General Mills, Inc.; and Howard Morgens, vice president of Procter & Gamble, were most important because they represented three of the largest American advertisers, and when they donated broadcast time and publication space out of their own tight advertising appropriations, the example was made for all advertisers to see. Incidentally, Mortimer, Gale and Morgens, like Sterling, Graham and Cole, all served as chairman of the Council.

Among the agents, Louis N. Brockway, of Young & Rubicam; Léo Burnett, of the Chicago agency that bears his name; Henry Schachte of J. Walter Thompson Company; Chester J. LaRoche, of LaRoche, McCaffrey and McCall, Inc.; William R. Baker, of Benton & Bowles, also have served as chairman. Other long-time supporters of the Council were Henry G. Little, of Campbell-Ewald; Robert Ganger, of D'Arcy Advertising; William E. Lewis, of Kenyon & Eckhardt; William Reydel and John P. Cunningham, of Cunningham & Walsh; and, of course, David Ogilvy. But most important was the top creative talent their agencies contributed to successful Council campaigns to get out

She shot the ashes
off the Kaiser's cigaret

HER name was Phoebe Mozee and she was born in [?] County, Ohio, in 1860, and she could shoot the he[?] a running quail when she was twelve years old.

Once, at the invitation of [?] Wilhelm II of Germany, she kn[?] the ashes off a cigaret while h[?] holding it in his mouth.

When she out-shot the great[?] bition marksman, Frank Butl[?] fell in love with her and marrie[?] and they were ideally happy the rest of their long lives.

She could handle a rifle or a six-gun with an artist[?] surpassed by that of any human being before her tim[?] probably, since. And when she appeared with Sitting[?] and other notables in Colonel Cody's Wild West Show[?] thrilled your father and mother—not as Phoebe Anne O[?] Mozee but as "Little Sure Shot," the immortal Annie Oa[?]

Annie Oakley, the poor back-country orphan girl who [?] her way to world-wide fame, was the very spirit of per[?] independence. That spirit is just as much alive in our ge[?] tion as it was in hers. It is among the great assets of ou[?] ple—and our nation. And it is one very great reason wh[?] country's Savings Bonds are perhaps the finest invest[?] in the world today.

Make that investment work for you! Increase your per[?] independence and your family's security, by buying [?] regularly—starting now!

    ★   ★   ★

It's actually easy to save money—when you buy United States Series E Savings Bonds through the automatic Payroll Savings Plan where you work! You just sign an application at your pay office; after that your saving is done *for* you. And the Bonds you receive will pay you interest at the rate of 3% per year, compounded semiannually, for as long as 19 years and 8 months if you wish! Sign up today! Or join the Bond-A-Month Plan at your bank.

For your own security—and your country's, too
invest in U. S. Savings Bonds!

Annie Oakley was one of America's famous frontier characters who was put to work selling United States Savings Bonds.

the vote, recruit for the Peace Corps, contribute to CARE, prevent forest fires, stop school dropouts, explain the problems and the possibilities in the mental health program, maintain Savings Bonds sales, and so on and on, in a total effort that today represents $300 million worth of advertising yearly.

These are some of the collaborators and some of the results of their collaboration in Ted Repplier's mobilization of advertising in the public service. This was not an altruistic undertaking; its sole purpose was (and is) to use the best means available to communicate some of the common problems of our time that must be met and overcome.

It would not be fair to close this chapter without mentioning two other individuals whose work in the formation and later operation of the Advertising Council resulted from their insistence upon the responsibility of advertising and advertising people to serve the public that supports them.

The first of these (if only alphabetically) is Frederic R. Gamble, recently retired president of the American Association of Advertising Agencies, an organization which he headed for twenty-two years. His members didn't always follow through on either their protestations or their promises; but Fred Gamble was vigilant, and when they slipped up they were in for some sound advice; the misdeeds were rarely repeated. On the other hand, the racier members of the advertising colony were effectively barred from what has been called the fraternity. (I understand it is against the law for anyone to be barred from a trade association if he is a member of that trade; so perhaps the fast-buck operators in advertising are merely not encouraged to join. I only know they are not included.)

Fred Gamble's adroitness was developed at Knox College at Galesburg, Illinois, and polished at Oxford, where he went as a Rhodes scholar in 1920. As an advertising salesman for the *Saturday Evening Post* in its heyday he acquired a nice sense of dignity, which he managed to impart in good measure to the advertising agency business of the A.A.A.A. members.

Paul West, the president of the Association of National Advertisers, was Fred Gamble's counterpart across the advertising table. It was he who enlisted the advertisers to support the Council, and he acted as its treasurer through all the years that Gamble was its secretary.

In a peculiar way, Paul West's job with his constituents was a good deal more difficult than Fred Gamble's. They both had the same problems of presenting the exigencies and obtaining the required response. But Gamble was dealing with agency principals who could make the desired decisions, while West's members were often organization men on somewhat lower levels. Fortunately for him, West's membership did include such men as Mortimer, Gale and Morgens, Tom Young of United States Rubber, Stuart Peabody of the Borden Company, and Russell Z. Eller of Sunkist, all of whom spoke confidently for their top management, and they gave the others strong support to stand on.

Paul West died in 1965. Fred Gamble has become a gentleman farmer, eyeing the advertising scene from New Jersey; a scene that both these men painstakingly improved.

Up, Down and Up Again

THE company's volume rose in 1947 to more than $50 million, keeping it in the top half-dozen of American advertising agencies, where it did some original work.

A Pepsodent toothpaste contest (to choose "My Favorite Brunette") broke all previous records with more than three million entries — each with a tab from a Pepsodent carton — a total which I believe stands as the largest to this day. Our advertisements for Kotex, addressed to teenagers on subjects of dating and grooming, now posted higher readership figures in many instances than the best-read editorial features in the magazines in which they appeared.

Robert Anthony, a white-haired, distinguished-looking waiter in the Empire Room at the Palmer House in Chicago, became the most photographed Negro of all time as the butler in a series of advertisements for Walker's De Luxe bourbon whiskey that would run in newspapers and magazines for a decade — or until a small group of militant Negroes informed the Walker company that the pictures of Robert Anthony as a servant demeaned the race. As a result, the proud old man was discharged from a service he loved, and Hiram Walker lost a venerable unofficial trademark.

The expurgation of Robert Anthony resulted in our engaging Ludwig Bemelmans to draw a series involving his own stylish waiters and fastidious butlers. But Bemelmans was busy with his gallery pictures, and it turned out that he merely signed the drawings that his friend and agent Irvin Metzl adapted from the rough sketches made in our own art department by the impish Orville Sheldon.

"After all," said Bemelmans, who considered the whole thing a lark, "there is no forgery. The signature is entirely genuine, and quite worth the money."

In radio, Frank Sinatra, who had abandoned Lucky Strike in a fit of petulance to sing for one of American Tobacco's competitors, returned to the Lucky Strike *Hit Parade* where he had first turned the squealers on. Pepsodent's Bob Hope and Pall Mall's Jack Benny were radio's most indestructible stars, together with Arthur Godfrey, whom we presented night and day for both Frigidaire and Toni. It was part of the Godfrey myth, and perhaps the part he most enjoyed, that the commercials he read were his own; that like Fred Allen before him, he loathed the advertising agency writers and had nothing to do with them. But the truth is that Arthur Godfrey read the Toni and Frigidaire commercials exactly as we wrote them for him, simply filling in the few spots that we left for his own enthusiastic comments.

Martin Gang and his Hollywood law partners, together with Don Belding, saw to it that our relations with the stars left little to be desired in a world where bickering over contracts and other business details is incessant because it is incumbent if not on the performers themselves then by proxy upon their agents. Hollywood is an almost impenetrable thicket of tangled purposes and personalities that Emerson Foote and I were glad to leave to Don Belding, whose Oregon country shrewdness was backed up by some of movieland's most sophisticated legal brains.

Another useful weapon in Don Belding's arsenal was his long, intimate friendship with Hedda Hopper, the Hollywood columnist for the *Chicago Tribune*. A word from Hedda caused many a difficult star or starlet to stop, look and listen to reason at contract time.

But these were to be the least of our worries.

On Sunday, March 21, 1948, Emerson Foote flew from New York to Chicago to say to Don Belding, who had flown from Los Angeles, and to me that he wanted to resign the American Tobacco Company account!

George Hill, Jr., who was again in charge of advertising, and whom we had thought sure to become president of the company, had suddenly resigned his $280,000-a-year job in open disagreement with Vincent Riggio, who had succeeded the elder Hill — presumably as regent. The mild-mannered, short, moustached Riggio had been an outstanding salesman for the tobacco company, and while he lacked his predecessor's Jovian authority, he seemed a man of quiet dignity and grasp.

Some said Vincent Riggio had silently resented the close association of Foote and George Hill, Jr., with George Washington Hill and his own exclusion from the advertising scene. Certainly I had never seen him in a meeting at which the senior Hill presided. But whatever the facts may have been, Riggio, who had been vice president for sales, now became president for everything, just as George Washington Hill had been. In resigning, George Hill, Jr., had made no statement of his plans. However, the press speculated on a proxy fight and the possible unseating of Riggio as president in favor of Hill.

Foote's decision to resign, he told us, took no account of the newspaper reports. "I am simply convinced," he said, "that it is no longer possible to do the kind of advertising for Lucky Strike that built the brand.

"Mr. Riggio is not an advertising man. He doesn't even want to talk about it. Whatever we submit we have to leave with him 'to think it over' and the word at the tobacco company is that he takes it home to get his wife's opinion. Lucky Strike is headed for disaster, of that I am convinced," Foote said. "On the other hand, in spite of the hide-and-seek operation our relations are pleasant enough. The account is not in danger, as far as I know. You can keep it if you want to. I just want out. I worked for Mr. Hill too long to go along with Mr. Riggio's indecision."

To keep the account or to give it up could have been a major dilemma. Foote, Cone & Belding, put together so precipitately, had been expected from the beginning to tear apart. And here was a natural parting place. But Foote and Cone and Belding were determined to stay together. This was something we never talked about, but it was always in our minds. Now, if Emerson Foote wanted to resign the tobacco company account, for any reason at all, then Don Belding and I agreed that we should. There was no argument.

Relinquishing almost a quarter of our total business, simply because it was incompatible, was decided upon in a matter of minutes. Whether or not Foote was right that we could have continued to work on Lucky Strike and Pall Mall advertising if he removed himself from the picture, I do not know. I am only sure that this was a possibility to which we gave not the slightest consideration. On Wednesday, March 24, following our Sunday breakfast meeting, a press conference was held in our New York office, and the announcement was made.

The resignation created advertising's greatest sensation. Coupled with speculation about George Hill, Jr.'s, suggested proxy fight (which never came off) the press had a fine old time. The New York *Times* made the story a major feature. The *Wall Street Journal* front-paged it. *Advertising Age* gave it seven columns; and *Tide* carried Emerson

Foote's picture on its cover, above the caption "For the advertising business a $12 million lesson." Foote's picture also appeared in newspapers from coast to coast. The idea of giving up twelve million dollars' worth of any kind of business was a new kind of advertising news. But it was Emerson Foote's answer to *The Hucksters*.

The thing I regret most about the American Tobacco Company resignation is the publicity that accompanied the agency's decision. It was a private matter between two companies with a history of long and profitable association. It was embarrassing to Vincent Riggio, and to Paul Hahn, who was president of the tobacco company subsidiary that was our client for Pall Mall cigarettes, to make it a public thing.

Pall Mall was assigned to Sullivan, Stauffer, Colwell & Bayles on the same day that Ben Duffy secured the Lucky Strike account for Batten, Barton, Durstine & Osborn.

Soon afterwards Lucky Strike embarked on a campaign that George Washington Hill would never have approved. Instead of the basic reason why Luckies were superior, or should have been, which was the fine tobacco story, built up over a period of years and well accepted, the public was now exhorted to *Be Happy, Go Lucky*. Momentum kept the brand going for a while, but then it began to slip. Soon the slide became precipitous, and it has never been halted. Recently, Lucky Strike advertising offered the doubtful proposition that *Luckies don't taste like Luckies any more!*

Despite the dramatic resignation of one of the largest accounts ever to change hands in the advertising agency business, Foote, Cone & Belding showed no decline in volume in 1948. With the addition of the Watchmakers of Switzerland and the International Latex Corporation (Playtex girdles) it slightly more than held its own.

But even more than the effect upon the agency of these new names on its roster was the introduction by one of our original clients of a product that was destined to do battle with the giants of the soap industry — and win. This was Dial deodorant soap.

After testing in Omaha and Oklahoma City, Dial was introduced in Chicago in a fashionably illustrated full-color page in the *Chicago Tribune* that was scented with $1,600 worth of Dial's own delicate perfume. This was mixed in the blue ink, and it dispelled immediately the notion that a deodorant soap had to have a strong, clinical smell. Lifebuoy had been asleep at the switch. Once again a good new product would take the play away from a less effective old one; no amount of advertising could reverse the trend.

The Kleenex pocket pack was another newcomer in 1948, and the advertising was immediately effective.

This was also the year of the Kotex moving picture, *The Story of Menstruation*, which the agency devised and which Walt Disney produced to explain the life process to teenage girls (and boys too, it turned out) in schools everywhere. It was one of the first public service films, and more than six thousand prints have been made of it to show to some thirty million intermediate and high school students. There is no advertising in it.

Later in the year, Hallmark, our greeting card client in Kansas City, replaced *Radio Reader's Digest* with its *Playhouse*, and *Variety* raved about the first performance, which was a dramatization of Edna Ferber's novel *Cimarron*, with Irene Dunne in the principal role; James Hilton, the author of *Goodbye, Mr. Chips*, was Hallmark's host. Lum and Abner, the bucolic comics, went on the air for Frigidaire. Altogether, Foote, Cone & Belding was responsible for eight hours and fifty minutes of radio time weekly (without American Tobacco) and the agency's programs consistently ranked high in the listener averages according to the Nielsen Index, which measured listening by electronic devices attached to radio sets in a cross section of the nation's homes.*

Television was still only a blur on the horizon. Commander Eugene MacDonald, president of Zenith Radio Corporation, had summoned me to get him some fresh film from our West Coast client, David Selznick, for a test of his phonevision, with which he hoped to promote pay-TV. The Commander was unsuccessful, but as this is written his successors continue to fight for the concept.

---

* Nielsen audimeters now are connected to 3,500 television sets in a similar structured sample of householders, and the results constitute the industry's semi-official count of viewers.

The Way Things Go

THE year 1950 began with the transfer of one of the original Chicago office accounts to New York.

In the previous fall the Pepsodent Division of Lever Brothers Company was moved from Chicago to New York and now the advertising account followed. When Foote, Cone & Belding was formed, the Pepsodent Company was owned by Albert D. Lasker and Kenneth Smith — whose father had first associated himself with Mr. Lasker in 1916. In mid-1943, after Charles Luckman, Pepsodent sales manager, had become a part owner and executive vice president, the company was sold to Lever Brothers, and Luckman, who went with it, soon replaced haughty Francis Countway as the British Lever's American chief.

Had not Charles Luckman had something like this in mind two years before, I have no doubt that Albert Lasker would willingly have made him the heir to Lord & Thomas instead of Foote and Cone and Belding; they were that close. But Luckman had other ideas, and the sale of the Pepsodent Company to Lever Brothers was made shortly after Albert Lasker's retirement from the agency.

Chuck Luckman had been a highly publicized prodigy; he was a master salesman and an accomplished showman. Now as Lever Brothers' top executive in America he carried Countway's tradition of autocratic direction of the huge enterprise that was centered on the Charles River in Cambridge, Massachusetts, beyond the limit of staid Boston understanding. Everything he did was showy and, characteristically, he replaced a number of Boston's favorite Lever Brothers people with outlanders of his own choosing.

Boston disliked what it considered to be Charles's brash manners, and his distaste for Boston was no less; he made up his mind to move Lever Brothers headquarters bodily to New York, and he did this with lofty disdain. The magnificent Lever House on Park Avenue was planned by Luckman himself (he had studied architecture at the University of Illinois) and by Skidmore, Owings & Merrill, to start a revolutionary trend in American architecture. Lever's was the first of the great glass office buildings. But Chuck Luckman didn't wait for it to be finished before moving away from Cambridge and Boston. Lever Brothers took temporary quarters at 61st Street and Park Avenue, and its Pepsodent Division was moved there, too, from Chicago. Pepsodent advertising was moved to Foote, Cone & Belding in New York at the same time, and a number of members of the agency's Chicago staff went with it.

Our disappointment over the Pepsodent transfer was assuaged with the completion on May 1 of the remodeling of an old loft building in Superior Street to house the agency's Chicago offices. The plans had been drawn almost a year and a half before the move was actually accomplished. But the owner had first to erect a new building for his own use. Thus we did not begin our remodeling until the premises were vacated in the late summer of 1949.

The original rough plans were made by us. Then we retained the architectural team of Harper and Louise Richards to proportion and design what we had planned and to do the interior decorating. The result was thoroughly satisfactory.

The Foote, Cone & Belding building was the second ever to be devoted entirely to an American advertising agency, and much was made of this in the trade journals. What only the venerable N. W. Ayer & Son, Inc. had done before, in Philadelphia, now was equaled in Chicago. One might have thought from the press reports that the old six-story red brick building suddenly had been touched by genius. And, in a way, it had.

The Richardses' concept was one that combined dignity and utility without any of the ordinary sacrifices. The building was the first in Chicago to be completely air-conditioned. It had an auditorium that seated 250 persons comfortably. It had a pleasant, roomy cafeteria. It provided 149 private offices, each as nearly the same size as the window spacing would permit. The Richardses had designed a democratic building, and, while we didn't foresee this, it had the immediate effect of making all our people feel like partners. The turnover of employees in any company is one of the plagues of the business, and now we had almost none.

When invited to dinner, should you be—

☐ Sure of the date ☐ "Fashionably" late ☐ Formally togged

You were positive Mary's mom had said *this* Tuesday. ("Dinner . . . a few special friends . . . do come!") Or did she mean *next* Tuesday? Double-checking would have spared much confuddlement. Saved barging in, a week ahead, to find the family rehashing Sunday's roast! Better not be "hazy" about certain *other* "dates", either. Or the kind of sanitary protection to choose. Remember, Kotex prevents revealing outlines. Those special *flat pressed ends* let you glide through any occasion — with a heart light as helium!

Are you in the know?

If he's just an acquaintance, best you—

☐ Try siren tactics ☐ Pay your own fare

Your friendship's merely casual. Comes along a bus — and suddenly your purse develops lockjaw! Why scrounge? A happenstance meeting doesn't mean he's bound to pay your way. Best you pay your own. And on "trying" days, it's smart to discover "your own" absorbency of Kotex. You'll see — by trying *all 3* — whether Regular, Junior or Super is the one just right for *you.*

Which can be a threat to poise?

☐ A callous heart ☐ A callused heel

We're talking about those beat-up loafers she's wearing. The soft shoe routine is fine — 'til they get too loose; then, being slip shod can cause a callus on the back of your heel. Shoes should fit snugly. Protects your looks, poise. Of course, at *problem* time, poise and Kotex go together. For that exclusive *safety center* gives extra protection you can always count on.

To help that sun tan "stay put"—

☐ Take a hot bath ☐ Take a breather

The sun's dyed your hide to a fetching sepi Now you'd relax in a nice hot bath. B unless you'd fade that glamour-hue — wa two or three hours. Taking a breather 'twi beach and tub can help your hard-earned ta stay put. And on "those" days, don't l *comfort* do a fadeout! See how long the so ness of *Kotex* stays — because this dowr napkin *holds its shape.*

More women choose KOTEX than all other sanitary napkins

Have you tried *new* Delsey toilet tissue — the only one that's fine and firm and soft — like Kleenex tissues. Each tissue is "clean-cut" to tear off evenly — no shredding, no waste. And Delsey's double-ply for extra strength.

KOTEX, KLEENEX AND DELSEY
ARE REGISTERED TRADEMARKS OF THE
INTERNATIONAL CELLUCOTTON PRODUCTS COMPANY

This extensive magazine campaign was essentially an adaptation of radio's audience participation program. It asked the reader to answer questions.

A few months after we moved into the Superior Street building, the authoritative magazine *Office Management* named it the outstanding new office building of the year to house fewer than five hundred persons. The award for the best building to house more than five hundred persons was made simultaneously to the new United Nations building in New York City. We were in good company. However, our joy was soon turned off.

In October the agency suffered a major blow. Don Belding and I were called to New York and informed that Emerson Foote must retire from the business. He had experienced a long series of illnesses. He had been hospitalized on numerous occasions. In fact, he was in the hospital then. "And he will be in it again if you don't relieve him of the responsibilities that slowly weaken his resistance, then knock him out," the doctor said.

Even though he had been away from the business for extended periods for almost two years, we had always known that he would be back. If there was any slack during any of his absences, it was always caught up when he returned; and Foote, Cone & Belding in New York had maintained its pace. "Now," said Albert Lasker, who was closer to Emerson Foote than to either Don Belding or me, "now you are going to have to go it without Mr. Foote. If you don't," he said, "you will be responsible for his health." This was a responsibility we had no right to assume. Whatever might be the result to the company, we were bound to proceed without Mr. Foote.

It would be wrong to say that he took the affairs of the business more seriously than either Don Belding or I did, but it would be wrong also not to acknowledge the fact that life in advertising in New York was more strenuous than life in advertising in Chicago or Los Angeles or San Francisco. As in every other business except moving pictures, success in New York is the goal which the most capable and intense advertising people seek to reach, and the game can be rough.

This is not to say that the rules are any different; but only that the players are probably the best in the world, and the competition is fierce and unrelenting. Also, because advertising was a major New York industry, with its comings and goings discussed at noon in every mid-Manhattan bar and restaurant and chronicled at length in the daily press, it was difficult to get away from. It was tightly tied to radio, just as it would later be to television; and broadcasting, like the theater, had its heartbeat in New York. There was not a single production company in Chicago; and Los Angeles was little more than an infrequently used extension on the telephone line that ran directly from New York to Hollywood. For just these reasons, Foote's job was harder than either Belding's or mine, and it took its toll as it took out of Foote, Cone & Belding one of the industry's most capable practitioners.

Thus the first break in the partnership occurred through circumstances beyond anyone's control; and it was to protect Emerson Foote's interest against any losses that might ensue from his leaving that his stock in the agency, which was in exactly the same amount as Belding's and my own, was purchased by the corporation and subsequently sold by it to a number of the other members of the organization. None of it was acquired by either Belding or myself.

The loss of one of the original trio of managers, who was manager of the office with the greatest potential, could have been a mortal blow to the entire enterprise. But neither Belding nor I took time to worry about this. We both began to spend more time than ever in New York, to lend whatever help we could to the staff that Foote had assembled.

It was here that I learned from Belding that a reasonably endowed person can do a great many more things than he may think if only he will get at each one as it comes up and not waste time fretting about the complication and how much time it will take.

As a result, the company's volume even in this unhappy year showed a good increase. Hallmark and Frigidaire took to television with regular hour-long broadcasts. The cereals division of General Foods placed the advertising for several new ready-to-eat products in the Chicago office. Anahist, the first of the antihistamines, was assigned to Foote, Cone & Belding in New York. Hughes Tool Company became a client of the agency in Texas, and a fifth domestic office was opened in Houston.

London and Pepsodent

ONE of a number of invitations I couldn't decline as chairman of the American Association of Advertising Agencies was to go to England in the summer of 1951 to the first International Advertising Conference to be held after World War II to accept a challenge to advertising by the Rt. Hon. Lord Beveridge, whose Keynesian criticism of contemporary business methods had been harsh and uncompromising.

The famous Beveridge Plan — the first of the so-called cradle-to-grave welfare programs — was under bitter denunciation by businessmen everywhere, and it was expected that Lord Beveridge would make his remarks at the conference an outright attack upon advertising rather than a challenge to it — unless the challenge would be to its existence at all. The chairman of the conference was the Rt. Hon. Lord Mackintosh of Halifax, who, for his golden toffee, was one of Britain's largest advertisers.

But such a fact was not counted on to deter Lord Beveridge. As it turned out, this white-haired, white-faced man could not have been more pleasant. I had expected to encounter a thunderer; what I met was a soft-spoken, pensive individual who had some sensible questions to propound. "Do you know," he said when we sat down to breakfast with Lady Beveridge before the meeting, "I find advertising fascinating. I ask myself why it seems to be paid so much more attention even when it is frivolous than serious writing in the press or even the most thoughtful, carefully prepared speeches. I ask myself. And I ask you," he added.

"May not the reason be," I replied, "that advertising uses a language almost of its own; that is usually simple and direct; and that its object is usually to invite agreement rather than to win an argument?"

"You mean," Lord Beveridge said, "that the serious writings and the speeches may be too intellectual or too theoretical to be personally appreciated and accepted, while advertising is more practical?"

"Yes, I do," I said. "Although the difference may not be in the language at all, but only in the use of the language."

"I wish that advertising could be pressed against some of our social problems," he said. "To help them to be understood in their full context, and in the matter of alternative consequences. Some of my own proposals have been so badly presented in the daily and periodical press that on that evidence I would resent them and reject them myself."

"There is one important difference," I told Lord Beveridge, "between advertising and press coverage. In advertising, the words and the interpretation of the proposition that is presented are the advertiser's own, and he is responsible for them. In reportage these are subject to someone else's interpretation, to the editor's evaluation of the relative importance of various items, and to the limitations of space. This is a vital and frequently overlooked difference; and advertising is not used often enough to carefully and completely explain the issues of public interest. Press and broadcasters almost always *edit* the arguments they present."

I am afraid I was giving a lecture. But when I explained the purpose and the workings of the Advertising Council, to promote various undertakings in the public interest, the pleasant old gentleman began to see that advertising could be used in a manner that he had not known to exist.

When it came to delivering the expected challenge to the conference, Lord Beveridge gave what turned out to be largely a resume of our breakfast-table conversation. This was without attribution, to be sure; but I couldn't have been less concerned about that. He made a strong case for the use of advertising to aid the consumer in his choices and to explain and support social change and development; and his principal admonition to the twenty-five hundred delegates from two dozen countries was to see that their advertising told nothing but the truth. This was a challenge that I found it easy to accept, and I did it with dispatch, and left the convention.

Not since the *Haxtum* tied up at the Queens Docks at Liverpool in the summer of 1920 had I set foot on British soil, and I was anxious to see the operation that had grown from Harry Berk's spadework under the direction of his successor, Brian MacCabe, at Foote, Cone & Belding, Ltd.

The offices were in a house in Berkeley Square that had been reserved throughout the war for General Franco, and the house was in much the same shape, with only a few partitions knocked out to make bathrooms and closets into offices and others thrown up to make small rooms out of large rooms. The layout was something less than ideal.

MacCabe, on the other hand, lived up to his billing. He had been an Olympic athlete, and a British hero of World War II. Wounded at El Alamein, when his tank was shot up by Rommel's panzers, and invalided home, he joined the paratroops as soon as he was recovered, and eventually was dropped behind the enemy lines during the final assault upon Berlin. He was just the kind of fighting man to head an American advertising agency in England.

Our difficulty was not that English businessmen didn't like Americans, but only that they weren't sure anyone could quite trust an advertising agent. Since modern advertising was an American development, this made the American agency a matter of serious question.

When the advertising of British Overseas Airways Corporation (BOAC), a government-subsidized account, turned up at Foote, Cone & Belding, the agency's future was forecast in unexpected terms, and MacCabe had made the forecast come true.

Realizing that what English advertising lacked was some of the polish of the American strain, he imported Russell Insley, a topnotch writer from Foote, Cone & Belding in San Francisco, to direct the advertising production. Realizing, also that the London office should have a strong British flavor, the rest of the staff was made up entirely of English men and women.

The London office was something to be proud of. But it wasn't in me to appreciate it. For despite what I considered a creditable performance at Westminster, I was dejected and distressed.

On our arrival in London the day before, to the tumult of a welcoming brass band at Waterloo Station that turned out to be meeting the boxer Sugar Ray Robinson, I received a most shocking cablegram. It was from Belding in New York.

"Pepsodent account," it said, "transferred today to McCann-Erickson."

In any such personal business as advertising, accounts are bound to change hands. But it is heartbreaking to lose one you have worked on for a long time and to the limit of your ability. Pepsodent was that kind. The reasons why advertisers and advertising agencies become unhappy and dissatisfied with one another are, as I have said, many

Its cleaner, brighter **Taste** *means*

cleaner, brighter teeth! **New Pepsodent,** *the only tooth paste*

containing **Irium,** *removes the film that makes your teeth look dull —*

uncovers the natural brilliance of your smile!

Use Pepsodent twice a day — see your dentist twice a year

Here was an attempt to put glamour into Pepsodent printed advertising, to go along with hard-selling radio commercials. Note dress length.

and varied. But the one that is most frustrating of all to the agency is the sweep of the new broom that is often the first objective of a new advertising or sales manager. Worst of all, this usually takes a little time to accomplish. You know what is going on. You know the result is almost inevitable. Still you hope and strive against it. Nevertheless, you feel the blow when it hits you with all the shock and pain of something totally unexpected.

So it was with Pepsodent. Charles Luckman was gone. A new advertising manager wanted an advertising agency of his own choosing. Nothing we could do was deemed satisfactory. Even a brilliantly conceived media plan (one that turned the sales tide for a much weaker Pepsodent when the account was returned to Foote, Cone & Belding four years later) was blandly turned down. We were "out" months before the actual announcement was made.

I wish I could remember that advertising manager's name; but I can't. I can't even remember what he looked like. For along with the share of Lord & Thomas that I inherited from Albert Lasker, I fell heir to a mental block that he had developed to immediately forget the name of anyone in whom he had been disappointed. In a matter of weeks after the sale of the Pepsodent Company to Lever Brothers, he had forgotten the name of Charles Luckman, who engineered the transaction; this was the man who only shortly before could have had Lord & Thomas had he wanted it!

Part of my unhappiness in London was because I tried to tell myself that had I been in New York I could have saved the account. I wanted to blame the 4A's for my being away. But this was no excuse. Anyway, I knew very well that the Pepsodent decision had been made when the new advertising man was hired.

It was merely easier to announce it when I was out of the country.

When Charles Luckman ceased to be the head of the Lever Brothers American company, Franklin J. Lunding of Chicago was made chairman of the Executive Committee. Lunding, a lawyer whose administration of the Jewel Tea Company had made it one of the leading U.S. food retailers, was a happy choice — particularly for Foote, Cone & Belding.

On the night of my return from the London advertising conference, I bumped into Lunding in the observation car of the Twentieth Century Limited.

"I am sorry," he said as we rolled out of Grand Central Terminal, "sorry for what happened at Pepsodent."

"You should be," I replied. I felt that we had been treated shabbily. But I thought Lever had come off much worse. None of the new management people at Pepsodent knew the problems and the opportunities that faced the brand as well as a number of our people who had been associated with it for years. "For one thing," I said, "Pepsodent's future lies in the supermarket and your people are devoting all their energies to selling the druggists. What they can't seem to get into their heads is that toothpaste sales from now on are going to be made in food stores. If Pepsodent doesn't have the chain food store business, the supermarket business, pretty soon it won't have any. To put the brand's fate in the druggists' hands is to condemn it to death."

Frank Lunding knew that if what I was saying about the division's preoccupation with drugstore distribution was right, the future of Pepsodent would indeed be bleak. He had helped to make it so. Supermarkets like the Jewel stores were taking over more of the proprietary drug business every week, and Colgate was capitalizing on the fact. Colgate had won leadership by sending the bulk of its production to the armed forces during the war. They had taken toothpaste to thousands of men who had never used a dentifrice before; now they were putting it where most people shopped most often.

It is part of the advertising agency's responsibility to be aware of such things. But it is also part of the advertiser's, and I felt that the Pepsodent division was failing to keep pace with the changes in buying habits.

That Frank Lunding agreed I had no doubt. But that he would follow up our conversation with some direct action involving the agency came as a pleasant surprise.

In no time at all I received a telephone call from the Jewel chairman. "I think Jerry Babb would like to see you," he said. Jervis Babb was the man Frank Lunding had installed as Lever president in New York.

"Why?" I asked. The president of Lever was one of the last persons I wanted anything to do with.

"Maybe you'll be surprised," Frank Lunding said. "If I were you, I'd bandage up my bruises and have a talk with Jerry."

This I did. And Foote, Cone & Belding was immediately appointed for the advertising of Lever Brothers' Spry, a vegetable shortening that was the second largest-selling brand in the country, second only to Crisco.

"Later," Babb said, "we'll return Pepsodent to where it belongs. In the meantime, help me get Spry on the track." As it developed, Spry was to sink gradually into obscurity as the easier-to-use liquid shortenings took over the market. But by that time Lever had appointed us for the advertising of Imperial margarine, and true to his promise, Jerry Babb had returned Pepsodent advertising to our care.

Death of a Giant

On May 31, 1952, Albert Davis Lasker died of cancer in New York City at the age of seventy-two. He had not been ill very long.

Ever since the day when we walked together out of the office in the Palmolive Building in Chicago and paused to watch the sign painter removing the name Lord & Thomas from the transom above the door, Albert Lasker had taken a lively interest in Foote, Cone & Belding. I had seen him regularly and often. I had almost never been in New York that I hadn't visited him either at his white-carpeted office in the Chrysler Building or at his magnificent flower-filled home in Beekman Place; and I always saw him during his infrequent visits to Chicago. While, as I have said, he had no financial interest in Foote, Cone & Belding, and refused to advise it, he wanted to know about every good and bad thing that affected the firm's fortunes. He rejoiced when we did well, and he commiserated with us over our unhappy experiences. Fortunately, during his lifetime the latter were few.

One day, sitting in his Beekman Place drawing room, above the East River, I reminded him of his reply when someone had asked him to assess the chances of Foote, Cone & Belding as his successors and he had said that if we made it people in the business would declare that he had trained us well; if we didn't, that we couldn't make it without A. D. Lasker.

"Ah! But I knew you wouldn't fail," he said. "If I'd had the smallest doubt, d'you see, there would have been no Foote, Cone & Belding. D'you?"

That Albert Lasker could win on either side of any argument I never questioned. Or that he sometimes argued against his strongest beliefs just for the thrill of winning against any comer. Mr. Lasker often pretended to be proudest of his shrewd instincts. But this, I think, was an argument, too, for argument's sake. What was his above all else was an extraordinary intellect that powered an interest in many things.

He talked finance with Bernard Baruch and painting with Berenson, with the same competence. He argued about the theater with John Golden, and the movies with Samuel Goldwyn. He talked golf with Gene Sarazen and Bobby Jones, air power with Alexander de Seversky, and politics with David Lawrence and Arthur Krock and Walter Lippmann and Wendell Willkie and Harry Truman. He debated radio and television with General Sarnoff and William Paley and discussed medicine with the Menningers and Lowell Coggeshall and Morris Fishbein, the professionals, and baseball with Branch Rickey. He could talk prizefights or merchandising with equal authority with Bernard Gimbel. Or labor relations with Anna Rosenberg and Madame Perkins. And he did. And in between, he talked with me about business and the role of advertising and the destiny of both together whenever I visited with him.

Albert Lasker was one of the most prolific of modern Renaissance men. His interests were all-encompassing, and his knowledge was enormous. His death came too soon, for his faculties were strong and his work was not finished.

The example he set for Emerson Foote and Don Belding and me, and the dozens of other men and women of Lord & Thomas who became the people of Foote, Cone & Belding, was the example of involvement. Albert Lasker was never, except in the case of Foote, Cone & Belding, merely an observer; he was always a participant. He was always ready to stand up and be counted; and when he changed his mind he experienced no qualms at all in admitting this. He went from a long career as a staunch and active Republican over to the side of Harry S. Truman because he believed in Truman's advocacy of social security and government leadership in the various fields of public health and welfare — particularly in research. This was a man to follow. And each of us tried in his own way.

One of Albert Lasker's active roles was as a trustee of the University of Chicago, where his counsel was sought frequently by Chancellor Robert Maynard Hutchins, and thoughtfully given. The university that John D. Rockefeller and William Rainey Harper founded in 1891 was perhaps the most liberal of all the world's great universities and it was constantly the target of heated conservative attack. Since the attacks often centered around Hutchins, whose wit was incendiary, it was necessary that the university have a volunteer fire brigade to put out the recurring flames, and Mr. Lasker was a leading member of that organization.

Before he moved from Chicago to New York, and shortly before Chancellor Hutchins retired, Mr. Lasker announced his resignation from the board. Later I took up where he left off.

After working on a brochure for the University's Council on Medical and Biological Research with Dr. Charles B. Huggins (later a Nobel Laureate), I had become a member and, subsequently, chairman of that council. The brochure was something for which F. W. Specht, president of Armour and Company, had generously volunteered my services, but the end result was clearly beyond anything that either of us could have foreseen. Late one afternoon in November of 1951, just after I had been persuaded by Charles Mortimer to become chairman of the Advertising Council, I was called on by the distinguished lawyer Laird Bell and Hermon Dunlap Smith, president of Marsh & McLennan, the international insurance brokers, and invited to become a trustee of the University itself.

I mention Laird Bell and Hermon Smith because they indicate the caliber of this most unusual board. Today its membership of forty-four includes the chairmen of Chicago's two largest banks; sixteen of the city's leading industrialists; three noted attorneys; publisher and editor, respectively, of the city's two largest newspapers; and a scatter of important business figures from other parts of the country.

The makeup of the group was similar in 1951; it had much the same standing in the business community that the faculty was accorded in the academic world; and I accepted the invitation that Laird Bell and Dutch Smith brought from the nominating committee with a sharp sense of wonder. I could only think of my difficulties in becoming simply a university graduate; now to be a part of the education establishment!

I had promised to become chairman of the Advertising Council, and this would take a great deal of time, but I couldn't decline the University appointment; I was afraid that it might never again be tendered. As it turned out, it has been a matchless experience, during which I have served with four great men in the chief administrator's chair: Hutchins, Lawrence A. Kimpton, George Wells Beadle and Edward H. Levi.

The University of Chicago is by any measurement one of America's foremost educational institutions. It is a teacher of teachers, and its graduates exert a powerful influence on teaching everywhere; in a recent convocation advanced degrees were granted 745 students who had come from forty-six states of the Union and thirty-one foreign countries, and would, for the most part, return there.

It is my concept that the trustees of a university have two primary obligations. The first is to select the university administrators and the second is to support these administrators, and through them the faculty, by securing the funds that are required to maintain the institution at the level of its ambition. Education at every level needs understanding and protection, as well as support, and all this hinges on the help of trained communicators to make the needs known; it gains little from amateurs with even the best intentions.

Although there was no direct connection between Albert Lasker's association with the University and mine, I like to think that my continuing participation in its affairs helps to pay my debt to that illustrious man. I have been chairman of the board since 1963.

The fact is that Mr. Lasker was not the only advertising man who had served on the board of the University of Chicago. Albert W. Sherer of McCann-Erickson was a longtime member. William Benton, onetime president of Benton & Bowles, was another. And in my own time Earle Ludgin, proprietor of his own advertising agency, has been a valued trustee.

A good advertising man must have some of the qualities of an evangelist. He must have a conviction about the products and the services that he undertakes to promote, and this is no less true when the products are the products of education. For a man who once wanted to be a teacher my position in the University has been something of a switch. But it fits very well with my business. Advertising is certainly not pure education. But the two have much in common.

Aren't You Glad You Use Dial Soap?

IF success comes usually to men who are most knowledgeable about their concerns and most experienced in their pursuit, then Edward W. Wilson of Armour and Company was a striking exception. A keen-minded lawyer turned chemist, he was responsible for one of the most dramatic developments in American marketing history. For at a time when Procter & Gamble was pulling farther and farther ahead of Lever Brothers and Colgate-Palmolive, its principal competitors in the soap industry, and generating an advertising fund exceeded only by giant General Motors, Edward Wilson took on this biggest of the soapers and beat them at their own game.

This was a two-sided contest. On one side was successful formulation and manufacturing which are the result of tireless research and trial and error, and on the other side, advertising, in a time and place where each of the competitors had a convincing story to tell.

I am aware that it is fashionable in otherwise informed circles to depreciate the soapers' claims, and to insist that all soaps and detergents, like all brands of aspirin, are essentially the same. But this is true only in the sense that improvement in any given product may be quickly matched by a competitor. The important thing is that innovation is every large manufacturer's chief weapon of competition, for there is no other possible basis for continuing success. As it stands, continuing improvement in consumer products of almost every kind is as close as the world has yet come to perpetual motion.

Where advertising enters the picture is to make the improvements known, but the absurdities committed in their name must be admitted, for they are rarely out of sight or hearing. That they are not merely

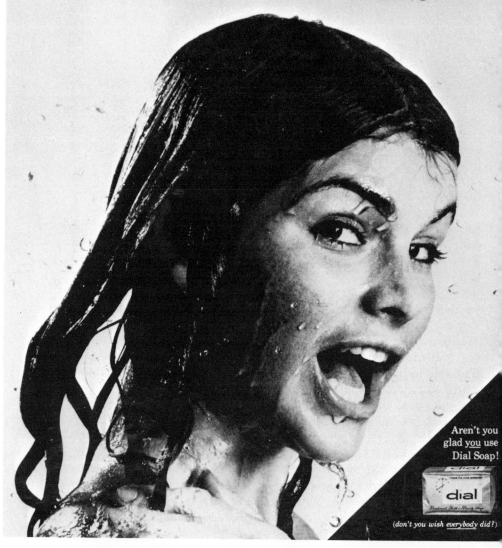

No doubt about it. The soap that stops perspiration odor best is Dial. Because only Dial has AT-7 to get rid of bacteria that cause trouble. So be sure, get Dial.

Aren't you glad you use Dial Soap!

dial

(don't you wish everybody did?)

From a perennial magazine campaign in support of Dial deodorant toilet soap. More than sixty possible variations have failed to top it in countrywide reader tests.

tricks to trap the unwary, however, should be borne in mind. The tricks are to attract attention to individual products in areas where almost all products are satisfactory; and the game of catch-the-leader is played both tirelessly and with wild stretches of imagination. That Ed Wilson did not follow in the path of the armored knight who chases dirt on horseback or the deodorant bar that *lets you feel really clean for the first time in your life* made him an unusual member of an industry that rarely departs very far from tradition.

In almost every other way the success of Dial soap is a success in the classic advertising tradition. Dial soap was established by proving that it had none of the strong antiseptic covering odor of Lifebuoy and yet actually destroyed the bacteria that make perspiration offensive. This was its opening promise, and it has never changed either its direction or its tone of voice. Change in either is one of the most debilitating of advertising practices, for it leads to excesses of every kind, the most common of which is discontinuing a successful advertising campaign simply because the advertiser has tired of it, or because of the start of a new calendar or fiscal year.

Wilson, the lawyer turned chemist turned marketing man, was unaware of this traditon of change, and Dial soap advertising has made the identical proposition for sixteen years, a period in which the brand has moved from fifteenth to first place among all toilet soaps in the dollar volume of its sales. Without doubt the world could have survived without Dial soap. But it would have been a far less pleasant world.

What are the facts about Dial soap as a product? Exactly what the advertising says. Dial soap stops odor before it starts by removing the bacteria that live on perspiration and cause its unpleasant odor in covered places (perspiration on your face or on the back of your hand is odorless).

The active ingredient in Dial soap is a bactericide called hexachlorophene which was perfected as a specific against athlete's foot during World War II, and incorporated in soap by Armour and Company and tested exhaustively at the war's end. In true storybook fashion, the discovery had been offered first to the established soap manufacturers, and to Armour only after the leaders had turned it down (presumably because they had something similar of their own in test). Frederick W. Specht, then president of Armour, encouraged Wilson to take it on.

"We really didn't know enough to turn down hexachlorophene," Ed Wilson recalls somewhat wistfully. "We didn't know that one rarely makes war on the big soapers; that the game is played by their rules because their research and development operations make them almost impregnable against any competition but their own.

"We just knew that we had the means to produce a very good new product. The question in our minds was whether we could sell it. Whether we could tell the story of our product in advertising that wasn't harsh and disagreeable as we thought Lifebuoy's booming 'B.O.' advertising was; and whether we could make the advertising investment to finance the introduction during the period when our sales would be small.

"The results in our test markets answered our questions in the affirmative. We believed we had a winner. And we took it to the public. Our advertising strategy was planned to convince the skeptical, and we have never changed it. It was right in its logic, and there soon was developed a very simple corollary to the basic proposition — the promise that Dial soap would stop perspiration odor before it starts was a brand-new promise. It had never been made before. Would the public believe it? Would they accept it that hexachlorophene was, indeed, what we said it was?

"Well, they did. As well they should have. For Dial soap was a real breakthrough. Also, it was a little better than we said it was, a little better than our advertising said, and people found this out for themselves and told others. Dial was a pure soap. It was also a mild soap. It had a pleasant, delicate scent. It lathered well, and because it was a hard-milled soap, it lasted much longer than most other brands.

"Altogether it was worth its high price of twenty-five cents for a bath-sized bar. It was worth it. But the market for a twenty-five-cent bar of any kind of soap was limited. This was what the big soapers believed. Then there began to appear in Dial advertising in print and through the air, in 1952 on Dave Garroway's television program and later during the first exciting months of the George Gobel show, an assumptive proposition that has been the basis of Dial advertising ever since.

"'*Aren't you glad you use Dial soap?*' the advertising asked. And then we added, '*Don't you wish everybody did?*'"

A girl named Catherine Haynie wrote that — not as a catchline, but out of her own conviction that there was no other soap anywhere that could do what Dial does. And Katie Haynie was right. Today Dial is one of the world's favorite personal products. And as the result of its large volume of sales, its price on the grocery store shelf is less than half what we thought at the start we would have to get for it.

One thing Ed Wilson didn't refer to was the personal success that was his as he shepherded Dial soap through the various crises of stiff price and prize and new-product competition. Neither cut prices nor prize contests nor new "miracle" products ever fazed him. He used coupons to meet price competition. He met prize contests with bigger prize contests (Dial has given away automobiles, airplanes, ponies, oil wells, race horses and even a uranium mine). But above all, Wilson saw to it that the quality of Dial soap was maintained and, whenever this became possible, improved.

When he retired from Armour and Company at the end of 1967 it was as president of this eighth largest of all U.S. corporations. His contribution there was measured in innumerable ways, for he was a perfect instrument for probing and pursuing the very original ideas that characterized the activities of William Wood Prince, Armour's chairman.

"One of the things we didn't know about advertising," Ed Wilson insists, "is that advertising campaigns wear out. Or that they are supposed to. We thought this was crazy. We thought changing successful advertising was like replacing a highly satisfactory salesman for no other reason than that someone else might do better. The result was (and is) that we have never changed anything basic about Dial soap advertising. To be sure, we have changed the format of our magazine advertisements from time to time and we have developed new television techniques. But we have never changed the fundamental advertising proposition. Or our tone of voice. Billy Prince and I were not gamblers."

One of the times Ed Wilson refused to gamble made my part in the continuing Dial story possible.

It has long been a practice of the very large advertisers to have more than one advertising agency. This is particularly true of multi-product manufacturers. General Motors employs seven agencies, General Foods employs five, Procter & Gamble, nine, and so on. Armour was for years an exception; they retained only Foote, Cone & Belding.

This was something that a high officer in the packinghouse division of Armour found unbearable. Calling Ed Wilson on the telephone one day, he declared that he thought the soap division should drop Foote, Cone & Belding and acquire a new advertising agency.

"Why?" Wilson wanted to know.

"Because Armour should have more than one agency," the packinghouse man said.

"Why don't *you* change, then?" Wilson countered.

"We can't," the other man said. "Foote, Cone & Belding does very good work for us."

"That," said Wilson, "is the way it is here, too. And we're not going to change." Nor did he.

Shortly after this telephone conversation took place, the packinghouse did replace our company, and quite, I think, for the reason advanced to Wilson, for there wasn't any other that Don Hause or David Duensing, the advertising men at the packinghouse, could discover. Anyway, five years to the day after we were replaced, by three other agencies (the man went all out), Foote, Cone & Belding was reappointed by the packinghouse. And again we began working for the whole Armour complex.

One thing I should add about Dial advertising is that scores of alternate campaigns have been prepared and tested, and some have tested well. But Wilson and Prince have stood firm.

"I don't want to disturb a successful venture," Prince insists.

To which Wilson adds, "When in doubt the best possible answer is *Don't.*"

When it began to be known that many dermatologists were prescribing Dial for minor skin troubles (especially adolescent acne) some of the Armour people wanted to advertise the fact. But Wilson refused. "Who," he reasoned, "wants to wash or bathe every day with a soap that is sold as a medicine? It is enough," he said "to say that many hospitals use Dial to bathe newborn babies. This is proof of its mildness."

When You Care
Enough to Send the Very Best

JOHN WANAMAKER invented the department store, Richard H. Macy discovered that the retailer's road to riches is apt to be most direct when he multiplies small profit margins by large-volume sales. Stanley Marcus, with his partner, Neiman, learned from their dissatisfaction with old prairie ways that high style is a matter of universal appeal, and a commodity no less salable in Dallas than in Paris.

Joyce Clyde Hall has been no less an innovator. Everyday greeting cards as we know them, designed to bridge the gaps of time and place between people, were his creation. And so was the introduction of style — both classic and contemporary — that makes so many of today's cards minor works of art. Meeting J. C. Hall for the first time, one would hardly have suspected this tall, spare plainsman (a man Grant Wood might have painted) to be the leading architect of America's social correspondence. But this he was; and this he is.

This was a man who cherished the amenities, and he was sure that he could make them pay. Indeed, they had to. For Joyce Hall could no more have been interested in a profitless undertaking, unless it were frankly eleemosynary, than in a business whose only aim was to make money. He had to have a large measure of satisfaction to sustain his interest, and he worked day and night to maintain it. He was alert to every new development in merchandising. His frequent trips to New York with his department heads were serious explorations into the fashions of the future; and he never failed to return to Kansas City brimming with new ideas. When the rest of the greeting card industry still was concerning itself with Christmas cards and valentines — and prices — he was reaching out for new ways to make cards fill greater needs and for new means to promote them.

When you care enough to send the very best **Hallmark Cards**

On rare occasions a picture clearly presents both the advertiser's proposition and a happy solution to a problem. This, for Hallmark, was one.

Even as long ago as 1944, when they wrote us they were looking for an advertising agency, there were five thousand different cards that bore the Hall trademark. Today there are fifteen thousand items in the Hallmark line, and Hallmark sales are in excess of eight million cards each day.

The prescience with which J. C. Hall has involved himself in various enterprises is something he would never admit. He looks upon the successful embarkation of Hallmark into the manufacture of playing cards and party goods and games and books and stationery, and candles and candy and toys, to say nothing about Hall's magnificent retail stores in Kansas City and on Fifth Avenue, in New York, as matters of course. When it comes to designing new greeting cards and other items in the growing Hallmark line, he will tell you that he has always relied on hunches, or as he likes to say, "the vapors of past experience." These he refers to as "things that I have a hard time explaining. But I know when I am right." And he does. "There is something in the past fifty-eight years that is telling me," he confides with a little smile.

This is probably true. But a good deal of what Mr. Hall refers to as experience is, in fact, a disciplined instinct that I believe is the most important of any man's faculties after only his ability to see and hear. Instinct may be applied to many things, and since its application is practically instantaneous, this allows time for more considerations. It multiplies a man's capacity for making decisions at the same time that it increases the odds that he will make each choice of action the right one under given circumstances.

In the case of Joyce Hall these circumstances range from contemplation of additions to the Hallmark line, to relations with Hallmark's employees and its retail dealers, to the building of a huge new business and residential complex in downtown Kansas City, and back, for example, to a new menu suggestion for the plant cafeteria, whose food and surroundings for enjoying it are superb.

Good food, as a part of good living, is a matter of Mr. Hall's everyday interest, and he is as respectful of his employees' appetites as he is of his own. One Saturday when I was lunching with him in the cafeteria, under the gold crown chandeliers, I observed that he was toying with a piece of chocolate cake that was clearly not in the Hallmark tradition. It was dry and crumbly and obviously stale.

"Where did *that* come from?" I asked him, "in the midst of so many good things."

"Oh," he said, "this is something I was supposed to sample last Tuesday, but I've been away all week."

It was plain that he felt entirely capable of passing judgment even given the delay. And I have no doubt that he was; his instincts are not impaired by small ravages of time.

This thoroughness in the master of Hallmark is not lost upon the members of his personal staff. Several months after Foote, Cone & Belding was retained by J. C. Hall to direct the company's advertising, C. E. Goodman, Donald Gray and John Oakson, the top echelon of the company's executive corps, were discovered to be checking the agency's references.

"What, please tell me," I asked John Oakson, "are you people doing? Don't you know that Mr. Hall himself hired our company?"

"Of course we do," Oakson replied, "but somebody remembered that we each were given three references to check, and Mr. Hall just might someday look in the files for the results."

Joyce Hall's greatest interest lies in the pursuit of excellence, and it dates from the day when he decided that the colored postcard was a paltry thing, and that the world was ready for something much better.

Valentines had long before combined words and pictures into ready-made messages of fun and frolic, and Christmas and Easter cards had begun to appear in some volume. But Mr. Hall looked beyond the valentines (of which he owns what is considered one of the world's great historical collections) and the other special-occasion cards, to the unfilled and unexplored need of millions of men and women who find it impossible to put their feelings on paper at the times they most want to. Under the pressure of their emotions they often lose the power to communicate at all, and many a message they want to send is never posted.

It was into this void that Joyce Hall moved in 1930 with characteristic confidence in what his instinct told him. The time had come for the everyday card, to help celebrate birthdays and anniversaries, to take notice gaily of engagements and weddings and births, to send congratulations as well as condolences and sympathy; to wish friends well under every kind of circumstance or contingency.

Thoughtfulness was the key, and Hallmark cards were designed to provide the varied means to express this. Nor was it enough that Hallmark should develop a large stable of writers and artists to provide the choice. It wasn't very long before Mr. Hall was reproducing words of cheer and felicitation from a whole anthology of English poets, from Chaucer and Shakespeare to W. H. Auden, and in America, from Emerson and Longfellow to Archibald MacLeish.

Classic art from museums and famous private collections later were made available to the public on Hallmark cards; and now the selection includes Michelangelo and Leonardo da Vinci, Brueghel, Cezanne, Monet — whoever's work is colorful and in keeping. Nor has the contemporary world of words and pictures been overlooked. The Hallmark and Crown that appear on the back of all Hallmark cards are applied also to creations of Ogden Nash and Paul Engle, Grandma Moses, Walt Disney, Saul Steinberg, Cecil Beaton; even Salvador Dali.

Mr. Hall's own favorite was Winston Churchill. The two men were firm friends. A number of Churchill's paintings have adorned Hallmark cards, and a fine seascape and a glimpse through a procession of stately halls in Blenheim Castle hang on the walls of Joyce Hall's private office. Except for the latter, which were gifts, Churchill received a high price from Hallmark for his works. But Mr. Hall has been extremely careful about the use of these. When a collection of Churchill paintings went on tour in the United States, he took all the Churchill cards out of the company catalogue and forbade his salesmen to let any Hallmark dealer tie in with the exhibit. In an equally restrained spirit, Mr. Hall never allowed the well-known Hallmark symbols to appear on the special Christmas cards that he printed every year for General and Mrs. Dwight D. Eisenhower.

It is easy to agree with a competitor that "when J. C. Hall does something he goes all out." He has upgraded the entire greeting card business. He has created a new service to the public. And he has gone beyond this. His contributions to the content of television have been unmatched by anyone concerned with broadcasting.

The step from radio into television at the end of World War II proved longer than most advertising people had expected. Television turned out to be something quite different from radio-with-pictures, which was the way it was conceived, and it quickly became apparent that radio techniques and most radio people had no place in the new medium.

Television belonged to the genre of the motion picture. Whereas radio depended upon the listener's imagination to picture people and places and most of the action, television left no more to the imagination than the moving pictures. It was a medium both explicit and complete, in that it could deliver into any home anything that had ever been put on the theater screen. Still, it took time to make the most of this, and in the years immediately following World War II, television was little more than vaudeville brought into the country's living rooms.

Soon, however, experimentation began in earnest, and Foote, Cone

& Belding found itself deeply involved in the excitement. Toni sponsored the ineffable Arthur Godfrey and Dial sponsored Dave Garroway, two of the rare exceptions who made the transition successfully from radio to TV. Roy Rogers, the so-called king of the cowboys, was enlisted to help sell Post Toasties and Krinkles. Sid Caesar, the comedian, who led in the early audience totals, helped sell Libby's pineapple. Kleenex aired *Fun for the Money*, a comedy quiz program. Frigidaire sponsored the ambitious *Pulitzer Prize Playhouse*. Hallmark was dabbling in drama with a version of theater-in-the-round under the direction of Albert McCleary, who brought to television the cameo use of the close-up, with little or no dependence upon sets.

But Joyce Hall was not satisfied with either his own efforts or the broadcasters'. In the beginning Mr. Hall, like most advertisers on television, sponsored regular weekly features. The first of these, beginning in 1951, had been a series in which the actress Sarah Churchill (the daughter of his friend) interviewed a procession of notables from the stage and screen, and from politics, on their lives and interests.

This was followed in 1952 by a series of biographical sketches that dramatized little-known events in the lives of famous people, and came logically to be known as the *Hallmark Hall of Fame*. Sarah Churchill continued to appear regularly, under the direction of Albert McCleary. Rosemary De Camp, John Barrymore, Jr., Edward Arnold, Joseph Schildkraut, and James Arness, were other stars. Scripts were written by Robert Mason Pollack, Jean Holloway, James Truex, Rod Serling.

This program continued into the following summer with gratifying results. Hallmark was acclaimed for its serious efforts, and research showed the preference for Hallmark cards among greeting card buyers to be something like nine to one over the next leading brand. Also, the Hallmark slogan, *When you care enough to send the very best,* proved to be one of the most readily identified advertising phrases in the country; surveys showed it to be second only to Coca-Cola's *The pause that refreshes.*

But Joyce Hall still was not content. He didn't feel that he was doing all he could for his audience. He felt that the entertainment he was providing lacked substance. Ever since he had sponsored Gian-Carlo Menotti's *Amahl and the Night Visitors*, the first opera written for television, on Christmas Eve, 1951, Mr. Hall's restless urge had been at work. The *New Yorker* had called *Amahl* a "lovely and wonderful thing to see and hear." It attracted so much attention from viewers and the press that Hallmark was to present it seven times,

Joyce Hall (RIGHT) with the author at an anniversary dinner meeting held on the roof of the vast Hallmark plant in downtown Kansas City.

and to pioneer the use of sponsored network color with the performance of *Amahl* on December 20, 1953.

Encouraged by the reception the opera received, Hall took another deep plunge when, in April 1953, he broadcast Hallmark's own
production of *Hamlet* with the celebrated Shakespearean actor Maurice Evans, starring under the direction of George Schaefer. This was
the first television "special": the first two-hour program of entertainment ever done in prime time preempted by a network from its
regularly scheduled advertisers. It was also the first work of Shakespeare ever to appear on the TV screen. *Hamlet* was a triumph for television and a triumph for Hallmark. It was followed in January 1954
by a two-hour production of *Richard II* and in November of that year
by *Macbeth* — both of which had Evans in the title role. The audiences were small by television standards even then, but the critics
were enthusiastic and the *Hall of Fame* took on a new character and
a new cachet.

Now Joyce Hall's mind was made up; he would use television only
for such programs. No matter what anyone else might do, he would
no longer sponsor a weekly program. He felt the cost of broadcasting
was such that no one could afford programs of real excellence fifty-
two times a year. Furthermore, he said he didn't need the frequency;
it was wasteful.

"We have decided," he said — and sent the agency to argue the
point with Robert Sarnoff and Sylvester L. Weaver at the National
Broadcasting Company — "that television time should be bought by
us only when we need it most (which is just before Christmas,
Easter, Mother's Day, graduation time, and so on), rather than fitted
to an inflexible schedule of weekly time periods.*

"We have also concluded that a longer-than-hour dramatic show,
produced with the greatest possible skill and the finest available talent,
will dominate the evening on which it appears, and be remembered
much longer than any ordinary program. Last and most important,"
he said, "we believe that the American public is more than willing to
accept and appreciate serious drama in worthwhile numbers."

Sarnoff was not at all sure that J. C. Hall was right about the
numbers. But Weaver, who was the adventuresome president of NBC
at the time, saw another opportunity. He saw the long-run advantage
to the network of preempting time from regular advertisers for special
shows and special sponsors. This opened up many possibilities. Most
of all, however, Weaver was intrigued with the idea of presenting

---

* He was counting on the carryover, for actually, half of all greeting cards sold
are "everyday" cards. Christmas cards amount to about ten per cent.

the classics on television, in prime time, to increase the stature of the medium. He knew that the audience would seldom, if ever, reach the heights, but he agreed with Joyce Hall that it would be a very selective audience and it would answer television's most demanding critics.

Thus was the television "special" born and nurtured because Joyce Hall refused to accept a pattern of programming that he thought was wrong for Hallmark and proposed an alternative that appealed to all the interests involved.

Alice In Wonderland, with the late Bobby Clark and Martyn Green, Elsa Lanchester and Eva Le Gallienne, was the first of the ninety-minute and two-hour programs that resulted, and that continue to this day to be television's most ambitious and most honored series.

Mr. Hall's successful insistence that the *Hall of Fame* should present the very best in entertainment is borne out in two lists that are unlikely ever to be duplicated in the glamour of the names they contain.

The first is the roster of authors whose works have been broadcast. These include, in addition to Shakespeare and Menotti and Lewis Carroll, and in the "order of their appearance," George Bernard Shaw, Elmer Rice, Emlyn Williams, Ferenc Molnar, Garson Kanin, Lillian Hellman, Jean Anouilh, Robert E. Sherwood, Gilbert and Sullivan, Marc Connelly, Mary Mapes Dodge, James Costigan, Frederick Knott, Elmer Harris, Sam and Bella Spewak and Cole Porter, Eugene O'Neill, John Balderston, Maxwell Anderson, Henrik Ibsen, Ludwig Bemelmans, James Hilton, Henry Denker, Edmond Rostand, Laurence Housman, Sidney Kingsley, Noel Coward, James Lee, John Hersey, James M. Barrie.

The second is the list of stars who have appeared on the *Hall of Fame.* These are again in the order of their appearance; Rosemary Kuhlman, Maurice Evans, Sarah Churchill, Barry Jones, Joseph Schildkraut, Judith Anderson, Reginald Gardiner, Ralph Bellamy, Dennis King, Teresa Wright, Vivian Blaine, Hal March, Joan Loring, Melville Cooper, Julie Harris, Walter Slezak, Cyril Ritchard, Roddy McDowall, Lilli Palmer, Siobhan McKenna, Anthony Franciosa, Mary Martin, Paul Douglas, Joan Greenwood, Greer Garson, Franchot Tone, Sidney Blackmer, E. G. Marshall, Eileen Heckart, Boris Karloff, Eli Wallach, Basil Rathbone, Charles Boyer, Katherine Cornell. Also, Theodore Bikel, Alfred Drake, William Warfield, Claude Rains, Rosemary Harris, Tab Hunter, Peggy King, Christopher Plummer, George Peppard, Victor Jory, Julie Wilson, Carol Channing, Jessica Tandy, Edna Best, Helen Hayes, Lloyd Nolan, Burgess Meredith, Piper Laurie, Hume Cronyn, Jason Robards, Jr., Lee Remick, Dame Edith Evans, James Daly, Kim Hunter, Keenan Wynn, Thomas Mitchell, James Donald, Tony Randall, Dorothy Stickney, Mildred Natwick, David Wayne, Miyoshi Umeki, Paul Ford, Gladys Cooper, George Rose, Trevor Howard, Richard Burton, Charlton Heston, Maureen O'Hara, Bert Lahr, Stanley Holloway, Alfred Lunt, Lynne Fontanne, Peter Ustinov, Geraldine Page, Jean Simmons, Claire Bloom, John Forsythe, Raymond Massey, Pamela Brown.

The programs have received more than sixty national awards for their excellence, including six Academy Awards for the best dramatic program of the year, and Joyce Hall himself was honored by a unique Academy Award in 1961, the year Hallmark presented a second version of *Macbeth*, filmed on location in Scotland. It was the first and only award to a sponsor. "Thank you, Mr. Hall," the Academy said, "for caring enough to send the very best in television."

Television has two publics, and Joyce Hall realized this and did something about it. His programming was aimed at thoughtful people or, as he said, "at the people other people follow"; and follow they have, in a rising stream, into thousands of department stores and card shops where Hallmark cards are offered for sale.

Actually, we know that during almost all of the *Hall of Fame* productions, more than half the available audience is attracted to something else, something much more popular, more in the television idiom of the cloak-and-dagger, wild, wild West or situation comedy, all written to formula. Fortunately, less than half of the national audience is quite sufficient to supply the preference for Hallmark that sustains its leadership.* Less fortunately for the less than half, television is programmed at almost every hour for the majority.

Anyone who can afford it can make a movie, and there are various means and places available for showing that movie. Anyone can write a book, and even if he has to publish it himself, there are plenty of presses available to print it. Anyone can start a magazine or newspaper, and many people have. But only those people can get into television who can be allocated by the government a channel for broadcasting that is not already in use. Since there are very few of these, television is to all intents and purposes a closed industry in which its chief product, which is entertainment, is planned for the majority of set owners. The same little home screen that may thrill us with *Elizabeth the Queen, Death of a Salesman, An Evening with Fred*

---

* Hall of Fame programs average about sixteen million viewers.

Astaire, or a thoughtful news analysis by an enlightened commentator, fills the hours between with quantities of unmitigated and almost unbelievable rubbish. Hour after hour is taken up with programs that copy other programs that weren't very original to begin with, and these are repeated again and again.

It is small wonder that some of the top audience programs in many weeks turn out to be moving pictures that may be anywhere from eight to thirty years old. These are usually more entertaining than the formula comedy and drama that is turned out today by the television program factories. Indeed, it has become fashionable to call the advertisements that punctuate the common run of these programs the best part of television. This last, I am afraid, is a rather sophisticated view. I daresay also that it applies to a relatively few commercials, for many of these continue to be either dull and tasteless or terribly overdrawn. They pay out for most advertisers simply because they are inescapable for large numbers of people; they are like the proverbial drops of water that wear away a stone.

It would be wrong for me to pretend that I am not interested in the large audiences to which most television is directed. I have to be, for competitive reasons, and my company buys all the viewers it can get for most of our clients. J. C. Hall is the exception.

As this is written, Foote, Cone & Belding is contracting for approximately $110 million worth of time (and talent) annually for twenty-odd advertisers on such programs as *Rowan and Martin's Laugh-In,* *The Dean Martin Show, The Jackie Gleason Show, The Ed Sullivan Show, The Smothers Brothers Comedy Hour,* and *Ironside*; and we have placed commercials on most of the mystery series of the past ten years, including *Naked City, 77 Sunset Strip* and *The Untouchables,* and such weary Western extravaganzas as *Wagon Train, Bonanza* and *Rawhide*; also *Ben Casey* and *Dr. Kildare*; and the Andy Griffith, Lucille Ball, Danny Thomas, Bob Hope, Jack Benny and Red Skelton shows.

These are listed to keep the record clear. They are, or have been, among the networks' most popular programs. Some of them, also, have become suggestive and nasty — and I shall return to this unpleasant subject.

Why has the *Hall of Fame* not been copied? It has. But not successfully. *Hallmark Hall of Fame* is an exception to the common rules of television because Hallmark is an exception. It has no advertising competition. It sets its own standards, and it cannot be challenged as long as it sticks to them. Besides, who could uphold them as well as Shakespeare or Shaw?

Five-Cent Package Makes
Two Full Quarts

ONE day late in the winter of 1953, Charles Mortimer informed me over a lunch table in New York's Barclay Hotel that our services would no longer be required by General Foods. My disappointment took my breath away. But Mortimer hadn't finished talking. "We have just concluded a deal," he said, "to acquire an important company in Chicago. It will be run not as a division of General Foods, but as a subsidiary. Our ruling on General Foods agencies does not affect subsidiaries. So, if you would like to handle the advertising for this company, which is called Perkins Products Company, I am prepared to assign the account to Foote, Cone & Belding in Chicago."

Perkins Products Company was something I had never heard of, but if it meant some kind of tie to General Foods, I wanted it, and said so. "You must know," I told Mortimer, "that this is like a lifeline. To be dropped by General Foods is nothing like losing the Pepsodent account, for that company was in such trouble that discharging the agency was part of the ritual of failure. Being let go by General Foods could only say to all advertisers, 'These people just don't rate with the other General Foods agencies, with Young & Rubicam and Benton & Bowles.' From that you have saved us, and I promise you that you will never be sorry."

Mortimer said, "I'll tell you something else. The man you will be working for at Perkins is a man named Parlin Lillard, who is a bundle of energy, and a man with a passion for action."

The Perkins company that I had never heard of turned out to be one that one of our own New York men, A. J. Becker, had turned up and turned over to Lillard. The company was the manufacturer of a soft drink powder called Kool-Aid. When Mortimer arranged to buy Milo Perkins's company for General Foods stock valued at $40 million, Perkins became that company's second largest stockholder, second only to Mrs. Marjory Post Hutton Davies, whose father had put the giant firm together. Charlie Mortimer had made his best buy, and Parlin Lillard was just the man to put in charge of it.

A five-cent package of Kool-Aid was a small envelope filled with mild-flavored powder that, when sweetened with sugar and added to two quarts of water, provided a pitcher of homemade grape, orange, lemon or berry-juice drink — artificially flavored and colored — that was a child's delight. Prior to the arrival of Lillard on the scene, half the flavor in Kool-Aid went up the factory chimney. You could smell it for miles around the plant, and it was said that so little taste was left that an adult could only consume the sweet, colored water by intravenous injection. Lillard changed all that. Leaning on his knowledge of General Foods methods, he applied the flavor-sealing process used in the manufacture of Jell-O, and suddenly Kool-Aid had lasting flavor, too. The additional cost was more than made up by a reduction in the amount of powder required to produce the superior drink.

Soon, America was drinking Kool-Aid to the extent of thirty-five glasses per year for every man, woman and child in the country.

In addition to the improvements that grew out of Lillard's knowledge of production, which is a characteristic of good management, Kool-Aid was the beneficiary of a lucky break in advertising. This came about when Marvin Potts, the agency's chief art director in Chicago, amused himself at a picture-taking session by drawing with his finger, on a frosty pitcher of purple grape Kool-Aid, a happy, smiling face. Thus is many a great advertising idea come by — by purest chance. David Ogilvy put the eyepatch on the man in the Hathaway shirt as a gag to amuse a photographer, and found that he had given a dashing character to Hathaway shirts that they had never had before. Potts, in the same offhand way, had stumbled on an idea that became central to all Kool-Aid advertising.

Added to the fact that a five-cent package made two full quarts, children found the picture irresistible.

Soon the smiling pitcher was the feature of the Kool-Aid package as well as the printed advertising, and the feature of each Kool-Aid television commercial, in which two animated Kool-Aid kids found their favorite drink in strange and romantic countries all over the world. These were among the first one-minute complete stories in television advertising, and acceptance of their promise that "Kool-Aid tastes great" was so widespread that Kool-Aid stands by the thousand blos-

Happy ending to the Easter Parade—that's Kool-Aid, the only soft drink with the smile of pure refreshment. A 5¢ package makes two quarts. Still the most for your money in flavor and fun.

Advertisements like this, in cool inviting color, in Life, *told parents that Kool-Aid was pure and good, and backed up the TV appeal to the kids.*

somed in place of the traditional homemade lemonade stands with which so many children welcome the warm days of summer.

Another item in Lillard's success, which came as usual from not accepting what *couldn't* be done, was the extension of the Kool-Aid season. Under Perkins the product had been sold only in hot weather; every unsold package was removed from the grocers' shelves after Labor Day and Kool-Aid was not returned there until the middle of the following June. This was altogether too little exposure to suit Lillard. He and his hard-driving sales manager, a blond, moustached young man named Bob McLean, inaugurated a series of display contests for the grocery store owners and managers that they couldn't resist, with the result that they kept Kool-Aid in stock throughout the year, and sales responded without regard to temperatures.

Parlin Lillard's enthusiasm, like all extravagant enthusiasms, occasionally led him into difficulty, but the most bothersome of his troubles was in no way foreseeable. It concerned a new product called Kool-Shake.

Kool-Shake was a flavor additive that did for milk what Kool-Aid did for water, only more; for in addition to flavoring it, Kool-Shake actually thickened the milk, as ice cream thickens a traditional milk shake. Home use tests indicated a high level of acceptance for the product. Children liked it, and their parents welcomed it as a way to get balky youngsters to drink milk without making faces.

Under these circumstances the grocers greeted Kool-Shake eagerly. Distribution was excellent. The advertising began, on television and in the Sunday comics. The whole country responded. Initial sales were beyond our expectations. Then, as suddenly as they had begun, sales stopped.

No amount of advertising seemed to make any difference. No mass displays in stores could move so much as a case. Kool-Shake, the overnight success, was a next-night failure for no reason that anyone could fathom. Certainly the children's taste had not changed. Nor had the parents' problem. Nor was the product different in any way from the one that had been so successfully tested. What, we kept asking ourselves, was so right about Kool-Aid that was so wrong about Kool-Shake? Finally the answer unfolded. When families that had been so pleased with Kool-Shake in the first tests were offered Kool-Shake again they were reluctant to accept the free packages, and almost equally reluctant to say why.

It was Parlin Lillard who discovered the truth. Indeed, there was nothing wrong with Kool-Shake, either as a concept or as a product.

Its troubles were economic. Whereas a five-cent package of Kool-Aid made two quarts of refreshing drink with only the addition of water and ice (practically free) and sugar (a staple in any kitchen), a ten-cent package of Kool-Shake required an additional ten or more cents worth of milk to make two glasses of milk shake.

Thus Kool-Shake was costing at least ten times as much for a glass as Kool-Aid! Moreover, with most families getting only two or three deliveries of milk weekly, the making of Kool-Shake put an uncomfortable strain on the supply, and made the cost and the bother of replenishing it at odd times a recurring nuisance. The combined factors of high cost and conspicuous annoyance were more than any product could stand; some very attractive advertising couldn't help it at all.

Sobered, but even more determined by the failure of Kool-Shake, Parlin Lillard shortly came upon another ready-mix that proved to be a winner because he was alert now to the necessity to check out every unfavorable possibility for its proper weight in the assessment of chances.

The new mix was called Good Seasons, and it contained various dry ingredients for superb salad dressing. Bob Kreis, head salad chef of the Brown Derby restaurants in Los Angeles, had made this to pass out in small envelopes to customers who asked for his recipe for Caesar salad. This was easier than telling them; besides, he wasn't about to give away any secrets.

Nor did he to Lillard. General Foods paid the estimable Kreis, a tall, good-looking Swiss with a Swiss banker's financial acumen, a tidy sum for half a dozen of his recipes and for his supervision of the business at the start. Once again General Foods know-how made possible a fairly substantial and very profitable business where none had existed before. The ability to preserve flavor in some of the exotic herbs that Bob Kreis combined in his mixes was the thing Parlin Lillard had learned from the Jell-O division and perfected at Perkins.

Now it was providing a new generation of housewives with tastier salad dressings at sharply reduced cost — for the herbs and spices in the Good Seasons packages were designed to be mixed with the housewives' own oil and vinegar (in a distinctive mixing bottle that could be used also as a cruet).

The idea was accepted with enthusiasm and Good Seasons salad dressing mixes seemed an instant success. Then something happened. Sales slowed. But before they could stop, as they did with Kool-Shake, the once-burned Lillard set out to discover what the trouble was. Once again, he knew that there was nothing wrong with the product. Or was there? Was there something in the basic concept that someone had missed? To try to find the answers to these questions, the Perkins people and the agency team that was responsible for Good Seasons advertising took to the field; but this time we narrowed our activity to investigating the prejudices of women who were *not* buying our product.

In no time at all, and before slack sales could cause the removal of Good Seasons from the grocer's shelves, we had our answers. Good as the dressings were, they appealed not at all to that large segment of the market that was used to the sweet, thick, red concoction called French dressing that is made to amplify the bland taste of delicate greens and cover up the stronger taste of vegetables. We were trying to sell our true French and Italian style dressing mixes to a public whose tastes were based on heavy condiments, not so much to enhance flavor as to change it.

Our products were simply not tuned to the mass market. Television commercials that made the mixing of Good Seasons look like fun sold hundreds of thousands of women, but we couldn't sell their husbands or their children — most of whom didn't like salad to begin with, and accepted it only when it was thickly disguised.

The result was that we turned from the large audiences of television to the smaller circulation of the better class magazines and built our business among the discriminating families to whom the appeal of Good Seasons was almost identical to that which Bob Kreis had experienced at the Brown Derby. A near miss became a clear gain and I learned an important lesson: a product of frequent use can build satisfactory volume on the preference of a relatively small number of families; it needn't appeal to everyone.

In the fifth year of our profitable association with Parlin Lillard (and Edmund Fitzmaurice, who had succeeded McLean as sales manager), General Foods bought the S.O.S. Company, manufacturers of the second largest-selling brand of steel-wool scouring pads. Brillo was the leader. Brillo had captured the New York market where the use of the pads was heaviest (presumably because of the large fastidious Jewish population) and this reflected itself in total national sales.

As usual with Lillard, his first step at S.O.S. was to improve the product, and this he did by increasing the amount of soap with which each pad was impregnated. Still Brillo continued to enjoy almost ninety per cent of the vital New York market. The facts about the improved S.O.S. simply weren't impressing our prospects there.

And no wonder. Steel scouring pads are a subject of infinitesimal interest; actually they are a scratchy, unpleasant fact of life in the kitchen. One might doubt that a little extra soap could change the appeal of a prickly pad. But it did when the S.O.S. story was told with gentle humor.

The late Gertrude Berg, one of Broadway's most serene and comfortable stars, became our presenter, and when she put an S.O.S. pad in an electric mixer to whip up a mountain of suds it seemed the most natural thing in the world to do to demonstrate the extra soap in which we had been totally unable to interest anyone by way of argument.

When Mrs. Berg allowed that the demonstration was "kind of silly," but obviously also kind of fun, like jumping in a mud puddle, she had her audience firmly in hand, and the result was instantaneous. A product, at first the victim of extreme disinterest, suddenly had been brought to notice by a graceful lady who treated it with just enough respect. Any more would have killed the sale; it would have made steel-wool pads a matter of ridiculous concern (a concern that afflicts the advertising of many a commonplace product).

As it was, S.O.S. won over the New York market, and with its lead in other parts of the country, regained the number one position in the industry that it had enjoyed years before as the innovator. A persistent Parlin Lillard then rounded the rough ends of the pressed steel strands, and, in a final gesture, made the pads rustproof.

Recently, the government, for reasons that remain unclear after many readings, insisted that General Foods divest itself of the S.O.S. company, which ownership it held to be in restraint of trade.* Since anyone who wants to can go in the steel wool business, and most of the grocery chains have, I think the Justice Department acted capriciously.

Meanwhile, General Foods had moved the advertising of S.O.S. and the Kool-Aid products to New York where, after the development of some corporate conflicts, this was removed entirely from Foote, Cone & Belding.

---

* S.O.S. is now the property of Miles Laboratories, of Elkhart, Indiana, the makers of Alka-Seltzer and One-a-Day vitamins.

He Drew His Way from Rags to Riches

WHEN Albert Dorne wrote the headline *He drew his way from rags to riches* for his Famous Artists School of Westport, Connecticut, he joined the ranks of the great copywriters. There had been other captions on other advertisements for the school and they had been successful. But it was this one, in the New York *Times* Sunday magazine that hit the jackpot, for the body of the advertisement told how the same thing might happen to other struggling artists and would-be artists, too. There was no fooling about it.

That he himself was the subject of the advertisement caused Albert Dorne not the slightest embarrassment. He knew that the success story of a poor boy was one of America's traditional favorites, and his own part in this one was just a lucky break; he wouldn't have to pay someone else for a testimonial. The truth was that he had been a poor boy, brought up in an East Side New York tenement; he had left school at the age of fourteen to become a messenger in knickerbockers in the office of Marcus Loew, the theatrical magnate; and the talent for drawing that he had developed all by himself, after work on week days and on weekends, had made him one of the best-paid illustrators of all time.

We had worked together on the De Soto advertising at the Getchell agency, and Albert had illustrated one of the early barrel advertisements for Hiram Walker's Imperial whiskey, together with the whole series of wartime advertisements for Frigidaire. Now, in 1953, the same year in which we began to work for Parlin Lillard on Kool-Aid, we became the agency for Dorne's home-study school.

His was a solid concept. To begin with, he wanted the school to teach the basics. He wanted it to embody his own philosophy of drawing, which began with knowing how; where one went on from there he didn't care, but he believed that every artist had to know what he was doing. He had no use for art for art's sake. "It should be the purpose of all art to say something," he insisted. And he wanted to teach his students to say what they had to say clearly and with conviction. This, he knew, must be based on knowledge, and the first book in the course offered by the new correspondence school was called *What You Should Know to Become a Successful Illustrator*.

When Dorne first had the idea for the school he enlisted Fred Ludekens, who was freelancing in New York, to help him plan the course. It took them four months to outline the original eighteen lessons, which they then divided equally between them to be written and illustrated, a task that took two hectic years because they had their own careers to follow for their livelihood. It was during these twenty-four months, when Dorne and Ludekens together made a total of four thousand drawings for the course, that a brilliant idea occurred to them. Why not, they thought, enlist an additional eight or ten of the top illustrators to design a series of postgraduate courses to explain their own viewpoints and their own individual procedures and techniques?

These were the artists whose work they had reproduced along with their own to illustrate the basic course, and the special courses could be an intensive and exciting follow-up. In time this proved unsuccessful; twelve more lessons on top of eighteen were more than most students could absorb. But the idea was worth all the trouble it had taken.

The other artists were enlisted as regular faculty members and the school was able to use Norman Rockwell, Al Parker, Ben Stahl, Stevan Dohanos, Jon Whitcomb, Robert Fawcett, Peter Helck, John Atherton, Austin Briggs, Harold Von Schmidt and Gilbert Bundy, America's top-ranking illustrators, along with Dorne and Ludekens, to give the courses added character. Out of this came the name Famous Artists School, which was, after all, what it was; and its success from this point was phenomenal.

To begin with, the instruction was first-rate.* The printed lessons, which have been revised every few years to bring both text and illustrations up to date, are only a part of this. Most important has been the method of correcting lessons that Dorne and Ludekens developed to break all the old rules of correspondence-school operation and sub-

---

* Famous Artists courses are used as reference works in leading traditional art schools, both in the United States and abroad.

stitute personal instruction for general advice. The Famous Artists is a correspondence school in which the student secures almost as much personal attention as he would receive in resident art school classes. When each lesson from a student is received at Westport the drawing is covered with tracing paper on which a skilled instructor actually draws his suggested corrections in composition, perspective, light and shadow, and makes whatever marginal notes the work seems to call for.

From the beginning the school took on the character of the founders. To be sure, they had thought of the venture first as a moneymaking operation. Albert Dorne had had intimations that his life might be short; he had hoped to build up an estate for his wife. Fred Ludekens was also most interested in the business aspects of the undertaking. Fred had never been known to make a picture except to fill an order. But both men became intrigued with the school as a teaching institution. In the blossoming of so many of its students, they discovered a new satisfaction.

An early experience will demonstrate. A New Jersey woman who had purchased the course failed to send in her first lesson, but forwarded instead a large framed triptych representative of the golden gates of heaven. This was a vision, she wrote, that had come to her at a time of sickness, and sustained her and made her well; and in painting what she had seen she said she had kept a promise to the Lord.

The instructors at Westport were ecstatic. And so was Albert Dorne. "A magnificent primitive," he agreed. "And," said Dorne, "send the lady back her money. And tell her never to take a lesson again from anyone, as long as she lives. It could ruin her."

It is unknown to me whether anyone else ever had his tuition returned from the Famous Artists. But this doesn't matter. The school keeps after its students to complete their lessons, to discover the satisfaction that comes from knowing how and why; and hundreds of its graduates are successfully pursuing careers made possible entirely through its teaching. Others who, for one reason or another, fail to finish their courses (which now include not only commercial art and illustration, but also at one end of the spectrum, painting, and at the other, caricature and cartooning) turn up as knowledgeable amateurs.

In 1956, after three years, Foote, Cone & Belding was terminated by Dorne and Ludekens despite the fact that I had been a director of the school from its inception. I hadn't been able to devote myself to the advertising, for all the time that I could spare from Chicago was taken up in New York with our crisis accounts, and with a new addition to the agency's assignments, called Clairol.

Anyway, there is a large question in my mind whether I could have satisfied Albert Dorne. He was his own best copywriter. The "rags to riches" advertisement is one I don't think I could have imagined; and if I had, I doubt that I would have submitted it. It would have seemed too personal, and too much like Horatio Alger for this self-educated man whose aim had ceased to be wealth and had become that of usefulness.

There are many stories about Albert Dorne, and they are part of the legend that grew up around him. The story I like best has to do with the sound thrashing his mother gave him one afternoon when she discovered her fourteen-year-old sitting on the floor under a high brass bed in their tenement flat crocheting a doily.

The fact that he was smoking a fat cigar had nothing to do with the punishment; she didn't want her boy to be a sissy. But Albert was only exercising his large, strong fingers in the kind of meticulous detail that was to make him famous as an illustrator. His mother needn't have feared for her son's masculinity. Before he became an artist he tried boxing, as a preliminary fighter; and he was an excellent handball player.

Above all, he was part of the day-and-night scene in that fashionable enclave of New York City that lies within a half-mile radius of Park Avenue and 57th Street. Far north or west of Central Park I am sure he never ventured, nor south of 42nd Street. Those parts of the city held no interest for him. He lunched every day at the Waldorf Men's Bar, with Herbert Mayes, editor of *McCall's*, Raymond Shindler, a detective who fascinated him, Joseph Hirshhorn, the uranium king — who owns the world's greatest aggregation of the sculpture of Henry Moore; or some other of the artists and art lovers who made up his private collection of entertaining people. Albert Dorne's friends were men of unique talents, even to Hilner, the butler with whom he played pool at his country house at Peekskill, and Benny Leonard, the former lightweight boxing champion, who was his sparring partner.

Albert Dorne was a broad, muscular man built on the order of a Black Angus bull, with heavy eyebrows, who would have looked decidedly sinister had he not usually worn a smile. He was fearless, except where automobiles were concerned. He was nervous about them and there was one night when a taxi driver whom he had cautioned several times to drive slowly took his admonitions as a joke and brought him up short in front of the Stork Club on 52nd Street with screaming brakes.

"If you will step out here a minute, I have something for you,"

Dorne said. When the hulking driver did, Dorne laid him on the sidewalk with a hard left to the jaw. "Next time you want to pay attention," he said.

The fact is, I have never known a kinder man. He treated reasonable taxicab drivers and waiters and clerks in stores with the same consideration that he gave to his best friends. But he didn't trifle, and he refused to be dealt lightly with.

His only idiosyncrasy was in the matter of clothes. He dressed immaculately and very expensively. "*You* can wear any old thing," he said once to a friend. "You've got that Princeton look. That Brooks Brothers look. I've got to wear suits from the best tailor in town and custom-made shirts and shoes, just to prove to *myself* that I really have it made."

This was a man who thought out a lot of things, and came to a number of original conclusions.

After Albert Dorne's very sudden death in December of 1965, Fred Ludekens came out of retirement in California to act as chairman of the company of which Dorne's second-in-command, Gilbert Granet, was named president.

Following the pattern of the Famous Artists School, Dorne and Ludekens had added a painting school, whose faculty was headed by Ben Shahn; the Famous Writers School, under the direction of a former editor of the *Reader's Digest*, Gordon Carroll; and the Famous Photographers School, the chief of whose faculty is Victor Keppler. All of the schools have been developed on the pattern established for the original venture, with ten or a dozen of the best-known and most respected people in each field helping to build sensible, usable, exciting courses. Names everyone would know were Arnold Blanch and Doris Lee in painting; Richard Avedon, Alfred Eisenstaedt, Bert Stern in photography; and, as writers, Bennett Cerf, Mignon G. Eberhardt, Bergen Evans, Red Smith, Faith Baldwin, Rod Serling — each different, each exceedingly well fitted to the task.

Now the Famous Schools have acquired the leading home-study school of accounting, the Linguaphone Institute for the study of languages, and the Diversified Education and Research Corporation, which operates the Evelyn Wood speed reading schools throughout the United States. All of these have brought the little company that began on the floor of Fred Ludekens's living room at 300 Park Avenue, where Albert Dorne laid out his first suggestion, to an institution that the investing public values today at many millions of dollars, based on stock exchange quotations.

My own satisfaction as a director is increased by the fact that the schools, after a hiatus of several years, have again become clients of Foote, Cone & Belding. I, for one, am quite willing to admit that we couldn't make the advertising as well as Albert Dorne could, but it is apparent that Ludekens and Granet, two tough taskmasters, think we can do it better than anyone else.

Dries Clear as Glass, Never Yellows

KOOL-AID and Famous Artists were not the only important additions to the agency's list of clients in 1953.

Paper-Mate, the leading manufacturer of ball point pens, appointed Foote, Cone & Belding, in Los Angeles. The makers of Sea & Ski, a suntan lotion that filtered out the sun's burning rays, appointed the agency in San Francisco. And Kraft Foods and S. C. Johnson & Son, the family-owned company that is the world's largest producer of wax products, named Foote, Cone & Belding, in Chicago.

Paper-Mate pens became the standard by which all other writing instruments were judged. Sea & Ski ended for most people the necessity to use messy oils and unguents in what was usually a vain attempt to prevent sunburn; Sea & Ski did its job neatly and as promised.

These, however, were single-product assignments for what amounted to single-product companies, while Kraft was committed to a wide variety of food products, and S. C. Johnson & Son had as its mission to protect and enhance the beauty of every household finish, as well as the bodies of boats and automobiles.

For Kraft our first undertaking was the advertising and promotion of caramel apples, which was most interesting because in this effort Kraft was interested not only in selling its excellent caramel candies but also in helping to move mountains of apples as an assist to the growers. In the course of time our Kraft assignments have come to include miniature marshmallows (invented by Kraft to eliminate the sticky business of cutting regular marshmallows to recipe sizes), toppings, pasta dinners, barbecue sauce and, latest and newest, frozen entrees and desserts that show how good frozen food can be when it is made with love and infinite pains.

We have worked now for five Kraft presidents, from Grell Pound and Clyde Loftus to Gordon Edwards, William O. Beers and O. E. Swain. We have worked for Charles Wright and Chester Green in sales and planning; and for Jack Platt, Bob Davis and Jim Blocki in advertising. But all of us together have been working through sixteen years to promote the work of Marye Dahnke and Dorothy Holland and their eager assistants in Kraft's experimental kitchens to lighten the labor of women everywhere who have meals to prepare.

Our first challenge for the Johnson people was to successfully promote an automobile polish that was intended to replace one whose acceptance had been threatened by an overenthusiastic article in the usually careful *Reader's Digest.* No single product could do what the article claimed for this one, at least not with the ease that was pictured. Under the circumstances, the first sale was almost sure to be the last to anyone who had read the *Digest* article, and such was the reach of that magazine's circulation that there were altogether too few who hadn't. The warranty on each can of Car Plate was fair enough, but this was lost sight of in the clouds of editorial enthusiasm. Car Plate was doomed, and Carnu, another polish, was introduced to take its place.

Almost the first thing Herbert Johnson said to us when we were given the responsibility for Carnu advertising, was "You will never be asked to invent a reason for the purchase of a Johnson wax product. We will never bring a new product into the market that is not superior to its competition, and we will never keep an old product in the market that has not been improved to maintain its superiority."

Carnu was placed in three different test markets at three different prices: $.99 and $1.19 and $1.39 for 14 ounces of the identical product. The result was a clear preference for the higher price, and Herbert Johnson took this as a mandate. He reasoned that if a man with a new automobile, or an old one of which he was proud, wanted to give it the best possible care, the Johnson wax company would cooperate; if the man with the new car or the cherished old one wanted to pay the higher price, Johnson would make it worth his while. Carnu was reformulated to include a greater percentage of Brazilian carnauba wax, the size of the container was increased to 16 ounces, so that a price of $1.39 was justified, and Johnson had a new leader in the marketplace.

The advertising for Carnu, true to Herbert Johnson's promise, was not an advertising agency invention. It came directly from the first demonstration we saw of the product by a member of the Johnson research team.

"Watch it," said Peter Crane, as he applied the thick white film to the hood of an old Ford car, "Watch it shine the deep down color back."

We watched. We took note. We remembered the words. And we put them into advertising. *Watch it shine the deep down color back* promised a successful demonstration before any demonstration was made; when the promise was fulfilled Carnu became a success with each user.

Herbert Johnson has filled his life with artistic experience. He was a long-time patron of Frank Lloyd Wright, who designed both the monumental Johnson headquarters at Racine, and the spectacular Johnson home called Wingspread (now headquarters of the Johnson Foundation for International Studies) on the shore of Lake Michigan.

Another adventure in art was the assembly of the collection of contemporary American paintings entitled *Art U.S.A. Now*. Moving to the medium of the motion picture, Herbert Johnson commissioned Francis Thompson to make the three-screen film, *To Be Alive,* that was the greatest single attraction at the New York World's Fair 1964–1965 and now is shown daily in a theater built specifically for this purpose on the Racine plant grounds.

Like Joyce Hall, whom he resembles in both his outward shyness and his ultimate inward confidence, Herbert Johnson has lived not two different lives, one artistic and one in business, but a single existence in which all of his interests move forward side by side. Fortunately for the American housewife, she has been the most pressing of these.

Herbert Johnson is retired now. But his search for better means to protect all kinds of surfaces (from hardwood floors, for which the first Johnson wax was formulated, to modern plastics and still more modern synthetic fabrics) is carried on vigorously by his son.

Today, under Sam Johnson's direction, and with the sharp marketing instincts of William K. Eastham, Johnson floor waxes account for more than half the total of such products in use in America. The automotive products are just short of first place in sales; and Johnson's Raid, whose introduction marked the company's first venture outside the wax and polish field, leads in preference among all insecticides.

Klear, the largest-selling self-polishing floor wax, Raid, and Johnson's Off!, the leading insect repellent, and Glory rug cleaner all have been introduced with advertising by Foote, Cone & Belding. But much of the success of Klear, insofar as advertising was concerned, must be credited to Howard Packard, Johnson's president at the time, and now chairman of the company's finance committee. His singular con-

Most ordinary wax yellows your floors like this tinted glass.

Klear dries clear as this clean glass — never yellows.

Wouldn't you rather have Klear's lasting beauty on your floors?

klear FLOOR WAX
SELF-POLISHING
WON'T YELLOW ANY FLOOR

created by JOHNSON'S WAX

The demonstration in this advertisement for Johnson's Klear self-polishing floor wax told more in a minute than almost any number of words could have done.

tribution came at a moment when there was grave concern about television commercials in which the demonstrations were not at all what they seemed to be.

A classic example of the hanky-panky was a shaving cream commercial which purported to show a piece of rough sandpaper shaved clean with what was called a super-moist lather. When it was discovered that the sand was not glued to the paper in the demonstration there was a loud hue and cry, and the fact that perfectly innocent television commercials used such props as mashed potatoes for whipped cream only because real cream melted under the hot studio lights made no difference. Television fakery was under fire (as the sandpaper commercial and any similar ones certainly should have been); and the fire was heavy.

It was at this point that I received a telephone call in Chicago from Racine, from Howard Packard. "Do you know," he asked, "whether the dark glass panel that is compared with the clear glass panel in the new Klear floor wax commercial was really made by waxing? Or was it painted?"

"I'm sure it was made by waxing with old-fashioned wax," I said. "That is the way the commercial was written. That is the way it was approved."

"Well, I wish you would look into this," Howard Packard said. "I know that Klear dries clear as glass, never yellows, as we say. But I'm not at all sure that you can spread any floor wax on *glass* to demonstrate the fact. What I am afraid of is that you are using something else — something other than wax. And that we must not do."

I am still uneasy when I think of the next few hours. For I discovered that Howard Packard's fears were well-founded. Sure enough, it had proved impossible to wax the glass to make the approved demonstration, and the resourceful studio people had simply dipped the glass panel halfway into a strong, clinging dye, leaving the other half untouched. The fact that no dishonesty was intended was all the excuse they thought they needed. But I hate to think of the effect on the introduction of Klear if the harmless deception had been discovered and exploited by an eager press.

As it turned out, we remade the commercial to explain that one half of the glass panel was *tinted* to simulate the effect of ordinary wax while *clear* glass represented the result of waxing with Klear; and the promise that Klear never yellows any floor was accepted on the basis of the parallel.

Howard Packard had been brought up in Marshall Field & Company to understand the value of candor in advertising even when no offense was meant by failure to disclose *anything*.

Advertising is often fun to make, but when it comes out funny it is usually disastrous, for advertising, after all, is not a form of entertainment; it is serious business and the record of failure resulting from attempts at comedy is long and appalling. Humor is something very different, and its use in the advertising of Johnson's Raid insecticide has had nothing but happy effects.

Prior to the introduction of Raid, insecticides had been promoted in print and on the air with ugly warnings illustrated with hideous photographs or drawings of ants, flies, mosquitoes, roaches, silverfish, and the rest of the crawling and flying household pests, all in forbidding detail. This could hardly be the way, the Johnson people thought, to introduce any new product from a company whose principal interest had always been beauty. Beauty and long life had been its twin watchwords, and now it was in the ugly business of killing.

The dilemma was one that marketing couldn't solve, but advertising could and did — with one of the most cheerfully conceived series of television commercials ever projected on family screens. The medium was the animated cartoon, and the episodes (that now run to several score) dealt lightly, but fatally, with the plans and strategies under which bands of bold and determined insects set out to conquer the kitchens and pantries and breadboxes that were the strongholds of the protector, Raid.

How the stratagems of the grinning pests were planned, with ingenuity and saucy contempt for the adversary, made them a resourceful and not unattractive foe to be vanquished rather than ugly bugs to be exterminated, and the victories of Raid over the marauders have had all the elements of a continuing contest in which the mighty aerosol can is mischievously provoked into action and retaliation.

The last, in all cases, has rested on the effect of the Raid spray which sends the pests to a doom that is represented by headstones that appear in limbo, as lights flash and bells ring in the manner of a pinball machine, when someone has won. *Raid kills bugs and kills them dead* are the words with which each commercial ends, but the terms in each one have been set by the pests themselves with a great show of braggadocio which makes their undoing no less than deserved.

Allegory is something I would rarely recommend in advertising. But it made Raid the leader in insecticide sales in its first year, and Raid has never been headed. Perhaps it isn't so much the allegory as the fact that no one has much sympathy for a smart aleck — and that is what Raid's swaggering, needle-nosed challengers always are.

Our association with S. C. Johnson & Son could not have come at a better time, for it followed by only a few months a decision on my part that might otherwise have turned the agency's forward progress into a ruinous retreat. The result of my action, which was taken in haste and regretted ever since, was to deprive us of the first of three large accounts that were lost to the company between 1953 and 1955. This was the Toni account.

After Toni's early success and the sale of the company to the Gillette Safety Razor people, Neison Harris left advertising more and more to subordinates. Some of these were extremely able; some were not; and, as usual, the advertising agency had trouble with the latter. Like most young advertising men, they wanted to make their own imprint on the advertising of their products. The Toni twins, who had been invented by Robert Koretz, a director of the agency, and tracked down all over the country by Coralie Schaefer, the agency's talent scout in this instance, were declared passé by Toni's young advertising people. They wanted something new; "new" meaning a device that would bear their own unmistakable fingerprints.

They forgot that the Toni twins were demonstrators, proving beyond a doubt that you couldn't tell the twin with the Toni-curled hair from the twin with the beauty-shop wave. Toni's young advertising people wanted something more like the girls who dreamed they went about clad principally in their Maidenform brassieres. The difference was that the Maidenform advertisements used a striking device to attract attention, while the Toni advertisements used a demonstration to *prove* their almost unbelievable promise.

The young advertising people at Toni believed that their promise had been proved. They wanted to make some new advertising history, and they called our people stupid for not agreeing with them. That made up my mind. To disagree with our people was one thing; I did it frequently, and expected others to. But to call anyone with our record stupid was something I could not take. It smacked of the advertising agent of the novels, whose only contribution was to agree with his client.

I lost my head and my manners went with it. I didn't either call on Neison Harris or write him a decent formal letter. I picked up the telephone in my office and told him that our people on his account had been categorized as stupid, and that we were through — as of that minute.

"Wait," he said, "let's talk about this."

"There is nothing," I said, "to talk about. No one gets a second opportunity to rudely attack our people." With that I put the telephone down.

Next day I had a call from Carl Gilbert, the crew-cut, broad-shouldered Gillette executive vice president in Boston who had managed the Toni purchase. He wanted, he said, to talk to me about something that must be a misunderstanding.

"No misunderstanding at all," I told him. "And I don't want to talk about it." Nor did I. When Carl Gilbert came to Chicago to discuss the matter anyway, I refused to talk about it at all. It may be that I knew so well that I had been wrong in not talking the thing out with Neison Harris, so wrong in my abrupt decision and my rudeness, that I *couldn't* talk about it. Perhaps I was too thoroughly ashamed. My original anger and my subsequent insistence on maintaining it had cost my company a $6 million account.

How entirely unnecessary and wrongheaded my break with Toni had been was brought forcefully home to me again ten years after the incident, when the Gillette Company acquired the Paper-Mate Pen Company and turned it over to the Toni group to operate. Paper-Mate was, as I have noted, a client of Foote, Cone & Belding in Los Angeles, and when Neison Harris called to tell me of the purchase and the plans for operating Paper-Mate as a Toni subsidiary, I thought he was being extremely polite. But he was much more than that. "The thing is," he said, "we would like you to do the advertising for Paper-Mate, here in Chicago."

It was that afternoon that I gave him my long-overdue apology. I could have added that I had never lost my temper again; the price had been much too much to pay.

Only Her Hairdresser
Knows for Sure

In August of 1955 the agency was appointed in New York for what proved to be one of the most successful lines of products ever introduced in the cosmetics business. The name of this soon to be famous collection of beauty preparations for the hair was Clairol.

My own work with Clairol was in the initial stages, with Lawrence Gelb and his sons, Richard and Bruce, two very young graduates of the Harvard business school who took to the cosmetics business and to advertising as though these had been invented for them by their father. Lawrence Gelb was a chemist who perceived that one of the greatest opportunities in the beauty products field lay in giving every woman who was dissatisfied with the color of her hair the exact hue and shade that she wanted. Once the perception was verified, Larry Gelb set out in New York and Paris to find the formula to make his vision come true: to answer a natural urge that had been obscured by the poor products then at hand and by the certain stigma that was attached to the very idea of hair coloring.

It wasn't very long before a satisfactory product was achieved. But this was less than half the problem. Hair coloring in 1955 had about the same social standing that was accorded cigarettes and bright-colored lipstick before the first World War. About seven per cent of women used it, shyly and secretly, except for a few aging actresses who could be excused on the grounds of their professional requirements. Its open use by anyone else was shocking and in no way condoned. Dyed hair, as it was called, was abominated by all right-thinking women, and the suggestion that anyone you *knew* used a tint was unthinkable.

Luckily for the Gelbs, and for Foote, Cone & Belding, when the problem of selling Clairol hair coloring was presented to the agency, it fell into the hands of Leo Rosenberg, who had played such a significant part in the successful introduction of the Toni home permanent wave, and a shrewd copywriter named Shirley Polykoff, whose feeling about any woman's appearance was that it should be everything she could make it. Shirley Polykoff thus shared the Gelbs' confidence that Clairol could resolve a growing desire and a need if somehow its use could be made as acceptable as wearing lipstick. She could see no moral difference, and if Clairol produced a result which was pleasing, then she felt the story could be told successfully. However, she knew that we had first to break down the deep prejudice that existed; and she knew also that this had to be done subtly; it couldn't be done by arguing.

First of all, she was sure, it would be necessary to change the popular conception of the hair-color user herself; it would be necessary to somehow make hair coloring respectable. At the time, as Miss Polykoff remembers it, "Models appearing in advertisements for health and beauty products were slick, overly made-up, oversophisticated fashion types, so we decided that our ads should present a portrait of the girl down the block, or the model with her face washed, gleaming in the sun. This, in itself, was a new twist.

"Then we added a child in each illustration for rapport, warmth, and to heighten the aura of respectability. With the appearance of the child in every advertisement, the model became a mother, aunt, sister, teacher or any other figure the viewer might choose for herself as a symbol of good moral character and good taste.

"The copy? Well, if you've ever read it you know that Clairol copy is always reassuring. It talks to the reader (or the television viewer) sympathetically, like a friend who cares. Then smack in the middle of all this respectability, we placed the question, the bombshell *Does she or doesn't she?* and followed this with the flat statement: *Hair coloring so natural only her hairdresser knows for sure.*" The second sentence was designed to answer the question that would be in the minds of any new user of Clairol, the vital question that had so often previously been answered affirmatively and, presumably, with a large measure of guilt.

What happened to Clairol when this advertising appeared, and in the dozen years since, is history. It is enough to say here that today almost seventy per cent of American women use hair coloring, happily and with no attempt to disguise the fact, and most of them use Clairol.

Does she...or doesn't she?®

Hair color so natural only her hairdresser knows for sure!™

Sharing a child's fun or by herself, she sparkles! Everything about her fresh and shining...radiant as a new day. Her manner. Her looks. The way her hair catches and reflects light—like natural color at its loveliest. In a sense, she's discovered how to make time stand still. It's Miss Clairol, the surest, most effective way to cover gray, and keep color young and bright, and beautifully even.

Hairdressers recommend Miss Clairol and use it above all other colorings because their professional reputations depend on beautiful results. They find Miss Clairol the most effective way known to cover gray. And what's more, it keeps hair in wonderful condition. This, too, is why more women use it. So quick and easy. Try it your- **MISS CLAIROL** self today. *HAIR COLOR BATH is a trademark of Clairol Inc. ©Clairol Inc. 1965*

Even close up, her hair looks natural. Miss Clairol keeps it shiny, bouncy. Completely covers gray with the younger, brighter, lasting color no other kind of haircoloring can promise—and live up to!

That perfect ladies, indeed, mothers of children, like this one, colored their hair helped make hair coloring a standard procedure for millions of women.

Looking back, the story of Clairol appears smooth and uncomplicated, a clear victory for a good new product in a neglected field. But
the truth is that Clairol's prejudice-shattering advertising (again, in
every instance, a demonstration, like the Toni twins) almost failed to
survive the advertising censors. As the Gelbs recall it ruefully, "we almost went down to bloody defeat."

Instead of scheduling the beginning Clairol advertising in the
woman's magazines — *Vogue, Harper's Bazaar, McCall's* — it was decided to place the entire budget in a family magazine like *Life*, an
unheard-of thing at the time. But the way we reasoned, hair coloring
for the lady of the house was bound to be a family affair; the sooner
the whole family began to take it for granted, the better it would be
all around.

But *Life* turned the campaign down. "*Does she or doesn't she?* is
much too suggestive a question," the copy censors said, and they were
adamant.

Then we challenged this panel of males to research the advertising
among *Life's* women employees. When they did this, they failed to find
a single one who confessed to seeing anything but the intended meaning in the proposed question. Somewhat shamefaced, *Life* accepted the
copy exactly as written. Encouraged by the growth of *Playboy* magazine and similar ventures in ribaldry, the double meaning has found
its way into advertising. But it had no place and no part in the achieve-
ment of Clairol.

While the success of Clairol, which began to take shape in 1955
was the most significant development in Foote, Cone & Belding in that
year, the most satisfactory at the moment was the reappointment of
the agency to direct the advertising of Pepsodent toothpaste. There
is nothing so exhilarating to any advertising agency as the return of a
lost account, and this was one which, by a stroke of good luck, gave
us an opportunity to soar.

In a matter of weeks following our reemployment, a new sound
was heard in the air as millions of radio receivers poured forth the
syncopated words *You'll wonder where the yellow went when you
brush your teeth with Pepsodent!*

Nothing like this had happened since the early days of radio, when
the latest antics of Amos and Andy or the barbed wit of Bob Hope
were reported and repeated as a part of the life of each day. The only
difference was that this was strictly business. It was the first new approach to dentifrice advertising since Colgate had promised: *It cleans
your breath as it cleans your teeth*, and I wish I could say that the
reference to yellow teeth, a household bugaboo in my family ever

since I could remember, had come from me. But it hadn't. The words were discovered on a crumpled piece of tissue paper in a pile of discarded rough layouts when I remembered Stirling Getchell sitting on the floor of my office sifting the contents of my wastebasket, because, he said, "You might not know a good idea if you saw one." This was the way I felt about the people who had looked at hundreds of suggestions by which it was hoped to bring Pepsodent back into contention with Colgate.

Our people believed that Pepsodent was a superior cleanser. However, they knew that Colgate's wintergreen flavor was preferred as a breath sweetener to the strong taste of peppermint that was Pepsodent's chief characteristic, and they were looking for a proposition that would help to overcome this. I was looking for a completely different one. As far as I was concerned, Colgate had preempted the breath story, and I didn't see how we could beat it. Research showed that breath and taste were synonymous, and we had the wrong taste. I didn't see how we could successfully fight Colgate on Colgate's own ground.

Now, in the scrap pile, I saw that we didn't have to try. *You'll wonder where the yellow went* was an answer on a torn sheet of layout paper. When we took it in rough layout form for newspapers and on an equally rough record for playing on radio, I made the shortest presentation of my life to Milton Mumford, Lever's president, Edward Hicks, in charge of the Pepsodent division, and Bill Eastham, the peppery Pepsodent marketing manager who was later to go to the Johnson wax company; I remembered an early admonition from Walter Doty, and I remembered that it had been repeated by George Washington Hill, and I staked all I had on it.

"Gentlemen," I said, "I want to play you a record. It is one minute long. After you have heard this record I want to show you an advertisement, a single newspaper advertisement.

"I have no introduction. I have no explanation. I want you to hear the radio commercial, for that is what we have recorded, and I want you to see the advertisement, just as the public would hear and see these without briefing and without any comment from me.

"When l have finished I want you only to say yes or no. If you have to think this over, if you hesitate, then the answer will be no."

When I played the record, and before I could unfold the newspaper advertisement, Bill Eastham said, "How soon can you get it on the air?" He didn't wait for either Mumford or Hicks to say anything, and when they did it was only to echo his question.

You'll wonder where the yellow went was paraphrased by President Truman ("You'll wonder where the voters went"); a popular song was written around the question; and the sharp sales increase for Pepsodent came close to doubling its volume. Sad to relate, failure to meet the competition of the fluoride toothpastes that soon appeared on the market caused another long downward trend. But when that happened, we had been divorced once again by the Pepsodent division. Bill Eastham had moved on. And the girl who wrote the inviting line has never, so far as I know, been heard from since. But then, she hadn't the slightest idea what she had when she wrote it; it was only the rhyme that intrigued her. What I saw was a new, direct, penetrating approach to the problem of tooth cleanliness in terms of appearance. This was underscored by the use of the word "yellow."

Yellow teeth were something nobody wanted.

One of the advertising ploys that is deplored by critics as far apart on the aesthetic scale as the rip-roaring Mr. Vance Packard and the equally ebullient but much more urbane Mr. John Fischer, late editor of *Harper's*, is the flowering of knighthood and romance through the power of a dentifrice, deodorant, dandruff remover, mouthwash, hair tonic, etc., and I think their criticism is supremely silly.

I am quite in accord with the conviction that real-life romance is rarely found in a vial or a tube, but I am equally convinced that there is nothing harmful in pointing out the happy possibilities in getting rid of dingy teeth, unpleasant body odors, unsightly dandruff, and so on. This is merely the advertising equivalent of the typical love story in magazine and even hardcover fiction where traditionally girl meets boy, girl loses boy, girl gets boy again — or vice versa. To object to this time-honored plot in advertising is pure snobbishness.

Furthermore, who is to say that such advertising has not been primarily responsible for the clean white teeth, pleasant breath, and the other things that have made most American young people so much more careful in their personal habits than any other young people anywhere? In the matter of tooth care alone, it is likely that advertising of the romantic possibilities has had more to do with the healthy teeth of two generations of American boys and girls than all the admonitions and warnings of all the dentists in the land. Insofar as Pepsodent had a part in this, and insofar as Foote, Cone & Belding was in partnership with Pepsodent on two different occasions, this is a matter in which I take some pride.

You Can't Call It Edsel

On Monday, August 15, 1955, I was summoned to Dayton, Ohio, and informed bluntly that henceforth Frigidaire advertising would be made by another agency. On my return from Dayton, I found a note on my desk requesting me to call Mr. J. C. Doyle at the Ford Motor Company in Dearborn, Michigan.

This seemed to me a poor joke. While it might be of some solace to make up the loss of a General Motors account with an assignment from Ford, I couldn't believe that a discarded General Motors agency would appear very attractive to their greatest rival. I couldn't imagine who the joker might be; if he wasn't a joker, someone totally wrong in his estimate of my judgment. I threw the note away.

But next morning I received a call from an old friend in the Advertising Council. "Did you get my message?" she asked. "To call Mr. Doyle at Ford?"

"Yes, I did," I said. "But somehow your name was left off. What is it all about?"

"I really don't know," she replied. "I was merely asked to deliver the message. So please do telephone the nice man. I said I was sure you would do this."

Then a strange thing happened. When I got Mr. Doyle on the telephone, I said, "This is Fairfax Cone. I understand you want to talk to me." He said, "No, I don't think it is quite that way." That was all.

I immediately called my friend at the Advertising Council, and told her what had happened. "Let me try to get this straight," she said. "I will call you back."

Within a matter of minutes, she was again on the telephone to say,

"It is a matter of protocol. Mr. Doyle doesn't want to call a General Motors agency. But he would like you to call *him* if you would be interested in talking about the advertising for a new Ford automobile."

This I certainly was. A new Ford automobile had been the subject of rumor and surmise in business and advertising circles for months, and its advertising was expected to be the largest new assignment ever made to an advertising agency. So it was that when I telephoned Dearborn for the second time that morning, I was careful to say, "Mr. Doyle, I would like very much to see you when this is convenient."

"Like tomorrow?" he asked.

"Yes," I said. And so began my three years' association with Larry Doyle, who took his nickname from a fighting third baseman of the old New York Giants, but who was one of the gentlest men I have ever known, a gentleman in the best sense of the word, in perhaps the most competitive business of them all.

When I walked into Larry Doyle's office, in a temporary wooden building labeled Special Products Division, Ford Motor Company, I did this with an uneasy conscience.

"Mr. Doyle," I said, "I have to tell you something. The strongest credential our company had for you was washed away day before yesterday when we were fired by Frigidaire."

"That," said Larry Doyle, a tall gray-haired man with a strong face and amiable eyes, "could be the least of your worries. We have talked to a lot of different people about Foote, Cone & Belding," he said. "You were recommended by each of our other three agencies, J. Walter Thompson Company, Young & Rubicam, Kenyon & Eckhardt. We have also talked to publication and broadcasting people. And various of our folks have talked to a number of your clients — including some recently retired people from Frigidaire."

"Perhaps," I said, "you can find out why we were fired by Frigidaire."

"I think if I were you," Doyle said, "I would forget about Frigidaire and General Motors, and concentrate on Ford."

And this we did, harder I think than we had ever concentrated on anything before. We wanted the advertising for the new Ford car, and we wanted to show our defecting client that he had made a large mistake.

Every time I saw Larry Doyle in the weeks that followed our first meeting my confidence rose that Foote, Cone & Belding would receive the new car assignment. But always when I left him I ran into circumstances that changed my confidence to doubt. Larry Doyle had cautioned me to sit tight, and this I tried to do, remembering particularly who had told me. Then I would make a discovery, as when I learned that the Special Products Division had asked for presentations from eleven different agencies, and I would be edgy.

Finally, on the morning of October 17, 1956, after two months of preparation, Foote, Cone & Belding made its formal presentation.

If there was any surprise in this it came out of the fact that I had managed to talk Fred Ludekens into returning to the agency business, where several years' experience with Chevrolet advertising, as a consultant to Campbell-Ewald, the Chevrolet agency, made him a particularly exciting addition to our team. As a matter of fact, while the other contestants for the account had hired a number of men with automobile advertising experience, Fred Ludekens was the only newcomer to Foote, Cone & Belding who had any part in our planning.

Once again I was elated when our scheduled three-hour presentation ran to five hours as Larry Doyle, Richard Krafve, Doyle's superior as general manager of the division (and one of Ford Motor Company's brightest stars) the R. F. G. Copeland, who had been brought in from the Kudner agency to be advertising manager, asked us innumerable questions and told us not to worry about the time. We told our audience every pertinent thing we had crammed into a final three-hour rehearsal the day before, and they asked for more.

When they asked us who, precisely, would be responsible for the account if Foote, Cone & Belding were appointed, I said, "The seven men who have taken part in this presentation, headed by Fred Ludekens, Charles Winston, and myself."

Charles Winston had begun in Foote, Cone & Belding as a trainee. He was a graduate of Princeton University. He had served in the Navy in World War II and had come to work in the agency under unusual circumstances.

"There is a young man in the reception room who is very anxious to see you," my secretary had informed me one busy morning in the spring of 1946, when our offices were still in the Palmolive Building in Chicago.

"Is it about a job?" I asked.

"Of course," my secretary said.

"But you know we have just put on a half-dozen young men, and we really don't need any more."

"You need this one," she said.

The upshot was a long, intimate talk with the young man. He had thought hard about his future during the night hours at sea where he commanded a PT boat in the Pacific. He was bent upon a career in advertising, and he was determined that it begin in Foote, Cone & Belding.

My secretary was right (as most of my secretaries have been right about so many things through the years), and Chuck Winston began work in the agency the following week.

After a year in the inside training program, he became an assistant on the Hiram Walker account; then, and for a considerable period, an assistant on the Frigidaire account; and finally, account executive for the Johnson wax automotive products and Raid insecticide advertising. Also, Chuck Winston had inherited from his father half-ownership in a Chevrolet sales agency in Joliet, Illinois, so that he knew more than a little about automobile retailing.

Thus he was our logical choice to head the Detroit branch office that would be one of the requirements of the new Ford Motor Company assignment.

Three of the eleven agencies originally selected to make presentations to the Special Products Division decided that the account would demand more of their resources than they were prepared to invest in a single account. This should have reduced the parade of hopeful agents to Dearborn. However, twelve additional agencies asked to be included in the competition, and presentations continued all through November and into December.

When these were concluded, six agencies withdrew from the contest. Of the fourteen remaining, Doyle and Copeland began to look most carefully at the five largest: Leo Burnett, Inc., Chicago; Compton Advertising, Cunningham & Walsh, and Dancer-Fitzgerald-Sample, in New York; and Foote, Cone & Belding, Chicago. Each was asked to fill out a questionnaire containing some seventy detailed questions prepared by Henry Baker, a scholarly investigator lured to Dearborn from the campus of the University of Utah; and Larry Doyle and Bob Copeland began a series of visits to the five selected agencies' offices.

The seriousness that surrounded these visits gave rise to one memorable incident at Foote, Cone & Belding, where it was reported that one of our elevator operators had insisted that our early-arriving girls take off their shoes before entering his carefully vacuumed cage. "I can't help it if it's rainy and wet," he insisted. "This elevator floor is going to be clean when those Ford people get here." When later we told them the story of the zealous operator, Doyle and Copeland seemed to enjoy this more than some of our scheduled declarations.

With the decision of half a dozen agencies not to compete for the account because of the cost involved prior to the receipt of the first commissions (which were many months off) Larry Doyle had inquired of the American Association of Advertising Agencies whether fees were ever charged under such circumstances.* When he learned that there was no precedent for this it was decided not to pay any, and when Cunningham & Walsh, one of the three finalists suggested a fee of $475,000, Special Products turned to the remaining two agencies — Leo Burnett, Inc., and Foote, Cone & Belding. Meanwhile, the speculation that thrives in the warmth of advertising competition continued.

On December 22, Krafve, Doyle and Copeland made a second visit to the Burnett and the Foote, Cone & Belding offices in Chicago, and again my confidence rose. The gentlemen from Ford, which was the way we always referred to them, spent the morning and had lunch with the Burnett people, but they spent the long afternoon, and had *dinner* with the seven-man contingent of Foote, Cone & Belding!

This I construed as a favorable indication. The first year's advertising was expected to amount to as much as $15 million, equal to almost a quarter of our going volume, and Burnett's too, and I think both companies could be excused for looking nervously for signs. We had outlasted or outdistanced eighteen other agencies, which were, with the exception of Thompson; Young & Rubicam; and Kenyon & Eckhardt, the Ford agencies, and the agencies representing the General Motors and Chrysler cars, the best and the largest in the business. That was some satisfaction. But now only one of us could win.

Or was this really so? Charles Winston's diary took note of these succeeding rumors:

December 29. New Ford car account will go to Maxon, Inc., because of that agency's experience with Ford dealer advertising, and excellent TV commercials for Gillette Safety Razor.

January 10. Cunningham & Walsh assigned account because of outstanding advertising for Jaguar.

January 13. Young & Rubicam has agreed to give up Ford's Lincoln account and take on larger Special Products assignment.

January 19. Foote, Cone & Belding out because Cone planning to retire to California.

January 30. Dark horse New York agency made special last-minute presentation to Henry Ford II and will get the business.

---

* In the years since it has become customary for advertisers to pay adequate fees for work done prior to receipt of commissions; and this has become a conservative influence in the business.

During the period from December 22 to February 7, I heard from Larry Doyle only once.

The recurring rumors all were bad. In my brighter moments, I supposed that Leo Burnett was feeling the same unease; if I believed that the aggressive Burnett people had sent Leo himself to Dearborn to make a special pleading, I am sure that the Burnett hopefuls could believe that we had concocted some highly successful approach of our own.

But about the middle of January I could no longer stand the quiet that shrouded Dearborn. I wrote Larry Doyle to say that our own silence should not be taken to indicate any indifference; we were only hoping to be considerate under the circumstances of Special Products' difficult decision. His reply was a single sentence delivered by telephone.

"If I were you," Larry Doyle said, "I think I would stop worrying."

But then silence overtook Dearborn again.*

Until, on the morning of February 7, twenty-two weeks after my first conversation with Larry Doyle, he tracked me down at a meeting at the Paper-Mate offices where I was visiting with Neison Harris, and asked me if I could conveniently come to Dearborn the next day.

"With your principals, and your lawyer," he said.

That was how I learned that Foote, Cone & Belding had been successful in what was undoubtedly the most spirited agency competition on record. Although no speculative advertising had been asked for, research and planning time probably represented a total cost to the twenty agencies of no less than $500,000.

I have always thought that Larry Doyle had opted for our company in the beginning on the strong recommendation of the Thompson company and Young & Rubicam. Thompson, under the longtime direction of Norman Strouse, in Detroit, was the premier Ford agency, and Young & Rubicam, which handled Lincoln advertising, was (and continues to be) an organization with the highest possible professional standards. I had considered working for both of them in years past and I had many friends in the two companies. These included Stanley Resor, the president of J. Walter Thompson Company, as well as Norman Strouse and John McQuigg of the Detroit office; and Sigurd S. Larmon, president, and Louis N. Brockway, executive vice president of Young & Rubicam. They were decidedly on our side, I thought.

---

* A major reason for my concern was the departure of Harold H. Webber from Foote, Cone & Belding shortly after we had made our original presentation. Webber was one of the best research men I knew, and the Ford research people knew this, too. Webber had gone to work for Gardner Cowles, at *Look* magazine.

But Larry Doyle was a careful man, and a fair one, and if he did have some prejudice in our favor he saw to it that this was justified in open competition. As it turned out, it was probably our position as the first of the agencies to make its presentation that gave us whatever advantage we had with the whole Special Products screening group. Our presentation set the mark everyone else had to beat, and apparently none did.*

When the contract that Ford insisted upon with the new agency was signed on February 16 (to become the first contract ever entered into with a client by Foote, Cone & Belding) we were told that our initial task would be to come up with an acceptable name for the new automobile, which then carried only the designation E — which stood for experimental car.

There were all manner of things, ranging from hubcap designs to division letterheads, that awaited the name, and we went immediately to work on it. The introduction of the car was still two years away, but such is the lead time required to do almost anything in the automobile industry that the naming job was a crash program. This was not something that had been neglected in planning; a good deal of effort had already gone into the search, which had included commissioning a name from the Brooklyn poet Marianne Moore, whose most remarkable suggestion was *Bullet Cloisonné;* but now the quest was turned over to the agency.

Naming products is a source of constant and usually fruitless mental exercise in advertising agencies (where the client's wife or a guest at a dinner party usually suggests the name that is finally accepted) and naming the E-Car was no exception. All the staff members of all the offices of Foote, Cone & Belding (in Chicago, New York, Los Angeles, San Francisco, even London) were asked to make suggestions, with a prize for the successful suggestion of one of the new cars itself. The result of the competition was a list of sixteen thousand names, assembled in two hectic weeks. This was reduced to six thousand, then finally, at Dick Krafve's insistence, to ten.

There was only one name that we were told had been ruled out. "You can't call it Edsel," Dick Krafve said. "That is positive."

Henry Ford II and his brothers Benson and William Clay Ford had told Krafve and Doyle they didn't think their self-effacing father would ever have approved the use of his own first name; so neither would they.

---

* Burnett had a long last laugh. Shortly after the Edsel decision, our greatest rival beat us out in competition for the Allstate insurance account which continues to be one of Chicago's most desirable.

That, we thought, closed the matter and so we searched far and wide and finally arrived at four recommendations: Corsair, Citation, Pacer and Ranger, with Corsair our first choice. This, it was established in hundreds of sidewalk interviews, had a highly desirable connotation for the "young people on their way up" for whom Ford researchers and Ford designers had decided the new car was to be made.

Unfortunately, as it turned out, the Ford directors, pushing for a name to be used on some vital dies, and tired anyway of the search that had assumed such exotic overtones as Miss Moore's, took only a quick glance at the huge display of possibilities and the agency's recommendations, and decided that if they could have the Ford brothers' consent, they would call the E-Car the Edsel, after all.

Consent was forthcoming, despite the earlier dictum, and so the Edsel was christened in embryo with a name that was at once a surprise and a huge disappointment. As one of our people said, "The name Flab, which had been suggested by a wag in our London office, couldn't have been any less appropriate." Insofar as the public was concerned the name Edsel was devoid of any feeling of action or spirit. It was a proper name, like Elwyn or Ethelbert, and like them, it was faintly effeminate. It had none of the strength of Pontiac or Lincoln, or the spirit of Mercury; nor did it perpetuate a great name in the industry like Chevrolet or Chrysler — or Ford itself.

The enthusiasm that Larry Doyle summoned up from the depths of his chagrin when he announced the new name was an almost unparalleled histrionic feat. His acting was superb. He even pretended not to notice our dismay.

The trouble with the Edsel was almost everything.

This is a story of perfectly understandable corporate misjudgment that anyone who wants to read will find in all its excruciating detail in *The Fate of the Edsel and Other Business Adventures,* by John Brooks. I shall touch on it only as it pertains to advertising and the public reaction.

To begin with, the Edsel was designed to an intellectual formula, which is not the formula by which cars are bought. Ford Motor Company, with its Ford, Mercury and Lincoln automobiles, stood in proper relation to General Motors, and Chrysler Corporation with their Chevrolet and Cadillac and Plymouth and Chrysler Imperial lines, respectively, at the extremes of the price range, from low to high. The competitive difficulty lay in the failure of Ford's Mercury to compete successfully against the General Motors middle-priced trio of Pontiac, Oldsmobile and Buick, and Chrysler's Dodge and smaller Chrysler.

As young Ford-owning families grew in affluence and stepped up (as the saying goes in automobile circles) from low-cost Ford to a car in the medium-price range, they were most apt to move on to a General Motors car or a Chrysler car, and thus be lost as Ford Motor Company customers and owners. Mercury, for some unaccountable reason, did most of its competing with Ford itself. It was to remedy this unhappy situation that a new car was conceived, then abandoned at the outbreak of the Korean war in 1950. Two years later, as the end of that conflict approached, the project was resumed, under Dick Krafve's direction; and three years after *that* the experimental E-Car was presented by Krafve to an enthusiastic gathering of Ford's top management.

According to John Brooks, the effect of the introduction in the Ford Styling Center was "apocalyptic"; after a moment of complete silence when the clay model was revealed, the audience, "as one man, burst into a round of applause."

No one there could have foreseen that he was witnessing the first act of the greatest tragedy in American manufacturing history. During the two years that were to elapse between the unveiling of the new car prototype to the Ford executives and the finished Edsel's introduction to the public, all the circumstances of its being would have changed.

It seems questionable that any product of pure research into public attitudes and public prejudices and public reactions to hypothetical questions, without any admixture of independent and unfettered genius, could be anything but a collection of compromises, and this is what the Edsel turned out to be. It was like a painting painted by a committee or designed by a computer. However, it was not only the fault of the human computations from an incorrect input that brought about the Edsel's downfall. The public that had responded to the research, that had thought it knew what it wanted, suddenly had a taste for something decidedly different.

The day of the compact car had arrived; and it was too late to change the Edsel. All the dies were cast, literally, and it would take two years to change them.

One of the innumerable compromises out of which the Edsel was finally assembled resulted in calling the four series, from top to bottom, Corsair, Citation, Pacer and Ranger, and these names were emblazoned on the front fenders of the cars to add to the public's confusion. (That the confusion was not the public's alone was indicated later when one of the agency people took delivery of an Edsel that was labeled Pacer on the right front fender, and Ranger on the left.) The differences, which were primarily matters of horsepower and overall length and decoration, had little or no meaning to the public. They were aimed solely to meet the price points that had been established by Ford's middle-priced competition, but this was private strategy, and the public failed to react to it.

One either likes an automobile or one doesn't, and the decision is made instantly on the basis of appearance. There is no argument involved. It is a matter of instinct, and it is unalterable. The choice of an automobile is an extension of ego in most instances, and it must be satisfied. Only the purchase of a home represents a larger outlay for most families than their purchase of a car, and the latter is even more personal. Every prospective car owner must view himself at the wheel of the car in question, and he must find the view highly satisfactory. Everything else is secondary.

When on a blustery, gray day at Dearborn we were introduced to the long-awaited Edsel line, with models in each of the four series, I was much less interested in the panegyrics heaped on it by the understandably ecstatic Mr. Emmett Judge, chief of Edsel's product planning section, than in Fred Ludekens's immediate response.

Ludekens is one of the best designers I know. He is a better designer than he is an artist. He would know whether the Edsel was basically well designed or merely readapted and whether it was adapted from something good or something bad. Besides these considerations, which I thought of as both aesthetic and functional, Fred Ludekens had been closely associated, as I have said, with Chevrolet advertising, and he knew what that largest-selling of all American automobiles meant to its owners. This was the market, along with the mass of Ford and Plymouth owners, that we had to compete for as twenty per cent of them moved up each year to a car in the next higher price class.

For these reasons I was more concerned with Fred Ludekens's reaction than my own. I was prepared by my natural optimism and my prejudices in this case to be bowled over by the new car. And I wanted Ludekens the designer and Ludekens the automobile expert to be, too.

When he nudged me, as we sat together between a large number of our own and Ford people in the auditorium of the Styling Center, I knew what his answer would be, and when I turned in answer to his nudge, he slowly, almost imperceptibly shook his head. Had he been excited he would have jabbed me hard. Months later, on the night before the formal introduction of the Edsel on September 4, 1957, when I hopefully asked Robert McNamara, Ford vice president who was later to become an outspoken Secretary of Defense, how he felt about the new car's chances in the market, he replied without words, with the same slow shaking of his head that had indicated Fred Ludekens's doubts.

I shouldn't have been so shocked. For between the two headshakings a number of features that had been contemplated for the new car were eliminated because of their cost, and a number of opportunities to improve it considerably at no cost at all were disregarded. The Ford Motor Company from top to bottom was concerned by the abrupt change in the public taste and appetite that boded no good for the established leaders in the medium-price range of automobiles and promised still less for a newcomer; or, in the dim future of the Edsel, four newcomers.

The compact Rambler had become the industry's overnight success. It was a small, sober, decidedly unpretentious automobile, whose strictly offbeat attraction was its unobtrusive, uncluttered *lack* of personality. It was all value, and after the styling excesses of the years of the tail fins, it was a welcome relief.

This the Edsel was not. It seemed, in fact, to be only timidly more of the same old thing.

Chief feature of the Edsel's appearance from the front was a vertical radiator grille, which was of European extraction. However, this was somewhat less than totally successful, for unlike its European counterparts the front of the Edsel's hood was extremely wide, and the space between the narrow vertical grille and the fenders on either side had to be filled in with conventional horizontal chrome strips which merely served to straddle the fence between European and American design.

It was unfortunate (but not unexpected if you were aware of the resourcefulness of the General Motors and Chrysler sales people in such an emergency) that the Edsel's distinctive, slightly oval vertical grille should be referred to as a horse collar, which it did, indeed, resemble, or a toilet seat, which it didn't at all — until someone said it.

From a side view, the car was only a little more attractive. For while rear fender fins had been shunned by Ray Brown, the Edsel's chief designer, in their stead, the rear fenders were marked with large bullet-shaped indentations that extended forward a third of the car's length and were painted in contrasting colors.

It was one of our running arguments with our client that one color was quite enough for an Edsel. Ours was a conservative car for con-

This is the # EDSEL for 1958

"Proved by the longest, toughest test of all—

1½ million road miles"

No other car has ever been more thoroughly tested than the Edsel.

For high altitude performance, Edsels were pitted against the mountain passes of Colorado, where transmissions, carburetors and brakes had to meet demands far beyond all normal needs.

Checked and rechecked, Edsel test caravans ploughed through powdery alkali grit and 118° desert heat in Death Valley to test cooling systems, carburetors, air cleaners and oil filters. Here transmissions and rear axle gearing took a merciless beating—and passed every test by the most comfortable margins.

Edsel experimental cars spent months in city and cross-country traffic, testing engines, brakes, sound level, ride and handling in the kind of driving you do every day.

The Edsel passed every test in the books—and some never thought of before. That's why when you drive your first Edsel, you'll know the solid certainty of a finely built automobile.

1958
EDSEL

New member of the
Ford family of fine cars

Edsel advertisements and TV commercials, too, were simple and understated. But the Edsel was doomed by the introduction of the compact car.

servative people, but a rich car, too, as we saw it, and richness of appearance would be impossible with overembellishment of any kind. Our only victory, though both Larry Doyle and Dick Krafve seemed to agree with us, and Bob Copeland was neutral, was to have three-color options (tri-tones, these were called) eliminated from the list of choices. Two-toning was bad enough. My own Edsel was painted in a single tone of dark metallic gray, and it was the most admired Edsel I ever saw, for it had a certain dignity.

The rear view of the Edsel was in every way its best; the gullwing design that had suggested itself to Dick Krafve as he contemplated a folded paper airplane later was copied by both Ford and Chevrolet. But by this time the Edsel was gone, and no one outside the styling departments ever connected the facts.

Mechanically, the new automobile was notable chiefly for what was called its pushbutton drive, a control panel located in the center of the steering wheel, the traditional location of the horn. Five push-buttons kept the car in neutral, or sent it forward or backwards at a fingertip touch — or they were supposed to. It was part of the sad fate of the Edsel that almost nothing worked the way it should have. For one thing, the car was rushed to market in September, ahead of the introduction of competitive new models, so as not to be lost in the traditional annual fanfare; some of the imperfections that plague every year's introductory models might otherwise have been discovered before the cars got into the hands of the public. Then it was too late.

But the main trouble with the Edsel was not its failure to perform. Its major imperfections were adjusted and its minor shortcomings were eliminated — except for one thing. The Edsel had been tabbed an ugly duckling; and an ugly duckling it remained. When I went to get my own Edsel on the morning the cars were put on display in the showrooms, it was very early, and the lone salesman on the floor was talking on the telephone. Waiting for him, I climbed into a shiny blue Corsair convertible and thought how fine it was; I hadn't quite made up my mind to agree with Fred Ludekens's verdict. When the salesman finished his telephoning and sidled over to where I was flexing my spirits at the wheel, I said, "Pretty nice, don't you think?"

"Yes," the man said. "All but that goddam front end."

Almost three million people who visited Edsel showrooms all over the country that weekend, with every expectation that they were about to behold a miracle, immediately registered the same reaction. If their expectations had been great, and they had, their disappointment was greater.

If publicity and advertising could have made any difference, they would have made the new car a success. Under the direction of C. Gayle Warnock, who is one of the most resourceful of public relations men, the buildup for the Edsel was the most intensive in the history of the automobile business. For three years before its appearance, even before it had a name, the car had been a topic of paramount interest to every current and prospective automobile owner.

Advertising, too, had helped to keep the interest level high. Paid advertising for the Edsel began in the early summer of 1957 with a two-page spread in *Life* magazine that took off from Gayle Warnock's carefully nourished publicity. There was a difference in tone, however. For since we couldn't match the exuberance (or the imagination) of the reporters to whom Warnock, in the way of a wise public relations man, had released a few facts, we decided that the car itself must outdo the advertising, which we accordingly pitched in low key.

The initial advertisement said, in conservative type, above a photograph of a car that was little more than a blur, "Lately, some mysterious automobiles have been seen on the roads." And the signature, which is the second best-read element of any printed advertisement, reported: "The Edsel is on its way — new member of the Ford family of fine cars."

Between the headline and the signature, the matter-of-fact copy, such as we hoped to continue throughout Edsel advertising, read as follows: "If you happened to be up in northern Minnesota last year, it's just possible that you might have seen a covered car cruising smoothly along out-of-the-way country roads.

"You would know if you saw it, because this automobile didn't look much like the usual run of cars you find around Bimidji.

"Or maybe you were one of the few who chanced to see such a car soaring wide-open through the sand and mesquite under the high, hot Arizona sky.

"And recently, more than one filling station owner in the Cumberlands has forgotten to say, 'Fill'er up?' in his hurry to ask, 'Hey, what kind of a car you got there?'

"Edsel is the kind.

"Maybe you thought none had been built yet.

"But if you did you were wrong. For almost a year, the first Edsels have been chalking up miles. Miles of pavement and of no pavement. Of mud and slush. Of mountain and flatland. Of sub-tropic heat and sub-zero cold.

"Not thousands of miles. Hundreds of thousands.

"By the time it reaches your streets, the Edsel will be one of the best-tested, best-proved cars in automobile history.

"And that time is not far off."

A following spread in *Life* showed a hooded car entering the gates of the Ford Motor Company Styling Center, and the caption read: "A man in your town recently made a decision that will change his life."

This was "more than a business decision," the text continued.

"This man took his money, his skill, his business reputation, his whole future and — becoming an Edsel dealer — he staked it all on the new Edsel automobile.

"That took a lot of doing. But he had to be a pretty exceptional man in the first place, or he and the Edsel Division would never have gotten together. The men who build the Edsel don't want a lot of dealers. They just want the best.

"Which leaves only one question.

"With so much to offer, why is this man willing to tie himself and his future to a car that neither you nor any of your friends has ever seen as yet?

"The answer is simple. He has seen it. He has driven it."

Two weeks before the September 4 introduction another spread in *Life* showed a huge auto-transport truck moving through the dark loaded down with five shrouded cars, and the headline said, "These carriers with covered cars are headed in your direction."

Again, the text moved the story along that the Edsel soon would be uncovered.

"Early this week, a group of big automobile carriers cleared the yards of six giant U.S. plants and rolled out into the night.

"Balling the jack. Because their steel racks held something they had never held before.

"They were loaded with a new kind of car.

"With four series — eighteen models — of a new kind of car called the Edsel.

"And the delivery date is urgent.

"The Edsel makes its public debut in September.

"Maybe you'll see some of these carriers loaded with covered cars on your roads in the next few days.

"If you do you might call to mind what one of their drivers said before he started out. The driver lifted the cover on one of the Edsels in his load and looked it over very carefully. And what he said, plainly and forcefully, was: 'I want one of those.' "

Finally, in the week of the actual introduction, and for some weeks thereafter the advertisements were headed very simply, "This is the Edsel." The buildup had been so great that we felt we could do no better than to try to answer some very natural questions about the new car and let it prove itself in demonstration.

So far as anyone could tell, the strategy of plain statement was well conceived — and well executed by Robert Eck, who wrote all the copy, and by Fred Ludekens, who made the illustrations. The proof of the advertising, and the reams of publicity, was in the crowds, estimated at 2,850,000 people, that stampeded to the dealers' showrooms on September 4.

Nevertheless, the debacle that took place when the public discovered that the Edsel was made of the identical materials, and had the same four wheels and brakes and springing as other automobiles, and was an ugly duckling to boot, called for a change in the only thing that could be changed — which was the advertising.*

Down the drain went the chaste, conservative copy as quickly as we could get rid of it. I have always thought that if Larry Doyle had been in Dearborn we might have saved this (and even, perhaps, the Edsel) by maintaining for it a published and broadcast personality that would eventually have been recognized by that sophisticated segment of the public for which the car was originally planned. But Larry Doyle, who had spent almost the whole two years of our association in the field lining up dealers, now was in the field holding their hands, urging them to hang on.

Bob Copeland's activity as advertising manager was being directed from Ford public relations headquarters even during the final stages of the introduction. Fear of the compact car filled the air. The new Edsel was clearly out of step. Ford management didn't want to add to its troubles with advertising that varied from the accepted industry patterns. Worst of all, Dick Krafve's support was lost to the cause when he was transferred, and the Edsel was placed under the direction of James J. Nance (late of Studebaker), to salvage what he could from the wreckage.

Jim Nance tried hard, but when the Edsel Division became part of the Mercury-Edsel-Lincoln Division in order to effect sharp economies in January 1958, only four months after the introduction, Edsel advertising — directed by a new group of Ford executives from the corporate public relations department — became stereotyped in the worst possible form. Cliché piled on cliché, as substance was abandoned. A headline in the spring of that year read, "The most beautiful thing that ever happened to horsepower." And the subhead said, "It

* One of the many rumors about the Edsel had it equipped with bellows-type air springs, an exciting innovation that had to be eliminated because of cost.

steals the show wherever you go — the long, lean, powerful 1958 Edsel."
The rhyming subhead was not poetry enough; the final display line
in the advertisement, under the Edsel signature, read, "Of all
medium-priced cars, the one that's really new is the lowest priced,
too!"

By March, the plain tailored drawings with which Ludekens had
illustrated the earlier advertisements had given way to photographs
that tried to show the car in middle-income settings, and one headline read: "They'll know you've *arrived* when you drive up in an
Edsel." Another said: "Says you're going places. Step out of the
ordinary and into the car of the year — the magnificent Edsel."

In June, Edsel advertising reacted to the fighting concept that a
good offense is the best defense, with the promise that "The EDSEL
LOOK is here to stay — it has the new ideas next year's cars are copying." This obviously took someone's fancy in the M-E-L Division,
and it was followed with "The EDSEL LOOK is here to stay — and
1959 cars will prove it."

In July, the offensive was continued with the boast that "DRA-
MATIC EDSEL STYLING" was "bringing new distinction to American motoring."

By November, when the 1959 models were introduced, the division
had had enough of the Edsel look and its losing battle against the
compacts, and the 1959 Edsel was called simply: "An exciting new
kind of car."

"Here, at last," the frustrated Mr. Eck was forced to write, "is a
full size car that makes sense. It looks right, works right. And it's priced
right. The beautifully efficient Edsel gives you luxury without
overdoing it. Plenty of room inside without a useless inch in length.
It's a car that gives you all the power you can use but won't hog gas.
It's a car that won't look dowdy next year. It's styled to last. It's engineered to last. And it's priced with the lowest priced three."

This was followed by "1959 Edsel. Looks right! Built right! Priced
right! Makes history by making sense. Exciting new kind of car!
A full-size practical beauty. Roomy without useless length. Soundly
engineered. Powered to save. And priced with the most popular
three!"

But once again advertising had failed to persuade an unimpressed public. The last poor Edsel was bought by less than three
thousand people.

Incredible as were the painful gyrations of the second year and
the hopeless resignation of the final few months, I shouldn't have been
surprised. Once Dick Krafve was removed from the picture and Larry

Doyle went out into the territory to make up as best he could to the dealers, the Edsel part of the M-E-L Division was operated without leadership and without hope. Every move that was made was defensive.

As an opening gambit in television the Edsel had presented a spectacular hour of music, with Bing Crosby, Frank Sinatra and Rosemary Clooney, that had one of the largest audiences of 1957 (and later picked up several Emmy Awards), and it was the agency's plan to present a series of special programs of great audience appeal. We could have had six or eight of these during the year for the same price as an average weekly half-hour. But the Ford Motor corporate headquarters undertook to direct the program side of the Edsel's television activity just as they had the magazine and newspaper copy, and they made an unbelievable decision.

After the brilliant introductory show that many thought to be the most exciting of all the special programs to that date, Edsel broadcast advertising was placed on *Wagon Train*, an expensive Western series whose audience consisted almost entirely of youngsters and oldsters. *Wagon Train* had an audience that was, as if by plan, almost entirely devoid of the young executive-group families for whom the Edsel had been designed and manufactured. Thus was America's newest and, hopefully, its most advanced automobile advertised on the air solely against the background of covered wagon days when all the women wore shawls and the men shot dinner with their rifles.

When Albert Weisman, who was the agency's man in charge of public relations and publicity, told me that there was going to be a great Edsel prize contest in which the prizes were ponies, I didn't believe him. Experience with Dial soap contests had proved that ponies make very bad prizes. Most contest winners, simply by the law of averages, live in cities and in apartments. A horse is one of the least of their desires. But the M-E-L people didn't listen. The miserable pony contest, like the *Wagon Train* program, helped push the Edsel to its lamentable end.

If the Edsel was to be a success, if it was to reach the total of two hundred thousand cars sold annually which would make the venture profitable, then there would have to be sold no fewer than six to seven hundred cars each business day. This was accomplished only for the first two weeks. Then sales dropped to half that number, and they never recovered. In midsummer the only Edsel dealer in Manhattan gave up his franchise to take on the Rambler. It was a hint of dire things to come.

In December, Henry Ford II told the Edsel dealers on closed-circuit television that the Edsel was here to stay. But the evil portents continued to appear, and the rumors flew as the new year began. Finally, the inescapable fact emerged that only 34,481 of the new cars had been registered during the twelve months of 1958.

A modified Edsel was brought out for the following year, but it bore little resemblance to the original. Ford's retreat had been complete, and it was disastrous. The "new" Edsel, without either the distinguishing radiator grille or Dick Krafve's gullwing rear end, quickly was reduced to a manufacturing schedule of some twenty per day, and in November, it was quietly discontinued.

From the beginning in 1957 to the bitter end, there were 110,847 Edsels manufactured. Their net cost, including plant and equipment that was not salvageable, is estimated at $350 million. It is further estimated that the Edsel dealers who had listened to the siren song and shared Larry Doyle's honest enthusiasm for the new car lost another $50 million in the fiasco; and Foote, Cone & Belding was not unscathed.

After the Edsel was discontinued the agency was assigned the advertising of Lincoln, and this was continued for a year during which the Foote, Cone & Belding office in Detroit was dismantled and its sixty-odd employees redistributed among the agency's other offices wherever this was possible, and among its competitors when it was not.

A generous settlement by the Ford Motor Company, made in view of the three-year investment we were unable to recoup in the normal manner when the Edsel was discontinued, allowed us to break about even on our Dearborn experience, the best part of which was our associations. Dick Krafve, Larry Doyle, Emmett Judge and Gayle Warnock are our respected good friends. Bob Copeland, who had coronary trouble long before he ever heard of the Edsel, is dead of a heart attack.

Krafve is a successful business management consultant and a director in a number of the companies he advises. Doyle is retired; Ford wanted him to stay in the company, but he felt that the failure of the Edsel was something he had to share with the dealers he had recruited. He had told them, because he believed it, that the Edsel would not be abandoned; it was not in him to tell them, after all, that it would.

Unfortunately, there was as yet no redeeming Mustang for Ford people to talk about.

The Marvelous Money Machine

WHILE it would surely be wrong to blame television for the fiasco in Detroit, it would be equally wrong not to point again to the efforts of the National Broadcasting Company that resulted in applying the *Wagon Train* image to what we all hoped would be *the* mid-twentieth-century motorcar.

This I will always look back upon as inexcusable — and a breach of good faith when NBC executives sold the program, against the agency's best judgment, to Ford corporate management. It was the last program we wanted for the new car. But the television people thought only of the large audience they expected to provide. They were not interested in the product fit; they were not interested in what we had both learned from the Hallmark experience about program compatibility.

Television is a victim of many excesses. Chief among these is programming for the largest numbers of potential viewers as a matter of policy, a policy which the broadcasters find difficult to abandon because numbers have taken the place of excellence and what is most appropriate as the basis for network competition. But the television moguls chose to be rich rather than right at the outset. Prior to World War II, as I have noted, they lost control of radio programming to the advertisers and the advertising agents who advised the advertisers, and they were determined not to let the same thing happen in TV.

For this I do not blame them. On the contrary, I believe programming is the networks' responsibility. Nor is this where the responsibility ends. The medium has other bounden duties. One is to be free of any coercion from advertisers or anyone else; another is to be scrupulously honest — in its own behalf.

Two ugly chapters darken the record.

It was in the late 1940's and early 1950's that a series of traumatic events led to a pervading fear of the Communist menace in America and a grave concern over the possible penetration of Marxist subversion deep into our life. The particular events that followed the Berlin blockade in 1948 increased the emotional shock the blockade caused. And before the furor of the Alger Hiss spy case which followed could die down, eleven leaders of the U.S. Communist party were convicted of advocating the violent overthrow of the U.S. government.

That was in 1949. Then, in the three years following there burst upon the front pages of the newspapers the cases of Dr. Klaus Fuchs, and Julius and Ethel Rosenberg, who were convicted of passing critical information to the Russians.

In 1950 and 1951 the motion picture industry fell under the scrutiny of the House Un-American Activities Committee; and the radio and television networks soon followed. The HUAC investigation resulted in the expulsion of a group of screenwriters known as the "Hollywood Ten," and the witch-hunt began on both coasts.

By this time the broadcasting networks, carefully clued in, had developed blacklists of performers who had been charged with disloyalty by virtue of identification with alleged Communist activities, and it soon became a fact of life that any performer or other participant in radio or television whose name was included in "Red Channels" or any other of the unofficial blacklists would not be employed.*

Advertisers also were furnished with the lists and accepted the charges at face value. Hysteria was in the air. Actors and writers who had joined political organizations twenty years before during the depression, in protest against the economic breakdown, were listed as politically dangerous. To be sure, some of the groups they had joined did turn out to have Communist affiliations; and later, when the Russians were our allies, other members of the industry joined frankly Red sympathizers to support the Soviet war effort against Germany. Now all were lumped together with known agitators and alien agents; and individuals who protested the indiscriminate listings became themselves suspect in the process.†

Some of the performers tried hard to beat back the blacklist, but to no avail. A significant case was that of Philip Loeb, who played a leading part in the popular Goldberg radio series. Gertrude Berg,

---

* "Red Channels — The Report of Communist Influence in Radio and Television," published by *Counterattack*, New York, June 1950.

† David Susskind testified in a court case that an eight-year-old actress was blacklisted for being "politically unreliable" and Mark Goodman admitted that sometimes an actor would not be hired simply because his name was the same as that of a member of the Communist party.

the star of the program, resisted increasing pressure to discharge Loeb following his appearance before HUAC. After a period of more than a year of this resistance, he was finally dismissed. Not long thereafter he died by his own hand.

Many performers summoned to the various HUAC hearings took refuge in the Fifth Amendment and thereafter worked no more in either television or the movies. Their refusal to testify was presumed to be an admission of guilt.

A countervailing procedure became quite popular and was used by a number of artists. This was termed getting oneself "white-listed." To do this, the performer named all persons who had participated in the left-wing activities with which he had been charged. The circle thus widened, no matter what the degree of involvement of the accused, or even whether they had been conscious of any questionable associations.

One who was caught in the web was a radio and television star named John Henry Faulk. In February 1956, Faulk had a successful career regaling his audiences with folksy Southern humor and satire that was somewhat reminiscent of Will Rogers. Faulk was coming into his prime, and a bright future was predicted for him. However, he was also active in the American Federation of Television and Radio Artists (AFTRA). Shortly before, he had helped lead a winning fight to elect union officers opposed to blacklisting and, particularly, to an instrument of vicious blacklisters that was operated under the name of AWARE, Inc.

AWARE was the creation of Vincent Hartnett, a private detective, and Lawrence Johnson, a superpatriot who lived in Syracuse, New York, where he operated a chain of grocery stores. Together these two terrorized the broadcasting industry and a number of its important advertisers. Dozens of actors, writers, producers, and directors suddenly discovered that they couldn't get work because Hartnett and Johnson had listed them as Communist sympathizers.

In February 1956, Hartnett distributed an AWARE bulletin vaguely accusing Faulk of some such subversive partisanship. Faulk filed suit. CBS executives agreed that the charges were preposterous, told Faulk not to be concerned, and then fired him without warning later when he was vacationing in Jamaica.

Hartnett and Johnson had not let up. The network had been told, and the advertisers on Faulk's program had been informed by Johnson, that the products advertised on Faulk's programs would no longer be stocked in Johnson's stores, and the clear intimation was that Johnson's boycott would lead to others, perhaps nationwide. All this was done without a shred of evidence that Faulk had ever done anything but attack the blacklisters, nor did either the network or the advertisers on Faulk's programs make any effort to get at the truth of the allegations.

Six years later, when Faulk's suit came to trial, the jury asked whether it could award more damages than the plaintiff's attorney asked, then granted damages of $3.5 million, the largest award for libel in American history. Johnson died in a Bronx motel while Louis Nizer, Faulk's lawyer, was making his summation to the jury, and I don't know that Faulk ever collected more than a small part of the award. But had he got it all, it would not have made up for the desperate years when this talented and popular performer tried to support his family in a dozen ways in which he had no experience, and failed.

His friends, including Edward R. Murrow, the star commentator of CBS, made possible the eventual hearing of his case. But his career had been ruined by the Syracuse grocer who dealt in unfounded suspicion and hate.

Midwestern awareness of the devilish blacklists came late and it was fleeting.

The only programs for whose production our company was responsible in Chicago were the Hallmark programs, and none of the stars we featured were ever attacked. I have no doubt that some members of the supporting casts and some of the production staff were. But these people were interchangeable, and why they may have been changed by our producers in the studios never became an issue.

There were rumors afloat from New York and Hollywood about performers and others who were in trouble as the result of participation in Communist activities, but since there was no actual production of any important program in Chicago, the blacklisting never became a live question there.

I never saw a copy of *Counterattack* or one of the AWARE bulletins; and I must confess that I had no great curiosity about the lists of performers that we were required to furnish Frigidaire for submission to General Motors with respect to the *Pulitzer Prize Playhouse* programs. I was dimly aware that this had something to do with the Red scare but since no objection was ever made to any of the names we suggested I had no reason to question the practice.

What I learned later, of course, was that persons on the blacklist were carefully omitted from the casting or other production suggestions. The culling in this case was done by the network.

Nowhere was the indifference of the broadcasters to any but their dollar interests better documented than by their reluctance to deal forthrightly with the rumors that began to circulate in the spring of 1957 to the effect that some of the popular quiz programs that had appeared to be exciting exhibitions of rare and encyclopedic knowledge were fixed.

Time (April 22, 1957) questioned the bona fides of the quiz shows. So did *Look* (August 20, 1957). Even earlier, in December 1956, a contestant had made a complaint to the Federal Trade Commission that the television quiz program called *The Big Surprise* was not the true test of knowledge that it was supposed to be. The Commission investigated but closed out the matter after receiving an affidavit from the producer of the show which denied the allegations and discovering that the show was no longer on the air.

The Federal Communications Commission was first officially drawn into the possibility that a quiz show may have been deceptive in July 1958, when it received an allegation from a contestant implicating the producers of *Dotto*, a CBS network program made by an independent company. The Commission made inquiry of the network, and was assured that it had no previous knowledge of the deception, had canceled the program, and had arranged for closer inspection of all its shows.

Nevertheless, the rumors persisted, and in September 1958, a local grand jury was empaneled in New York City under state authority to investigate the matter. While the jury indicted no one and for some reason refused to make its findings public, the minutes of its hearings were finally made available to a subcommittee of the House Committee on Interstate and Foreign Commerce in October 1959, and open hearings there amply confirmed the rumors that had been dismissed by the networks as false and irresponsible for more than two years.

The most popular of the programs involved were *Twenty-One* and *The $64,000 Question*, and while there were variations in detail, all of the quiz shows had a single basic element in common. Contestants in various walks of life were asked questions and received prizes of money in varying amounts depending upon their success in answering questions of increasing difficulty or upon defeating other contestants in tests of knowledge.

In addition to these, there were also many other quiz programs: *$64,000 Challenge, Tic-Tac-Dough, Name That Tune,* and so on. But in each case the basic appeal of the show derived from its being presented as a legitimate test of intellectual attainment and memory. Metropolitan newspapers front-paged the weekly results of the principal quizzes. And why shouldn't they, when an immigrant cobbler earned a fortune by his knowledge of opera; when a jockey was an art expert, and a postal clerk knew everything.

It was clear that the essence of the appeal of the programs was their allegedly unrehearsed nature and the fact that the unlikeliest individuals were masters of all kinds of erudition. Much effort was made to emphasize this. The questions were represented as being so prepared and so guarded that no contestant could possibly know what questions he might be asked. Contestants were placed in glassed-in "isolation booths" to dramatize the fact that help was in no way available to them. On some programs, questions were drawn from envelopes delivered dramatically to the master of ceremonies by a vice president of a prominent New York bank, accompanied by uniformed guards; and it was solemnly announced that no hands had touched the sealed envelopes from the time the questions were composed and placed in the vault until the envelopes were opened in front of the studio audience.

It was a ritual that befitted programs costing three or four million dollars a year. But it was all for show.

Many witnesses before the subcommittee testified that they were intensively briefed before their appearance as contestants. In some cases they were told what the questions would be and what the answers were. In others they were given scripts to memorize and they were rehearsed in dramatic aspects of their appearance, the feigned despair and the agony of choice with thousands of dollars hanging in the balance. Questions were framed to keep attractive contestants on the air and so increase the audience, and to eliminate contestants who were less attractive and let the ratings lag.* It was also disclosed that the ritual of the bank vault meant nothing. After the questions were chosen for each contestant, those questions were taken to the bank, then brought to the program at the appointed time.

Top officials of the networks may not have known what was going on, but they could scarcely have been unaware of the published rumors. Nor should they have failed to make a serious investigation of them. The failure came from hearing what they wanted to hear, from being deaf to what they didn't. When the whistle blew, the programs were off the air. They had run their course, and they had served well the purpose of the marvelous money machine.

Robert E. Kintner, president of NBC, brushed off the disgraceful

---

* Not all contestants were helped in advance. Boxing expert Dr. Joyce Brothers, a psychologist, was a contestant the producers tried to get rid of, but she answered the most difficult questions that could be devised on the subject.

goings-on when he said mildly, "We were merely taken by a small group of deceitful people."

Thus did television excuse its culpability and its negligence.

That some of the deceitful people in the shocking affair of the fixed programs were advertisers and their agents was implicit in the testimony of a number of participants.

The executive producer, producer, and associate producer of *The $64,000 Question* swore that the briefing and manipulation of contestants on that popular program was at the desire and direction of the sponsor. Chief officers in the sponsor company vehemently denied this, and they were backed by one of the sponsor's agencies. The representative of another of the same sponsor's agencies said he believed that the exercise of some type of controls in quiz programs should have been known to "anyone with a certain depth of experience" in the television industry. And the advertising manager of the sponsoring company supported the position of the producers. He testified that strategy meetings were held weekly at which representatives of the sponsor indicated they wanted certain contestants continued and often made "urgent suggestions" that other contestants be dropped. Ratings were uppermost in everybody's mind, the producers said, and as ratings dropped, pressures for more controls increased. The principal method of controlling contestants, the producers said, was to determine what the contestants did and did not know and to ask questions accordingly.

The parade of contestants who admitted their complicity stood as the final indictment of the fixers whose cupidity would have been too much for carnival showmen.

Once again I happened to be far removed from the scene. None of the programs that were involved in the scandal was produced in Chicago; and had I been asked when they were at the height of their popularity whether I thought there was anything wrong with them I am sure that I would have answered emphatically in the negative. The rumors had stopped short of Michigan Avenue.

It was two years later, in October 1959, that the full story came out in the hearings of the House Special Subcommittee on Legislative Oversight. The time lag greatly softened the blow to the public, and the television networks received the mild censure in stride. Television had turned to the Westerns to replace the quiz shows, and *Gunsmoke*, *Wagon Train* and *Have Gun, Will Travel* held the top three places in the Nielsen audience ratings when the scandal broke.

The failure of television in the nasty business of the blacklists and the quiz show scandals was a failure of the networks.

At the station level nothing has been so disappointing as the absence of quality in local programming devoted to public affairs; and, again, the whirring wheels of the money machine are to blame.

Although there is no established price that has to be paid for syndicated film for broadcasting on local stations, there is a rule of thumb that puts this at about one hundred and fifty dollars for each half-hour for a market the size of Chicago, where four commercial stations may be bidding for the reruns. This might be only a little less than the cost of a studio discussion program or a simple musical show.

However, a station in a small market with only a single television station might well purchase the film for fifteen dollars for a single showing, while the production cost for a live program would be substantially the same as in the large market. The combination of the film's lower cost and its historically greater drawing power has made this the choice of most station owners most of the time.

To quote Ward Quaal, president of WGN Continental Broadcasting Company, Chicago, one of the most knowledgeable of the broadcasters, and my client, "A good public affairs program need not be divorced from entertainment. These programs should be produced with all the skill, verve, and appeal of commercial programming. If they are well done they can appeal to a long list of local advertisers." Ward Quaal's own success attests to the validity of his statement. But there is a vital corollary. "The qualities necessary for sponsorship," says Quaal, "are importance of subject, imaginative presentation, good production-direction-writing, wide viewer appeal, timeliness and newsworthiness. In other words — good television."

This is what most stations have failed signally to provide; not because of the unavailability of talent in most cases, but because the cost appeared likely to reduce profits. This last is the most difficult problem to face any businessman, but when the business is a public utility it is the public whose best interests should come first.

As I wrote in *Fortune* in July 1965, television has grown big and rich and flabby. Some of my best friends in business are in the broadcasting business, and while I wish them well, I am also distressed at what I perceive to be television's uneven success. Never have profits been better for the operators and never has the product of television, which is programming, shown less imagination or less promise. During television's twenty years, entertainment, which is the principal element in programming, has rarely been explored beneath the surface of old vaudeville routines and motion picture forms. And only the prospect of repeating all of last year's monotonous attempts at amusement could be more dismal than the prospects for entertainment in any upcoming season.

It is no wonder that serious critics view television darkly. And while I would like to be concerned with it as they are, on purely artistic and intellectual terms, there is another side to the matter that I cannot overlook. This is the conviction on the part of almost all viewers that there is nothing wrong with television that can't be blamed on advertising. As a result, criticism of advertising grows louder and it is more persistent than any other complaint about current business practice. Television is seen as the helpless victim of advertisers' cupidity. It is the advertisers, most people believe, who initiate all program changes; and who but the advertisers, they ask, are the perpetrators of those ghastly commercials?

To suggest that such questions may be a soothing accompaniment to the march of the broadcasters to the vaults is simply to point to the obvious. Advertising is a ready scapegoat. This is a subject to which I shall return; and with a recommendation. Meanwhile, I want to refer to another shortcoming of the broadcasters.

Beginning with broadcasting by radio, a large section of the adult public took to getting its news through the air. This was easier than reading a newspaper. For one thing, it didn't absorb all one's time; it was possible for a man to bathe, shave and eat his breakfast while listening to the radio. If he drove to work by automobile he could hear it all again. And his wife could hear the headlines too, while preparing breakfast and at the table.

The chief difficulty with this, and one not always recognized as the custom became widespread, was that the headlines were all the radio listeners ever got. There was no depth to the reporting, and there were no editorials or other means for interpreting the headlines or commenting upon their significance.

Now, along with its failure to experiment in entertainment (or anything else except the documentaries that are broadcast all too infrequently) television is reproducing radio news with little added but the picture of the man or woman who is reading the headlines, or a brief interview with the principals in the action and a picture of the scene. I purposely omit as exceptions such interview programs as *Meet the Press, Issues and Answers* and *Face the Nation* because they are so confined in time that they rarely do more than scratch the surface of any subject. The fact that the programs are unrehearsed makes the guests wary and equivocal; understandably, they do not wish to be cornered; and the time (usually a half-hour) is so short that very little is ever resolved.

In the six years since his death, no one has taken the place of Edward R. Murrow. Eric Sevareid of CBS comes closest, for his comments are both shrewd and penetrating. Frank Reynolds of ABC is thoughtful and courageous, although afflicted with a voice of doom. But Huntley and Brinkley on NBC and Walter Cronkite on CBS, together with their various on-the-spot reporters, rarely do more than repeat the headlines — even though they may come from London or Prague, via satellite, or from Saigon.

This is partly a matter of time. Since television must appeal to everyone, it must cover all the news, and this means that there is no time to develop any of it. Still, it seems a pity that television should add so little to the knowledge of a people whose ignorance of what goes on in the world both at home and abroad, and why some things go on and some others do not, is often abysmal. There is too much at stake to have nothing but the headlines to go by.

The television reporting of the rioting in Chicago during the Democratic Convention of 1968 was an example of something less than conscientious, in-depth reporting. Admittedly the police were aroused, and admittedly they pummeled a large number of demonstrators and two dozen or so members of the press; the police were rough and they were tough, and they made mistakes. But so far as I know it was only these things that the world was shown.

What the television reporters could have told their audiences, had they done their homework, had they got into the ranks of the protesters beforehand, was that plans to incite riots and to bring about police action were carefully laid out and scheduled like a battle plan, and carefully followed.

Pictures of clubbing and thumping were real enough. But there was little mention made of the plans that were discussed and the threats that were openly uttered and published to disrupt the convention and turn the whole city into a shambles. Nor was there any reporting of the specific provocations that led up to the police action that was played and replayed on television during the fateful evening of August 28, and thereafter. Nothing was said about the taunts that were hurled at the police or the foul names they were called. No one was told that they were spit upon, or made targets for potentially deadly missiles and paper bags and bottles filled with excrement.

The riots of the previous April in Chicago were forgotten, and the failures of security at Dallas, Memphis and Los Angeles, as the television cameras, carefully set up where the action was promised, fitted neatly into the pattern the protesters had planned. The sorely provoked police reacted and overreacted precisely as hoped for, and so did the television cameramen and the TV commentators. Yet in the most publicized public disturbance in anyone's memory, not a shot was fired, not a single life was lost, not a serious injury sustained — by any of the combatants.

It would be a pleasant exception in the total coverage of the hideous events if I could report that the press as a whole had behaved with greater objectivity. But this was not the case. When some newsmen also were clubbed in the confusion, this was loudly called a challenge to the freedom of the press!

There is nothing new and startling about the bellowing of certain newspapers when it is their ox that is gored; their right to immunity from any charge of recklessness in reporting is long established; they tend to see what they want to see. They also tend to print what they want to print on front pages, and bury what they want to bury far in the back.

Had advertising been used with any such abandon as the reporting by the press and television, the advertisers who were responsible for it would undoubtedly have been haled before the Federal Communications Commission, with the press and television howling for their scalps.

No lying advertisement ever fooled so many people with half a story. One reason is that no newspaper or magazine, and no broadcaster, would have accepted it for transmittal. The shortcomings of the publishers and the broadcasters were, in this case, exclusively their own.

Momentum

THE years of the Edsel were not all bad. The agency continued to grow, and this it has done ever since. Also, under the direction of Robert F. Carney as chairman, Foote, Cone & Belding became a public company in 1962 and, three years later, saw its shares listed for trading on the New York Stock Exchange. I think Robert Carney helped establish the legitimacy of the advertising agency business as no one else had. Its books were opened to scrutiny and what the financial people saw was good.

Nevertheless, my own interest continued to be in the presentation of products, preferably new products but sometimes old products with new uses or a new personality, and I found ample scope for my interest in a succession of new assignments. Some of the companies that made these assignments were well known, some were branching into new fields, some were entering nationwide competition for the first time.

In the first category was Zenith Radio Corporation, where I was intrigued with a sign above each workbench on the production lines that read: *Careful, this may be the one you get.* Somehow, this seemed to me to guarantee Zenith's advertising promise that *the quality goes in before the name goes on.* Reason enough, I think, why Zenith is today the leading manufacturer of television sets.

It is Zenith's good fortune that the late fiery Commander Eugene MacDonald and the heir to his mantle, the sturdy Scotsman, Hugh Robertson, chose their successors well. Joseph S. Wright, Sam Kaplan and Walter Fisher, the present management triumvirate, maintain a standard of quality that is never relaxed. When Zenith advertising posed the question *Why not get the best?* it was echoing television servicemen everywhere; they were Zenith's incomparable salesmen.

Shortly after the Zenith acquisition in 1958, the agency was retained by the Dole Pineapple Company of Hawaii, by Trans World Airlines and by the Equitable Life Assurance Society of the United States.

TWA came and went. Dole and the Equitable came and stayed; and they have been joined by a long list of well-known names. Contac. Fritos. True cigarettes. Sunbeam. Peoples Gas. International Harvester. Sara Lee. Monsanto. Ralston Purina. Merrill Lynch, Pierce, Fenner & Smith, Inc. Falstaff Brewing Company and most recently, Sears Roebuck & Company.

In recalling the agency's appointment by the Dole Pineapple Company, I am reminded of the extraordinary result of one of the first advertisements we made for this new client.

Dole was the traditional leader in pineapple sales, and neither Libby nor Del Monte, the runners-up were seriously threatening Dole's position. But *all* pineapple sales were slipping — primarily because canned peaches were in abundant supply and selling at a much lower price than pineapple.

We turned at once to recipes that were new and easy to prepare.

One thing we had learned long before was that nothing is so useful in advertising to women as helping them with everyday problems, none of which is more tiresome than menu planning and meal preparation. Consider that the average housewife is faced with the question of what to serve for dinner more than three hundred times each year! When she asks her husband what he would like for a change, he is most apt to reply, "Oh, anything." And the lady of the house is left alone with her problem.

This is the reason why so much food advertising is recipe advertising. Food products manufacturers, like Kraft and General Foods, Armour and Swift, and even the biscuit people, maintain large kitchen staffs just to hunt down and try out new recipes that use their products to meet the endless anxious need.

The great difficulty is to invent recipes that will become standard and be used again and again. Chocolate chip cookies promoted by the Nestle people did just this. Kraft's caramel apples were another welcome suggestion (to the extent that thirty million sticks are furnished by Kraft to apple-dunkers every year).

Pineapple sales were, as I have said, soft when the first of our new advertising got under way, and it may have been this fact that made any expansion seem phenomenal, but the fact remains that a simple recipe printed in an advertisement in *McCall's* magazine caused a seismographic disturbance in grocery warehouses across the land.

Now-Zenith brings you portable TV's biggest picture... 21" Super Screen!

DIAG.

 (ACTUAL SIZE)

Above: *The Regis*, 21" diagonal Super Screen portable TV, Model Y2224.

See the widest, highest, biggest rectangular picture in portable TV. Now you can enjoy the first true 21" (diag.) picture... the biggest in portable TV... in a slim, trim, fit-anywhere cabinet. Yet inside, you get the complete Zenith Handcrafted chassis

for unrivaled dependability. Even the contact points in Zenith's Super Gold Video Guard Tuner are 16-carat gold for a brighter, sharper picture years longer.

See the complete line of Handcrafted Super Screen portables... at your Zenith dealer's.

See all the Zenith Golden Jubilee special values at participating Zenith dealers!

BEST YEAR YET TO GET THE BEST

ZENITH

The quality goes in before the name goes on

Television advertising for Zenith TV sets features the hand-crafting that makes these instruments unique. Printed advertising stresses picture quality.

The recipe suggested that the top be removed from a can of sliced Dole pineapple, the juice drained and replaced with lime Jell-O; then the can frozen, and the lime-pineapple mold pushed out, sliced and served on a dessert plate. The result was a run on lime Jell-O, and Dole pineapple, too; for although there was other pineapple in the stores, the first company to incorporate a new idea in advertising inevitably reaps most of the benefit. This was such that the recipe has been repeated as a reminder again and again.

Soon after Rolland W. Taylor, who had been a member of the Chicago staff, returned to Foote, Cone & Belding in New York after a stint at the Colgate-Palmolive Company, the agency was appointed for the advertising of another of the new products in the long line that has made my days in advertising so absorbing.

This new product, for the relief of colds, was called Contac. It was made by Menley & James, a subsidiary of the great Philadelphia pharmaceutical house of Smith, Kline & French, and it was their first venture into the proprietary drug field. The name Contac was a contraction of the words "continuous action," and this was what the amazing new remedy provided. Each Contac capsule, the advertising said, "contains 600 tiny time pills. Some go to work right away for quick relief. The rest are scientifically timed to dissolve slowly. They release their medication drop-by-drop into your bloodstream to give up to 12 hours of continuous relief."

This was a large promise, but Contac kept it. It truly worked wonders for most cold sufferers. It quickly became, and it remains, the largest-selling cold remedy, and Contac advertising has been filled with artful humor instead of ugly maps of the nasal passages and unpleasant obstructions therein.

I cheer for A. J. Becker, who named the contents of the multicolored capsules *Time Pills*. This was something anyone could understand.

Another proposition that anyone could understand was that *nothing shaves like a blade*, and when this was propounded for Robert P. Gwinn's Sunbeam blade shaver, which cut whiskers instead of squeezing them, as do conventional electric shavers, success came overnight.

Nothing in television advertising works like a demonstration, provided that it is dramatic; and the demonstrations that were developed to introduce the Sunbeam blade shaver were both dramatic and convincing. These were filmed without rehearsal, in Grand Central Terminal, in New York City, at the Powell Street cable car turntable in downtown San Francisco, and other equally unlikely spots for such a purpose.

"Pardon me, sir," our interviewer would say, stopping an early morning passerby at random. "Have you shaved this morning?"

"I have" was the usual reply.

"But will you try this shaver anyway?"

After twenty seconds, the shaver was emptied on a sheet of white filter paper to show a conclusive residue of beard.

"This," said our interviewer, "is what your razor didn't get."

No one could deny the proof on the filter paper, and Sunbeam shaver sales soared.

International Harvester followed Sunbeam into the agency fold, and advertising a huge assortment of large, expensive farm implements became a new experience and a new challenge to people who were used to the promotion of small, inexpensive packages of frequent purchase, or, at least things, like radio and television sets or electric shavers, that anyone could operate.

I know I have said that the American housewife is a purchasing agent second to none, and I meant this. However, I think it is also true that the farmer is even harder to sell. The housewife makes up her mind in a hurry, the farmer, whose purchases of equipment are complicated and expensive, tends to take an interminable amount of time. The housewife looks eternally for something new. The farmer has a built-in prejudice against change.

Thus it is the job of advertising for farm equipment (and construction equipment), as it is for automobiles, to present an attractive background for a dealer's invitation to a demonstration. The sale, in the long run, becomes a matter of personal salesmanship; advertising can only set the stage.

Returning to my office from a meeting in our boardroom late one afternoon in May of 1963, I found a note on my desk asking me to call a Mr. Lubin, a name I didn't recognize, at a number that meant nothing to me.

When I got the man on the telephone, he was highly irritated.

"I've been waiting for two hours," he said testily. "You're pretty damn hard to get hold of; particularly when someone wants to give you some business."

"I'm sorry," I said. "I've been out of my office."

"Well," said Charlie Lubin, who now introduced himself as the little baker of Sara Lee, "I guess I wouldn't be calling you if all you had to do was sit around waiting for your telephone to ring. It's better that you're busy."

That was a typical Lubin judgment. First he made it. Then he justified it. He was strictly an intuitive operator. If there was one thing that he thought less of than anything else it was research. He and Albert Lasker would have understood each other perfectly; both were completely satisfied with their own instincts. Charlie Lubin knew how to make cake and he learned how to freeze it and keep it fresh and delicious, better than anyone before him; he knew how to make it with butter when other pastry cooks said this couldn't be done (they said you had to use vegetable shortening); and he knew the rich tastes he was making his cakes for, and he couldn't be concerned with any others.

He had also made up his mind to hire Foote, Cone & Belding, even before he telephoned. And this he did, two days after the call.

The bakery at Deerfield, Illinois, where Sara Lee cakes go on wide belts from stainless steel gas ovens into a frozen-storage locker that could, by actual measurement, accommodate two regulation football fields, stands as a monument to Charlie Lubin's genius, for he planned every inch of it. Unhappily, after he sold his company to Nathan Cummings's Consolidated Foods, the two men disagreed on business procedures (but not on the quality of the cakes) and Lubin departed.

We were part of Charlie Lubin's team and it followed, as it usually does under these circumstances, that we would go, too.

Nathan Cummings has treated me well, but I miss the ebullient little man who built the world's largest cake bakery much more than I miss the business. His insistence on quality refuted all the arguments of the critics of business who so delight in downgrading the products of mass manufacture and mass distribution. Charlie Lubin made his cakes with fresh whole milk, fresh eggs, and fresh-churned butter of a higher score than is available at any grocery store.

One of the things that makes Sara Lee coffee cakes so rich and so good is the recipe for all of these that calls for a layer of butter equal in depth to the basic layer of dough. The combination is folded and rolled and refolded until the lamination represents sixty-four alternate layers of butter and dough, imperceptibly combined. Sara Lee pound-cakes, too, are half batter and half butter; Sara Lee layer cakes float on clouds of real whipped cream.

I rarely disagreed with Albert Lasker, and when I heard him say, many years ago, "I don't ever want a client who couldn't be successful without my help," I took this as gospel.

Now, however, I would amend it sharply to say that I don't ever want a client to whose business advertising is not vital.

This has long been the trouble with the beer business, and specifically, with local or regional brewers, whose principal dependence is upon their salesmen. They have depended upon their salesmen to keep the tavern keeper and the bartender in line to push their product across the bar to the ultimate customer. However, in recent years, the shift of a significant share of beer sales to the supermarket has changed this, and advertising for the national brands acts the very same way for beer that it does for any other consumer product.

Our experience with Acme beer in San Francisco, Gulf beer in Houston and Rheingold beer in New York, made this very clear. As long as beer was sold by the bartender, advertising was something the brewer did to please *him*. When beer began to be *bought* by the *consumer*, it was advertising that had to make the first sale.

Acme beer, once the leading beer in California, failed because it continued for too long to woo the wrong person. Rheingold, once the leading beer in New York City and its environs, sank almost out of sight in a very few years when a rapid succession of new managements failed to move the public by any of an equally rapid succession of new advertising approaches.

One of the reasons for my frequent trips from Chicago to New York over such a long period of time was my involvement with the fabulous Liebmanns: dear old Mr. Alfred, well past eighty years of age, who sat between his son, Philip, who was president of the company, and the brewery's second in command, the petulant Dr. Herman Schuelein, whose disaffection intermitted only at lunchtime — over beer and a marvelous collection of cheeses.

The splenetic Schuelein had definite advertising ideas, all of which were opposed by Philip Liebmann. And quite rightly, too, because the doctor's advertising ideas were at best primitive.

"Attack the other brewers," he would say. "What are you afraid of? Call them what they are! Crooks! Bandits! Frauds! How can they say their beer is good when only our beer, Liebmann's Rheingold beer is beer as beer should taste?

"Liars! Swindlers! Thieves!"

Whether Doctor Schuelein really wanted Rheingold advertising to go to such lengths, or whether he was simply trying to goad Philip Liebmann into abandoning the pretty girls who were chosen each year to be Miss Rheingold and to represent the brewery in all its advertising, I do not know. I am sure only that Philip Liebmann loved each successive Miss Rheingold more than the one before while the dyspeptic little doctor hated them all equally.*

---

* Only U.S. presidential elections accounted for more returns than the annual balloting for Miss Rheingold.

The only advertisement that Philip ever made for Rheingold beer that Dr. Schuelein liked pictured the doctor himself, marching his twin dachshunds across a large newspaper page, a salute to a distinguished brewer.

A serious misadventure in Southern California, where a successful sampling campaign produced nothing but dissatisfaction with Rheingold beer, led, after Mr. Alfred's death, to the reorganization of the company and to Philip Liebmann's departure from it. The effect of Philip's withdrawal is difficult to estimate. But as an omen of bad days to come, I think it was fairly clear. For throughout the industry the large, successful breweries are operated, almost without exception, by families long in the business and fanatically devoted to it; and Philip Liebmann's personally directed advertising turned up satisfactory sales for many years. That it failed ultimately is less likely than that beer tastes changed and Rheingold stubbornly did not.

Anyway, Anheuser-Busch and Schlitz, the undisputed leaders today, are operated by descendants of the founders. And so is the fourth largest brewer, Falstaff, which has brought Foote, Cone & Belding onto the national brewers' scene of action for the first time. Chief of operations at Falstaff is Joseph Griesedieck, grandson of the founder.

The temptation to accept the responsibility for advertising products and services whose appeal to any large segment of the public is questionable, or ones which are underfinanced, is equally great among small advertising agencies and the smaller offices of the large agencies.

Many more advertising campaigns have failed for lack of money than for any other reason. Still, attempts continue to be made to make skillfully employed dimes do jobs that would overtax dollars. I have tried to discourage these, and I am afraid there are some people we have turned down, and some we have given up, who believe that our decision either way was the result of an interest only in money. This has not been the case. Our interest is in legitimate businesses and products where all the elements point to the probability of success; and where, as I have already said, advertising is vital to that success.

During the twenty-five years of our corporate existence our Los Angeles and San Francisco offices have been involved in the coming and going of forty-six accounts in whose plans high hopes were the principal ingredient. Among these were several agricultural cooperative marketing groups whose existence depended entirely upon satisfying all the different wishes of hundreds of grower-members; all were encouraged by the success of the Sunkist orange growers; none seemed to realize that this was the result of using large advertising appropriations with consistency and professional skill. Most of the failures were in industrial and semi-industrial accounts where the chances for success were often dependent upon remote circumstances on which advertising had no effect.

Altogether these forty-six accounts represented almost two new ones each year. They stayed with the agency, or remained active, for an average of forty months and cost the company many thousands of dollars.

Advertising agencies have been notoriously lax in the management of their own affairs. Some observers have blamed this upon the absorption of agency people with their clients' affairs to the exclusion of anything else. I am inclined to put the blame on the nature of advertising agency people who, until fairly recently, were writers and artists and salesmen whose views of conservative business management were that it was nothing but a shackle to be avoided at any cost; and the cost was great.

Preferred Over All Others

RECENT years have seen the retirement of almost all of my long-time associates both within the agency and in our client firms, until only those who began as trainees in the agency and junior executives in our client companies are left.

Emerson Foote and Don Belding, of course, are long departed — Emerson Foote to devote his life to the twin causes of cancer and heart research and the world population crisis, and Don Belding to his own multiple interests in public affairs, to Freedom's Foundation and the Easter Seal organization, and as chairman of the Executive Committee of Schick, Inc. Bob Koretz, Milton Schwartz and Bill Forrest are longtime Chicago directors of the agency who are retired, and Robert Carney, the robust lawyer who played such an important part in its life and its success, works only as a consultant.

The agency will miss the regular employment of these men, and it will be different without them. How different is hard to tell, for advertising itself is changing. But, hopefully, the clients who are now in the eight- to twelve-year range of longevity will go on to approach the twenty-five-year partnership that we have had with Hallmark and Hiram Walker, and the even longer ones that Foote, Cone & Belding inherited from Lord & Thomas.

Sunkist is the oldest of all the clients of the two agencies together. It is now in the sixty-first year of continuous association with what I shall call the "Lasker companies." Kimberly-Clark is next, dating from 1923. Then come the First National Bank of Chicago, 1931; and Armour and Company, which appointed the agency first in 1934. Each of these companies is more exciting and more useful than when I first knew it.

Sunkist oranges have been painstakingly developed until they are sweeter, juicier and more uniform, and, by and large, cheaper. The First National Bank has found new ways and new means to instruct and to serve a public whose financial requirements have made banking, among other things, an important retail business; the First, in effect, rents money, and it rents to little people as well as big. Armour has transformed an uncertain and frequently unprofitable old-fashioned meatpacking business into an industrial complex whose products range from agricultural chemicals and pharmaceutical products to easy-to-store, easy-to-prepare canned meats, toilet soap and synthetic detergents.

The story of Kimberly-Clark is more of the same. When I was first introduced to John R. Kimberly, in Neenah, Wisconsin, in the summer of 1942, he was on brief leave from a wartime assignment in Washington. When he returned from that two-year engagement, there began an association between us that has spanned a generation of changes in business and advertising. Jack Kimberly's grandfather founded Kimberly-Clark to manufacture book paper and newsprint, commodities whose future and the profits therefrom he felt to be assured. But the grandfather was only half right. The markets for book paper and newsprint did grow, beyond anything he contemplated; but they were commodities, and like all commodities they tended to be purchased from the lowest bidder. The products were standardized, and there was no creative selling involved in their distribution.

The prospect was not one that intrigued the grandson. Despite his training for it (at the Massachusetts Institute of Technology) and his apprenticeship in the mills at Neenah, Jack Kimberly was not inspired by a view of the future that showed nothing but a struggle to reduce irreducible costs and cut prices to the barest profit levels. This was too grim for a man who dreamed, and in 1923 Jack Kimberly and Ernst Mahler, an inventive and resourceful papermaker who brought his keen mind and his heavy accent to Kimberly-Clark from Austria, teamed up to project paper pulp into paper *products*, and two new, revolutionary developments were the result.

These were the expendable Kleenex tissue and the disposable Kotex sanitary napkin. And it is doubtful if ever two new products gained greater acceptance in so short a time. It was only a few years before Kleenex tissues were substituted for cloth handkerchiefs by millions of cold sufferers and substituted for rags and towels by the nation's spillers; and in even less time Kotex napkins were adopted by a whole generation of women who gratefully accepted them as an unrivaled personal aid and comfort.

Don't put a cold in your pocket, was appropriate advice from a

Razzle Dazzling!

The Kleenex Boutique Collection

The Kleenex Boutique Collection is in ... and tissues have never been so glorious. Full-size tissues shockful of color. Splashful of scent. Stashed in name-dropping mini boxes. Four pow! pow! pow-erful ways to glow. Hot Pink. Bold Gold. True Blue. Avocado Green. With bathroom tissue to mix or match.

NEW PRODUCTS FROM KIMBERLY-CLARK

The introduction of bold colors into the world of tissues caused a change in preference that has all but eliminated the old plain-white sheets.

very red-nosed man on posters all over the country, and it took Kleenex tissues out of their original category of facial tissues for removing cold cream almost overnight, and spread around the globe as Kimberly and Mahler and their associates went on to make the tissues stronger and softer, and more absorbent, and appropriate for countless household and other uses. Kleenex tissues in the rear window are almost a trade-mark of the American automobile, and they are no less standard items in most businessmen's desks than on their wives' dressing tables.

Altogether, Kleenex tissues are preferred over all others, and their quality, which is quietly, constantly improved, is attested by the fact that they command a higher price per box than dozens of other brands that are available in supermarkets everywhere. The same thing is true of Kotex. Kotex is preferred over all other napkins; and the latest in a long line of innovations to increase protection at the same time that bulk is reduced is widening the gap.

With the frank advertising of so many personal products in general magazines, and even on television today, it is worth pointing out that this is not the way it always was.

In the beginning it took all the eloquence at Albert Lasker's command to gain acceptance for Kotex advertising even in the strictly woman's magazines. It was not the advertising *per se* to which the publishers objected, but what they considered the delicacy of the subject. They were adamant. But so was Mr. Lasker.

"Would you keep news of such an important development for millions of women, such a means for new freedom of action, such a milestone in hygiene, a secret?" he wanted to know. "Would you make this an under-the-counter product like contraceptives?" he thundered. "You don't know what you are doing," he repeated. "Depriving your readers of legitimate, important news."

After repeated similar arguments, the publishers took counsel, and Kotex advertising began to appear in print in the fall of 1924. It was far from explicit. But no product that meant so much to so many women could long hide behind a barrier of vague hints. It had to come out in the open, and it did, in skillfully devised advertising that spoke with clinical authority.*

Just now there is a considerable switch to tampons, or to the use of both napkins and tampons sequentially, and Kimberly-Clark is in the forefront of this revolution, too; just as they have spread their in-

---

* To this day the *New Yorker* refuses to accept advertising for Kotex. However, it also eschews advertising for girdles and brassieres, and numerous other things that its editors simply do not fancy.

terest in Kleenex tissues to include Kleenex paper towels, paper napkins — even paper uniforms and dresses — in all of which the endeavor is uppermost to make better products to deserve public preference. No one knows better than Jack Kimberly that preference is something neither money nor advertising can buy. It has to be based upon confidence; and confidence has always to be earned.

Jack Kimberly's retirement as chief executive officer of Kimberly-Clark Corporation in 1968, and the succession of Guy Minard and Harry Sheerin to the top management posts, marked the end of one of the very personal partnerships that began twenty-five years ago when a group of brave businessmen in Chicago took Albert Lasker's word for it that Cone, along with Foote and Belding, might be worth a chance.

The heads of Armour and Company, who were then the meticulous George A. Eastwood and Frederick W. Specht, who would rather have been an architect, and the great financier with the unimpeachable middle name, Edward Eagle Brown, chairman of the First National Bank of Chicago, all are gone. And so are their immediate successors, the scholarly Ed Wilson at Armour and Homer Livingston, chief custodian of the quarter-billion-dollar endowment of the University of Chicago, at the First. David Duensing leads Armour-Dial, as it is now called, and Gaylord Freeman is chairman of the bank.

Donald Hall sits in the president's chair at Hallmark. Sam Johnson has succeeded his father at S. C. Johnson. And Hiram Walker is in its third round of succession, with Clifford Hatch succeeding Burdette Ford, who succeeded Howard Walton, who succeeded Harry Hatch, who was Cliff's father and who put Hiram Walker-Gooderham & Worts together. In the Walker Division, Jack Musick is the successor to longtime president Ross Corbit.

Now Jack Kimberly's retirement and my own close the first chapter in the story of Foote, Cone & Belding in Chicago.

But this also, I think, points the way into the future. Kimberly-Clark was the first of our Chicago clients to earn clear preference for its products in the marketplace, and as it did this, first place in sales became my goal for all the products we would ever advertise. We haven't made it for each one. In several instances the aim of the advertiser has been somehow diverted. But we have reached our goal in most cases.

Advertising is a competition that one enters to win; and it would be a poor advertising agent, just as it would surely be an unambitious manufacturer or distributor, who would set out with any other end in view.

Forget everything you knew about macaroni and cheese

Instead, think of golden elbow macaroni deep in cheddar flavor (a whole can of creamy cheese sauce) — that's Kraft Macaroni and Cheese Deluxe Dinner

Deluxe is different—rich with enough cheddary sauce to melt all through the tender, smooth macaroni . . . fresh with flavor because you do the cooking. Tonight, have a Kraft Macaroni and Cheese Deluxe Dinner. There's no other like it!

Kraft Home Cooked Dinners
The quick kind you cook up fresh

Largest-selling dinners in the world are Kraft's "quick kind you cook up fresh." The number of hours thus saved to American housewives is incalculable.

Most important, there would be many fewer new products, for no other changes would be made in established products than to reduce their cost of manufacture. This would be a stalemate for hundreds of thousands of young people who annually enter into adult employment. They, too, should be able to look forward to involvement in the world of innovation, and the building of preference.

"Preferred over all others" are good words to work for in any endeavor. In advertising there are none that are equal. For they mean that the product in question has been accepted at full value by its intended public, and that the advertising that informed this public of the product's promise has served them both well.

The satisfaction that the people of Foote, Cone & Belding have felt in the success of Kleenex and Kotex, Sunkist and Dole, Toni and Clairol, Contac and Dial, Kool-Aid and Klear, Raid and Off!, Hallmark cards, Kraft dinners, and Zenith television instruments—all of which are preferred over all others — makes any broad criticism of advertising meaningless and unthinking. The simple questions remain. How else could any large number of people have been made aware of the solutions to problems these trade names embrace? How, without advertising, could any of these products have presented their comparisons with the products they were made to supersede? What, without advertising, is industry's means of communication?

Part IV

The Men on the Cover of Time

A GATEFOLD cover on *Time,* for October 12, 1962, pictured, in a montage of men and some of the products they advertised, a dozen of the leading figures in the agency business. With one or two possible omissions these represented the largest agencies, and the most important advertisers; and in what is often thought of as a young man's business, only two were under fifty years of age.

Here was Norman Strouse, fifty-five, the studious successor to the stately Stanley Resor as head of J. Walter Thompson Company, the agency for Ford, Kodak, Radio Corporation of America, Pan American Airways, and enough other front-line companies to make it the largest advertising agency in the world with total billings that year of $380 million.* Alongside Strouse was Thompson's chief challenger, Marion Harper, Jr., forty-six, whose plan for a great international network of agencies was bundled together under the imposing name Interpublic, and whose clients included Chrysler, Coca-Cola, National Biscuit, and Humble Oil & Refining Company.

Third largest of U.S. agencies was represented by George Gribben, fifty-five, the gifted copywriter who had but recently been made president of Young & Rubicam, agency for General Foods, General Electric, Arrow shirts, Borden, and Metropolitan Life Insurance Company, among others.

Here also was Charles Hendrickson Brower, sixty, who had succeeded Ben Duffy, who had succeeded Bruce Barton, inspirational author and silk-stocking congressman from New York, who had built

* The 1962 volume for almost all of these agencies has doubled in the years since.

the fourth largest American advertising firm, Batten, Barton, Durstine & Osborn, around such illustrious clients as American Tobacco, Armstrong Cork, Campbell Soup, Pepsi-Cola.

Oddly missing from the group was a shrewd, laconic New Englander named Ted Bates, sixty-one, whose fifth-place agency of the same name represented American Home Products, Standard Brands, and Colgate, and whose copy chief, Rosser Reeves, wrote the excellent textbook *Reality in Advertising*, which explained Bates's own brass-tacks philosophy. (Bates's advertising for Anacin or Ajax will probably never win a prize for style, but it has paid off much better than most in hard competition.)

Leo Burnett, chairman of the sixth largest agency, which bears his name, was pictured in front of the bright red Marlboro cigarette package which he had made famous, and a cock that was stretching to crow on a box of Kellogg's Corn Flakes, the nation's favorite breakfast food. Leo Burnett was seventy when *Time*'s cover was painted, but he is as active today as he was then, and sound advertising also for Schlitz, Allstate Insurance and United Air Lines proves this.

My own picture was next, representing the seventh largest U.S. agency. Foote, Cone & Belding in that year had a volume of $127 million, a shade behind Burnett, slightly less than half the Thompson volume. Its pictured advertised products were Dial, Clairol, Kool-Aid, and Sea & Ski.

Then followed Robert E. Lusk, sixty, chairman of Benton & Bowles, the agency founded by Chester Bowles, later governor of Connecticut and ambassador to India, and William Benton, who became a U.S. Senator, and is now publisher of the *Encyclopaedia Britannica*.* The principal accounts of Benton & Bowles were for various products of General Foods and Procter & Gamble. Harry Batten, sixty-five, was the next man on the cover, as chairman of N. W. Ayer & Son of Philadelphia, whose advertising for the American Telephone & Telegraph Company has long been one of the proudest campaigns in the industry.

The next three faces were those of Robert M. Ganger, fifty-nine, Henry G. Little, sixty, and John P. Cunningham, sixty-five, chairmen, respectively, of D'Arcy Advertising, Campbell-Ewald, and Cunningham & Walsh. D'Arcy was the agency for Anheuser-Busch (for Budweiser beer) and for the Standard Oil Company of Indiana; Campbell-Ewald had the largest advertising account ever conceived for a

---

* Next to Albert Lasker, from whom he learned his trade, William Benton has become the wealthiest of all the advertising agents. An offer of $100 million from Marshall Field, Jr., for Benton's *Britannica* in 1965 interested him not at all.

single product: $60 million annually for Chevrolet automobiles. Cunningham & Walsh was the agency for Texaco, Western Electric, and the telephone companies' Yellow Pages.

The last of the twelve on *Time*'s cover was David Ogilvy, whose agency, Ogilvy, Benson & Mather, was much smaller than any of the others except Cunningham & Walsh, but in many ways equal to any of them.* Ogilvy was an Englishman who had been a chef in a Paris restaurant and a door-to-door salesman in Scotland before he came to America to be an assistant to George Gallup, the pollster; following which he moved easily into the agency business. In addition to the famous Hathaway shirt man, David Ogilvy introduced the red-bearded Commander Whitehead for Schweppes, and proclaimed the loudest noise in a Rolls-Royce automobile to be the ticking of the clock on the dashboard. Ogilvy advertising had a memorability about it not only from what he said, but also from the literate simplicity with which he said it.

A second omission on *Time*'s cover was William Bernbach, the wizard who helped make the buglike German Volkswagen automobile a great American success, and whose advertising for Polaroid cameras, Avis, and Calvert Reserve, *the soft whiskey*, have become classics. Bill Bernbach, president of Doyle Dane Bernbach, started in retail store advertising (for Ohrbach's in New York) and he brought some of its intimacy and some of its daring into the national field. His advertising talked the way people talked, even to effectively making jokes where the sanctities of selling had never before been defied. When Bernbach prepared a Volkswagen advertisement under the heading *Think Small*, he began a new informal era in advertising that is still very much in vogue. The only trouble with this is that it requires a Bill Bernbach to keep it on its bearings; most of the imitators tend to make it much too giddy.

These were the men who headed the agencies that had made advertising history in the period that followed World War II and ran well into the 1960's. They were the men who headed the agencies that recognized the obligation of advertising to be responsible, and who set out to try to make it so.

They were the men who contributed the best talents in their companies to the work of the Advertising Council and who were most active in the affairs of the American Association of Advertising Agencies, which sailed a course close to restraint of trade to keep recognition away from agents whose performance was questionable. When the

---

* Ogilvy, Benson & Mather is now known as Ogilvy & Mather.

The men on the cover of Time, October 12, 1962. (TOP ROW, LEFT TO RIGHT) *Norman H.*
Strouse of J. Walter Thompson; Fairfax M. Cone of Foote, Cone & Belding; Charles H.
Brower of Batten, Barton, Durstine & Osborn; Harry A. Batten of N. W. Ayer & Son;
Leo Burnett of Leo Burnett; David M. Ogilvy of Ogilvy, Benson & Mather; Marion

doesn't

she?

arper, Jr., of Interpublic. (BOTTOM ROW, LEFT TO RIGHT) *George H. Gribbin of Young* *Rubicam; John P. Cunningham of Cunningham & Walsh; Robert E. Lusk of Benton &* *owles; Henry G. Little of Campbell-Ewald; and Robert M. Ganger of D'Arcy* *dvertising.*

4A's signed a consent decree ruling out the requirement that agencies retain intact the commissions allowed them by the media, all restraint was removed. But under the strong influence of the men who were pictured on *Time*'s cover, the moral suasion of the Association continued to be an effective influence.

From the above one might conclude that in my view the "good guys" in advertising have all been on the agency side. This, of course, is not so.

The main forces in the Advertising Council as it evolved after World War II were advertisers and media men as well as advertising agents, and it could not have succeeded without all of them.

Today, in addition to a board of eighty-four directors made up of advertisers and media and agency representatives alike, the Council works through an Industry Advisory Committee of fifty-six members drawn from the top drawer of American business.

The total of public service contributions of space, time and talent through the Advertising Council in the 1967–1968 fiscal year exceeded $304 million. This was broken down into $258 million in media contributions and $46 million in agency contributions; while the Council's own operating costs were a frugal $664,000.* The value of the Council can hardly be exaggerated. In its twenty-five years of unselfish activity it has made a cumulative investment for social profit that has passed the $4 billion mark.

Three of its directors, then and now, appeared on that 1962 cover of *Time*. They were Leo Burnett, Robert M. Ganger, and myself.

Many years ago, it occurred to Earle Ludgin, president of the agency of that name, in Chicago, that it would make an interesting feature for a 4A's meeting if an agent were to choose a group of current advertisements made by competitors that he would like very much to have made himself.

When Mr. Ludgin broached the idea to me, I agreed that it would be fun and I offered to try to get Leo Burnett, who was my favorite man in the business, to make his choice.

I should have known better.

"Look," said Burnett, leveling, "did it ever occur to you that I just might want to solicit one of those companies someday, and how it would look if they reminded me that I had chosen their advertising as something I wished I had done?"

---

* Principal campaigns continued to be for Aid to Higher Education, American Red Cross, Better Schools, Forest Fire Prevention, Highway Safety, United Fund, U.S. Savings Bonds, U.S.O.

There was no answer to that. And it could have done for me, too. But when I told Ludgin, he replied that since I had agreed that the idea was a good one, it was up to me to perform the act; and I did. In fact, I did it again and again until it became almost a yearly exercise, and until my lists began to be looked upon almost as awards to the best advertising, no matter how carefully I stated that these were only advertisements that I would be pleased to have made.

This last, however, was not enough for my old friends at *Time*, for in their issue of August 17, 1959, three years before the gatefold cover ran, there appeared a selection of the advertisements that *Time* called my "favorites of the past decade," limiting the field to magazine advertising and excluding my own company's.

What interests me most about these, ten years later, is that each one stands now, as then, as an example of first-rate advertising. Seven of the ten campaigns continue to this day without any significant change.

Pillsbury cake mixes, under the headline *Who, Me?* superimposed above a photograph of an almost life-size chocolate masterpiece, a promise that *anyone* can bake a cake just like it. All one needs is the magic mix. And so it has proved.

Hathaway shirts advertising came next, and my example was the initial appearance of the man with the eyepatch who put a real man in place of a clothing-store dummy into such advertising for the first time.

Jell-O advertising through the years has occupied itself with subjects as diverse as wide-eyed hungry children, weight-watching adults and animals out of the fairy tales of Andersen and Grimm, as means to illustrate its continuing promise of good-tasting, easy-to-make puddings and pie fillings. The advertisement here bore the heading *It's National Jell-O is a Bride's-Best-Friend Week.*

Johnson & Johnson's Baby Powder came next. Under a softly-tinted photograph of a mother and child, the caption read *Fragile . . . Handle with Johnson's,* and it seemed to me that there could be no more thoughtful advice. It was the restraint in this case that delivered the promise.

Polaroid Land cameras were something new in 1959. They were new in principle, and new in the results anyone could achieve. It was the results that the advertising stressed with pose-and-fire portraits of famous people; and so strong was the personality of the advertising that it needed neither headline nor signature. The proposition was complete without either one.

Kraft jams and jellies advertising was also a demonstration in print. There were the delectable fruits *grown moist and tender in the long*

summer sun, ready to be quick-cooked in Kraft's own special way.
What more could anyone ask?

Armstrong linoleum advertising illustrated once again, in my opinion, that a sound approach need never be changed but only varied. Armstrong's promise was what one can do in a house, or a room, even an attic, with a little imagination and with Armstrong's help.

Examples of all of these continuing campaigns are current in the weekly or monthly magazines and on television (except for Hathaway, which appears only in print).

The three other series I chose in 1959 were the *Ladies Home Journal's*, wherein you were variously and humorously reminded never to underestimate the power of a woman; Life Savers, the candy mint with the hole; and the program advertising of the Columbia Broadcasting System which called attention to their great Sunday afternoon musical offerings. These served their various purposes; and each has been replaced.

Incidentally, eight of these ten campaigns were made by agencies represented on the 1962 *Time* cover. The Pillsbury advertising came from Leo Burnett; Hathaway from Ogilvy, Benson & Mather; Jell-O and Johnson & Johnson from Young & Rubicam; Armstrong from Batten, Barton, Durstine & Osborn. The *Journal* advertising came from N. W. Ayer & Son; the CBS advertising from McCann-Erickson (Interpublic); and the Life Savers campaign from Young & Rubicam.

The Polaroid advertising was made by Doyle Dane Bernbach, whose president should, as I have said, have been included on that cover. The Kraft advertisement was made by Needham, Louis & Brorby (now Needham, Harper & Steers) of Chicago, an outland city that *Time* had already flattered with two portraits.

The men on the cover of *Time* in October of 1962 were still a little dazed by television.

The idea that the program was the thing prevailed throughout the industry, and this was understandable. Sponsor identification was still an important measurement of value, and this held down the interest in commercials.

It was generally believed (although there was no real evidence to prove it) that the public was mildly annoyed by the advertising; and, to tell the truth, the sponsors themselves were. The commercials were a necessary evil that the advertiser chiefs left to the Indians while they concentrated on the programs. Being in show business was a grand and glorious experience to a lot of men who should have known better.

Eventually the growing cost of television forced a sobering change in their thinking. Sponsor identification was lost in a maze of products whose advertising was crowded into thirty-second segments, twelve or more to the hour, and, despite the opening and closing announcements ("billboards"), nobody cared who the sponsors were. In the beginning, the sponsorship of both hour and half-hour shows was most apt to be devoted to the advertising of a single product. Then this was divided between two advertisers for two products. But as the cost kept rising as more sets came into use, alternate-week sponsors began to divide their time between two products. Thus a single half-hour came to carry commercials for three or four products, plus one or two more in billboards and closing credits.

Now the commercial became important, and new attention was paid to each one. The integrated commercial, which had been a favorite of the advertisers ever since Jack Benny acted out Lucky Strike commercials on radio, suddenly had no place in the new medium. Commercials that might appear anywhere there was a time spot for sale had to stand on their own.

The sight of undistinguishable vapors coursing through the sinus canals, hammers pounding away at the cells of the brain, and leaky faucets dripping acid into troubled stomachs followed each other with a dulling insistence that was relieved for the most part only by such gay impossibilities as fairies who came out of the sky magically to make laundry whiter than white — unless it was colored, in which case the laundry would be brighter than bright!

This was the era of what were called "exaggerated graphics," and the exaggerations were apt to be ridiculous. Still, there were exceptions. There was a marvelous demonstration of the Remington electric shaver in which a stiff black brush and a fuzzy yellow peach were shaved with equal ease and a smooth result. There were the great Chevrolet commercials where driverless cars maneuvered through the streets of New York and Paris and floated through Venice canals. There were the Raid commercials (from my own company) where an army of sly and mischievous bugs were pitted in a continuing series of contests against the implacable insecticide. There was the Bufferin commercial whose only action was the movement of the second hand of a watch counting off the sixty seconds in which the fast-working analgesic would become effective in relieving headaches. Happily, now there are a good many more like them.

The men on the cover of *Time* had been largely responsible for the taming of advertising, and for harnessing it to the requirements of a productive society. They had insisted upon the probity of advertising until this was not easily breached, and they had brought printed advertising to a new degree of understanding and acceptance. It was no longer often questioned, for it didn't need to be.

But advertising is a fast-moving stream. And if, as James Young has said, it is a self-purifying stream, it also needs constant attention. Television has made this abundantly clear. This, then, becomes the province of the successors of the men I have been talking about. Norman Strouse, George Gribben, Harry Batten, Henry Little and Jack Cunningham are already retired, and successors are being groomed for the rest, all of whom, with the exception of Marion Harper and David Ogilvy, have passed the age of sixty. Together they have a good deal that is good to look back on. As a result, their successors have a good deal to look forward to that can be much better.

It is impossible, of course, to say who will succeed to the top position in each of the agencies when the rest of my friends and associates in the agency association and the Advertising Council are retired. However, this does not mean that I have no idea what kind of men these will be, for I have a good idea.

By and large, they will be much like the individuals in my own company who are today the younger officers and directors, and the managers of our offices. Typically, these are veterans of World War II, who joined the agency as trainees soon after they were discharged from the armed services, and either came directly to Foote, Cone & Belding or had one other job, where their view of advertising caused them to decide upon this as a career.

When the agency business was young and the services the agencies rendered were personal and uncomplicated by the intricacies of marketing, or product or media research, the agency proprietors were not apt to share ownership that was largely of their own making. Lord & Thomas had been owned almost entirely by Albert Lasker, and this was as it should have been because he had built the business through his own efforts and he had made himself responsible to the agency's clients.

When Foote, Cone & Belding came into being the situation was different. Now the men who had represented Albert Lasker were responsible, and they were responsible not simply to Foote, Cone & Belding, but to the partnership of all of them together. For this reason, as soon as the individuals whose names were on the letterhead felt sure that the business was going to stay afloat, they offered half their shares to the men who had come with them from Lord & Thomas at the beginning; and, in time, a dozen of these became directors in the new company.

When Foote, Cone & Belding became a public corporation in 1963, all the holdings of Mr. Foote and Mr. Belding had long since been repurchased by the corporation and distributed to other members of the firm, sold to them at book value.

One of the newsletters that pretend to look inside advertising, as they do a number of other businesses, maintained as early as 1955 that "Cone had quietly been purchasing stock until he had virtual control of the agency." The truth was, I had sold more and more of my original 32 per cent of the shares to my associates, and when the public offering was made, my ownership in the company was less than 6 per cent. A number of men had acquired shares that were worth small fortunes.*

Among these were three onetime trainees who had become officers of the company, and I believe their progress through the agency is typical of the business as it exists today, where training in advertising is thorough and the results carefully measured, and where the total experience is generously seasoned with free public service.

First of the trainees to become a director was Charles Winston, who was successively general manager in Detroit and Chicago and who, in 1967, was elected president of Foote, Cone & Belding at the age of forty-eight.

Second of the triumvirate of early trainees who have become directors of Foote, Cone & Belding, is Arthur Schultz. Two years ago he was made executive vice-president and general manager in Chicago. Schultz is forty-seven.

The last member of this group is Robert Trump, who became a director at the same time. Trump, forty-eight, is chairman of the Chicago office plans board, which is responsible for advertising strategy for all Chicago office accounts.

Another early comer, Richard W. Tully, who joined the agency in 1947, was made chairman in 1967. Tully is forty-eight.

(Some of these titles have been changed as a result of corporate reorganization but the position of each of the men at the top of the agency structure is the same.)

The continuity of these men is not unique to Foote, Cone & Belding in Chicago. It prevails in the other offices of this agency; and the personnel records of J. Walter Thompson Company, Young & Rubicam, Leo Burnett, Batten, Barton, Durstine & Osborn and most other leading agencies would be entirely consistent with our own. Longtime employees Danny Seymour, Edwin Bond, Ed Thiele and Tom Dillon

---

* Now, although Foote, Cone & Belding is a publicly owned company, approximately two-thirds of its shares are owned by employees.

have already succeeded Norman Strouse, George Gribben, Leo Burnett and Charlie Brower, respectively, in the above-mentioned companies, and a similar succession is underway in many another.

It is simply a fact that as the agency business has matured, it has become attractive to better-educated and more serious men. They have found it increasingly more challenging and more rewarding and they have built their careers with a minimum of job-switching.

There was a time when advertising was something a manufacturer did merely to keep his name before the public. Now he advertises in order to keep his business alive and moving forward. As advertising has become vital to our system of communication, it has called for more and more of the skills that are taught in the graduate schools of business at such universities as Chicago, Harvard, M.I.T. and Stanford, and it attracts some of their best students.

With their much better-trained staffs and their much better-trained client organizations, the advertising agencies have achieved a degree of stability that is in sharp contrast with the quixotic nature of the business prior to World War II, and this goes back again to the necessity for advertising in a free-choice economy.

There is also the fascinating area of public service with which advertising began to ally itself when the Advertising Council was formed, and this has become an increasingly satisfactory outlet for scores of agency people as their unique talents have been discovered and put to work. The extent to which they combine advertising as an element in the economy with advertising as a social force will be the measure of the advertising men of the future.

Advertising is one of the most pervasive of all the forces that persuade us. Even when it is used for purposes that are evil it cannot be eliminated. But it can be used overwhelmingly for good. That it will be is every sincere adman's wish.

The Mandates

THE deepening interest of agency people in public affairs has brought a new dignity and a new sense of purpose to their total activity. In my own early days in the trade, advertising people were rarely brought into community activities except to help secure publicity for fund-raising campaigns, and they didn't do this very well.

The trouble was that advertising and publicity operate in widely divergent ways, and while advertising may have in it elements of publicity, publicity can rarely be controlled and directed with the end force of advertising. Publicity tells what is going on and what the circumstances are; advertising tells what one may do, or should do, to join in the activity — and how and when and where.

Publicity is always proposed hopefully. There is never any assurance that the project that is involved can be publicized as planned. This is up to the media; it depends on whether or not they have space and time available for the publicity and, actually, how acceptable it is to them in view of their own interests. Advertising, on the other hand, appears as the advertiser wants it to, for once the media have agreed to accept it, they cannot change it. Thus, advertising planning is firm planning; and it was this that the advertising industry, and particularly the advertising agency representatives, brought to the support of many community activities and, particularly, to their financing, for the first time.

The work of the Advertising Council on a national basis is now mirrored all over America at the local level.

In Chicago, advertising men and women sit on the boards of the Community Fund, the Welfare Council, the Red Cross, the Lyric Opera,

the Art Institute, the Crime Commission, the principal educational organizations — which is to say, the University of Chicago, Northwestern
University, De Paul and Loyola universities and the principal hospitals;
there is no civic undertaking in which they are not now included among
the planners. It is possible that the activity of advertising people in
public affairs is somewhat greater in Chicago than anywhere else in
the U.S. But if this is true, it is only because the Establishment in
Chicago, far from being closed, has been open for many years to anyone whose interest in the city is both educated and unselfish.*

The principal challenge to advertising people everywhere is to
move toward professional status. Technically, this may be something
they can never achieve, but they can observe professional rules and
they can maintain professional standards. Obviously, this begins inside
the business, for whatever may be done outside it will not make up
for any lack within.

Once upon a time it would have been challenge enough simply to
clean up advertising, to make it truthful and to make it useful. But as
most people now know, dishonest advertising has become a small part
of the total. The requirement of most advertised products to produce
results as promised is inherent in the economics of the marketplace;
it is not a matter of the advertiser's morals. As I have said, it is virtually
impossible to sell a bad product twice to the same person, and the
number of products that can succeed as a result of one-time sales
is limited almost entirely to products of infrequent purchase such as
automobiles, heating systems and major appliances that are sold, for
the most part, in person-to-person confrontation by live salespeople
and not by advertising.

But if honesty in advertising has become the accepted standard, the
question of good taste continues to plague the industry. In the beginning of this book I referred to the extremely poor taste of a great deal
of book and moving picture advertising and to political advertising
that oversteps what I consider to be the bounds of decency. I mentioned also the excesses that occur in the advertising of health and
beauty products. Almost all of these are matters of tasteless presentation.

Somehow there must be a better way to present a mouthwash on
television than to show a distraught, tearful teenager screaming
at her escort at a party "You said I had . . . *bad breath!*" Or a frantic
woman reporting to a friend that her husband insisted that her "breath
was a major cause of air pollution."

---

* The most prestigious of Chicago business and professional clubs is the Commercial Club, limited to 160 active members chosen for their public interests and
their public service. Presently the club membership includes six advertising agents.

Obviously there is nothing immoral about this kind of thing. Nor was it advertising that first brought it forth. It is part of the permissiveness of our times, and the crudeness that filters into advertising from books, movies, plays and television entertainment where no subject is too intimate or too delicate to be exploited for laughs or for tears.

Under the circumstances of a general breakdown in the authority of schools and the church to preserve social standards, it can hardly be expected that advertising will pick up the pieces and put them together again. But it can, and it *should*, be made with the obligation in mind to raise the standards of our manners and our conduct and not to accept these at the scornful level of a rude and frequently vulgar generation. This is not to say that I believe the hippies and their fellow travelers have been responsible for the breakdown. On the contrary, I hold them to be a result of it. But they are also its clearest manifestation.

Advertising always follows, it never leads. Nevertheless, it should be used in the best traditions of our society and not the very questionable postures that evolve from time to time. One of the worst of the offenses of advertising in this area of bad manners is the denigration of competitive products through the use of odious comparisons, sometimes joking, sometimes deadly serious. I am perfectly aware that depreciation is the basis of both nightclub humor and many a sales person's strongest ploy. But this doesn't alter my view that advertising should never stoop to conquer. To see that it doesn't is the second charge that I would make to the successors.

It ties closely to the first, to play a personal part in community affairs; and it leads directly to the third, which is to use advertising as an educational force.

For sixteen years the *Saturday Review* has made awards to a growing number of advertisers and agents who have taken advertising beyond the call of duty to explain and argue and defend and attack all manner of good and evil aspects of our life and times, and some of their efforts have been so successful that the critics' failure to note them can only be put down as calculated and irresponsible.

Much of what I am talking about is called institutional advertising, and it appears in several forms. One of them is public relations advertising and another is public service advertising. The longtime Weyerhauser campaign in magazines (now also on television) which explains the company's program of reforestation is a prime example of the first, for it is a direct answer to the charge of lumbermen's contemptuous destruction of national resources. The Caterpillar Tractor

Company has used its advertising to explain reclamation projects in which its products are engaged and to point out ways in which other communities and municipalities can look forward to public improvements of a similar nature. This I would call public service.

In neither of these instances (and there are many more) is there any direct connection between the advertiser and his audience. He sells to someone else. The advertising is a matter of education and elucidation and the climate in which the advertiser's business is done.

Institutional advertising of a slightly different cast has been carried on for many years by the Metropolitan Life Insurance Company in the interest of better health; by Warner & Swasey, toolmakers in Cleveland, who have attacked inflation in all its many guises; and by the Container Corporation, which has presented the wisdom of the ages in a long series of brief quotations embellished with brilliant illustrations or even more remarkable abstractions.* These campaigns serve as strong backgrounds for the salesmen who must approach the advertisers' best prospects, very few of whom ever telephone an insurance company, a lathe maker or a manufacturer of paper cartons.

Advertising as a public service is another variation. It comes closer to the Advertising Council concept. There is no direct connection between the advertising and the advertiser's products, but the subject of the advertising is strongly connected with the advertiser's interests. Thus the Mobil oil company publishes powerful appeals to the public to drive safely so that they may continue to be customers. The Better Vision Institute of the American Optical Company and associated optical goods manufacturers warns against failing sight and blindness, and suggests how these may be avoided. General Electric explains the Pacemaker, the electric heart stimulant that is surgically implanted under the skin. International Paper Company presents both the joys and the lifetime values in reading. Seagram's distilling company advertises so that teenagers and their parents will understand that drinking is a pleasure that should be reserved for adults.

One may hope, and I do, that institutional advertising is just now getting its second wind, after the hiatus that followed the return to product selling in the aftermath of World War II. Except for their contributions to the Advertising Council, most advertisers took a hard-nosed look at anything not directly connected with product selling. When the *Saturday Review* began to make its awards, there was barely enough such advertising to fit a single category.

---

* When I once complimented the late Walter Paepcke on this series, he said, "I am afraid that you and I are the only two people in the world who understand it." But whether they understood it or not, I am sure that it set his salesmen apart just as he intended.

Now that institutional advertising is established as good public relations, I expect it to be used increasingly as an extension of private
relations — which, after all, is where public relations begin. The only
danger that I foresee is in overenthusiasm. This is something that
the successors should watch out for.

Despite what I have said about the values in public service advertising, I am disturbed by the television advertising by the American Cancer Society and the Heart Association in their attack upon
cigarette smoking, for I see in it the very same excesses in what may
prove to be a good cause that are condemned in an evil exercise.

That smoking may be harmful to some people to some extent I
have no doubt (so may eating sugar, or driving an automobile), but
that it is harmful to all people in the same degree has certainly not
been proved. There are millions of smokers who appear not to be
affected in any way except pleasurably; and I would like to see the
Cancer Society and the Heart Association admit some qualifications in
their sweeping condemnation of cigarette smoking.

To say that one minute of cigarette smoking is equal to one minute
of life, which the Heart Association has, is the kind of exaggeration
that would be loudly condemned in product advertising by the very
zealots who approve it for anti-cigarette advertising.

Surely there is a difference between individuals and their tolerance
of many things and so long as a number of eminent physicians believe
that there is a considerable difference in the incidence of lung cancer
in men and women, for example, I would rather listen to them than
to the emotional pleas of the crusaders.

This is not to say that I approve all cigarette advertising. I don't;
I simply object to the attack that has been launched in such general
terms on the products of an industry that are made legally and sold
legally up and down and across the United States. The next step could
be prohibition; and I remember the Volstead Act all too well. Meanwhile, I hate to see advertising used with such cavalier support for
an unresolved issue.

Great care must be exercised in choosing up sides.

Another field where it was once thought that only editorial treatment could educate and move the public is in the political arena.
Some very crude advertising was also used, but it was strictly homemade and consisted primarily of charges and countercharges that
rarely came to grips with real issues.

Today this, too, is changed, and not, in my opinion, altogether for the
better. While the prepared question-and-answer technique that was

first used on radio and television in the second Eisenhower campaign for the Presidency has been improved, the failure to develop the debates that were so important in the Kennedy-Nixon contest in 1960 has been, to me, a distinct disappointment.

I am quite aware of the reasons that were advanced by the Nixon campaign organization in 1968, but I find these cynical and unworthy. The former Vice President was far ahead, they said; to debate would be to give added exposure to his opponent. The strategy was undoubtedly shrewd, and I am sure that it worked. But it was hardly in the best public interest to eliminate the possibility of any direct confrontation between the two candidates.

The use of film clips was often candid and effective, but politics have not climbed nearly to the moral plane achieved by advertising at large in the two latest decades of this century, and political advertising exudes rude challenges and denigration. The 1968 campaign of Governor Wallace of Alabama was decidedly in the outmoded tradition of half-answered embarrassing questions. So was Richard Nixon's exploitation of the horrors of Vietnam, for which he offered only the vaguest relief, while the lengthy soliloquy by Vice President Humphrey on the subject of his retarded granddaughter was in questionable taste.

One might observe, I suppose, that newspaper editorials also are inclined toward unrelenting ridicule and abuse of opponents, and warm praise for every action of their favorites, during most political races. But we are talking about advertising; and as more and more political and public affairs advertising is prepared by competent and conscientious advertising practitioners, advertising will find its place as a more useful and dependable force.

Here it seems appropriate to mention the role of advertising in the hoped-for improvement in race relations, and I think this has been considerable.

To be sure, this was slow in coming. Up until very recently there was little or no representation of black people as users, or hoped-for users, of any of the products of general distribution. The reasons, I suspect, were twofold. In the first place, the blacks represented only 10 per cent of the population and something less than that proportion of buying power. Second, it was generally accepted that the white people shown in advertisements were the models most black people accepted for themselves.

It was only when John Johnson, the publisher of *Ebony* magazine, began to point out that the Negro market was a distinct entity that the advertisers' eyes were opened. The result was the development of a large number of advertising campaigns directed solely to Johnson's and other similar audiences.

Much more important, and fortunately, television opened the way to advertise to white and black people at the same time, and effectively.

Television ownership among black families is every way comparable to television ownership among white families; the circulation is there. But even more important is the nature of the medium that lends itself so admirably to brief vignettes that while they are on the screen absorb it totally. Thus the screen that shows a black housewife preparing a meal is every bit as important, and yet no more so than any one of two or three vignettes that feature white housewives. This was very difficult to achieve in printed advertising, where small illustrations tended to absorb the available space, and where these were devoted to the interests of the majority.

There is also a good deal of advertising on television that features children (advertising for toothpaste, peanut butter, cereals, cameras, shoes) and it has been both easy and, I believe, effective to use a combination of black and white children in an ever-increasing number of commercials.

On the other side of advertising, which is making it, the successors to my generation have a long way to go in the development and use of black talents. The hiring of blacks to fill what amounted almost to a quota rather than to develop young men and women for specific assignment resulted at first in hiring perfectly good (and not so good) applicants who often failed at the outset to match the job requirements that were so carefully set down and rigidly adhered to. Foote, Cone & Belding made this mistake along with numerous other companies.

Then we forgot about quotas, and began searching for interest and aptitude, and I think we are beginning to do well. As this is written we are eagerly awaiting the return next summer of seven young men and women whom we recruited because they had been editors of their high school annuals. They spent last summer in our Chicago office, half the time working at various jobs, half the time in an advertising "school" which we organized under the direction of a professor from Roosevelt University, and which was deemed a qualified success.

These seven young black students came to us with an attitude that clearly said, "Show us." They were suspicious of us as employers, for they doubted our motives; they doubted that our school was anything more than a charity front. When they found that we were looking for talent, and ready to seriously help develop *their* talents, the attitude changed radically, and before the summer was over several of the group were showing promise enough to make the project a success. Is this an indication for the future? I think it is. I hope our lead will be followed.

I have left to this point the all-important subject of television, wherein I believe the obligation of the successors is a joint one that involves programming no less than the advertising with which the programs are spaced and interrupted.

For one thing, it would be foolish to believe that advertising on the tube will ever rise to greater heights of taste and manners than television programming. Although certain examples of broadcast advertising represent a gain over some of the older patterns of broadcast entertainment, it is the latter and not the former that represent television to the American audience. Insofar as advertising supports this, it must share responsibility for it; and the practice at this point is not a pretty one.

Here I agree completely with Jack Gould, the uncompromising television critic of the New York *Times,* who on June 12, 1968, said, "Broadcasters automatically accept the role of leadership when they accept their licenses. Restraint in emphasizing violence and torture as ingredients of entertainment is both little to ask and long overdue. Television, obviously, is totally capable of broadening its scope in many other creative directions and reflecting the very best, not the worst, of our culture."

Unfortunately, or maybe fortunately, this is not where the matter ends. For while the responsibility for programming is indeed the broadcasters', support of free television lies solely with the advertisers. Theirs is the money that keeps the cameras grinding. Their acceptance of the broadcaster's programming or their refusal of it is the difference between success and failure for any broadcaster; and their willingness to support competing broadcasters entirely on the basis of audience delivered represents the rejection of responsibility that should be no less theirs than that of the broadcasters themselves.

There has never been another medium even remotely like television, and it requires a new set of rules for all of the participants. For the first time in history millions of children have been eyewitnesses to all the world's promise and all the world's horrors, with the latter, unfortunately, predominating.

The old vicarious thrills that lay in the pages of magazines and books and on the moving picture screen now are not vicarious at all. They are part of the living room scene, and the holdups and the tortures and the murders occur in close proximity and in detail as part of every day.

On the other side of the coin, also in the living room is the dream world of extravagant, exaggerated luxury, and it is from this that many an adolescent is returned to his own much less bountiful world with full knowledge of certain fascinating criminal means to rise above it, to escape its ugly reality. That the escape always ends in disaster on the screen is often anticlimactic; this aspect is usually dealt with briefly, and it is the thrill of the chase, with handguns flashing and blood spurting, that remains in the mind. Furthermore, it is generally a mistake that only a fool would ever make that trips up the swaggering hoodlum or outlaw who is the villain, or hero. He became too greedy or too careless; or he was really a stupid fellow.

While I hold the responsibility of the broadcasters to plan and produce their programs to be wholly without advertiser interference, I also hold it to be an obligation of the advertisers to look beyond the audience figures to the social implications of the programs they support.

It was not only the broadcasters who were deaf to the entreaties of Newton Minow, who as chairman of the Federal Communications Commission called television a "vast wasteland," a condemnation that is often repeated. The advertisers were equally oblivious to Minow's complaint. All were concerned with circulation, and not to provide it spelled disaster for the broadcasters, for they were caught in the advertisers' own competitive toils. The manufacturer of Dodge automobiles, for instance, could hardly accept a higher cost per thousand viewers of Dodge commercials than the makers of Mercury automobiles were paying for theirs; or the makers of Anacin more than the makers of Bayer Aspirin.

The problem today is to rid the air of some of the programs whose delivery of large audiences is achieved in disregard of thoughtful criticism and concern; and it is to this that all conscientious advertising people should address their attention.

Still, this is only one phase of broadcasting that cries out for correction.

The air belongs neither to the broadcasters nor to the advertisers. It belongs to the people, and it belongs to *all* the people.

And just as their immediate predecessors were the prime movers toward honesty and responsibility in advertising itself, the men and women who are the driving force in advertising today should insist that the most dynamic of all advertising media shall perform in the total public interest. This means that side by side with their efforts to de-emphasize violence on the television screen, they should support and insist upon a reasonable amount of programming for the minority of viewers whose interests go beyond horse opera and crime shows and the witless and soporific entertainment that is called situation comedy.

There can be no doubt that a large number of television viewers are getting what they want. It is even probable that a majority of television viewers are getting what they want. But even if this is true, there is a sizable minority that is satisfied only at rare intervals and at odd times.

When almost three hours pass on an early fall Sunday afternoon with no other choice for the viewer than baseball and reruns of three or four crime and situation comedy shows, something is wrong. Nor is the average prime nighttime programming a great deal better. For half the year there is some kind of drama in hour or half-hour segments every evening. Too many hours are filled with Western outlaws and gunplay, although some deal with big-city and even international crime and murder; while the half-hours creak with current imitations of old domestic and other comedy routines. Then there are the so-called "big" shows in which a parade of guest stars, not quite attractive enough to have their own regular programs, repeat their special routines to the raucous delight of the studio audiences whose knowledge of the acts causes them frequently to drown out the comic punch lines in their eagerness to show off. It is quite possible to believe that the studio audiences (or the simulated studio audiences) are the worst part of television.*

Anyway, painfully revised versions of old favorites fill most of the nighttime hours for half the year; then previous chapters of the same programs (or even older series) fill the other half. At one time the thirteen-week summer period was used to try out and test new programs. But this apparently represented a strain on the money machine that was decided by the moguls to be unwarranted. Hence, they extended the thirteen-week summer period to something like twenty-six weeks and concentrated either on inexpensive substitutes or even cheaper reruns. (Recently the latter have been inserted more and more frequently into the regular schedules.)

I have argued in the past, and publicly, that there is some television programming that is very good programming. The *Columbia Work-*

---

* Any question about the cultural level of the studio audiences can be easily resolved by watching one of the late-evening personality programs, when the host takes his microphone out among the faithful for a little repartee.

shop series of 1967–1968, the *Hallmark Hall of Fame,* Jacques-Yves Cousteau's underseas explorations, the *National Geographic* adventures, the wonderful musical programs that feature Julie Andrews, Barbra Streisand and Herb Alpert and his Tijuana Brass band, and Jackie Gleason and Art Carney with their Honeymooners skits are examples; and the record of television's political and social documentaries contains some first-rate entries. But it is impossible not to argue that there is too much in television that is stupid and ugly and too much that is vicious.

Worse still, it is foolish to maintain, as the broadcasters like to, that you can choose your television, because you can't. You must take it or leave it, for better or worse. Furthermore, once you take it, you have had it, to the exclusion of everything else broadcast at the same time. Once you have missed a competing program, you most likely have missed it forever (unless it is a routine program, in which case it will be rebroadcast at regular intervals as long as the tape holds out). Otherwise the disadvantage is real, and the consequences are serious. The American public is getting its television purely and simply according to the money that is in it for the majority of owners and operators of television stations.

Unfortunately, we have no "little" television stations in the sense that we have the smaller magazines. (I omit the educational television stations because, with one or two exceptions, they are hardly comparable; magazines produced with the same ineptitude would barely make a second appearance.) The fact is that we have only giant television operations, fighting each other for their share of a $3.5 billion annual income. Television's great networks were developed solely to make money. Radio had shown the way, and it was paved with gold. Nor do I want to change it all. I am not a revolutionary. I only want the networks and the stations to put some of the profit back into the product.

To begin with, I want them to use their best talents to develop programs of adult interest that go somewhat beyond the late-night movies whose adult aspects are limited largely to the exploitation of sex and criminality, and to schedule these programs in prime viewing time. The networks have only to insist that the advertisers buy the networks' own selection of a diversified group of programs, trending heavily to the popular, to be sure, but including a reasonable number for the minority of viewers and charging the advertisers accordingly.

It is my conviction that while the ratings by which television is judged are quite adequate in measuring the audience of programs presently on the air, they leave serious questions unanswered about nonviewers.

The first question, of course, is why their sets are not turned on.

The second is what would change this.

These are not questions to be answered by reviewing the past, or even by a survey of the public today, with the replies fed into a computer for electronic analysis. The answers can only be arrived at as the result of serious endeavor by the networks to raise the level of programming in certain nighttime segments every week for several years, measuring the results not alone in number of viewers, but also very carefully with regard to the kind of viewers.

I, for one, would not be unduly concerned with occasional ratings (or audience) no more than half of the average for all programs. This would represent a cost of about five dollars per thousand viewers. Admittedly this is twice the present acceptable rate. But it should be pointed out that merely to mail a letter to a thousand viewers and take your chance on their reading that letter would cost *sixty* dollars!

Maybe the advertisers, as well as the networks and the stations, have had it, as the saying goes, too good.

It was almost ten years ago that I first urged the networks to consider what came to be called the magazine concept of television programming, in which they would design their schedules to include comedy, drama and popular music, and serious material, in reasonable proportion, and rotate the advertisers' messages through the full schedule just as this is done in magazines.*

I continue to believe this is the best possible solution to the problem of satisfying minority tastes. It puts the full responsibility of programming where it belongs, in the broadcasters' hands, and it obligates all advertisers to support superior programming on the basis of reasonable participation.

Although my suggestion was commented upon favorably in the press, it was dismissed by William Paley and my friends Frank Stanton at the Columbia Broadcasting System and Robert Kintner at the National Broadcasting Company, with the single terse comment from the latter that "it won't work." At the American Broadcasting Company, Leonard Goldenson thought the idea might be worth testing. But since I have never heard anything more about this, I must conclude that he was merely being polite to a fairly important cash customer.

* Louis N. Brockway of Young & Rubicam had suggested a form of tithing whereby advertisers might donate 10 per cent of their schedules to cultural or public service programming. But this, I feel, took away the broadcasters' responsibility. Anyway, with the current practice of buying commercial spots rather than programs, it would be impractical.

If evidence was needed to fortify the argument for quality in television programming, the Lunts furnished this when their production of The Magnificent Yankee *for Hallmark attracted 25 million viewers.*

Still, I believe this is the only way the minority of viewers, who would like to look at television for some kind of adult stimulation, are likely to be satisfied. The educational stations are poorly financed and understaffed; and try as they may to do better, most of their programming scales downward from mediocre. If, on the other hand, the networks, with their ample resources, backed by the advertisers, would undertake some of the same subjects and some of the same experiments, television might begin to satisfy even its severest critics. Surely there would be an advantage to most advertisers in reaching from time to time an audience that has proved to be unimpressed by the antics of Jim Nabors, Jerry Lewis and Jonathan Winters or the misadventures of Robert Culp, Bill Cosby or Efrem Zimbalist, Jr.

In any case, it it is not my wish to remove any of the popular series (except those where the *modus operandi* is violence) from their place in the regular nighttime schedules. I only propose that these be pre-empted once or twice in each thirteen-week period in order to insert a small number of programs with what I would hope would have more artistic dimensions. *

Perhaps I should point out that when I first broached the magazine concept of programming in a talk in Los Angeles (hard by the enemy camp in Hollywood) in February of 1960, the argument was advanced that the advertisers would never accept the rotation of their commercials because each wanted to have his own program, to be known as its sponsor, and not to be confused. Today, ninety per cent of national television is bought on a scatter plan, whereby the advertisers contract for one-minute commercial segments in anywhere from one to twenty or more different programs each week. Except for Hallmark, Chrysler, Kraft, Xerox, Monsanto and a very few other advertisers, none has any interest any longer in sponsor identification.

The magazine concept has at least got this far. After all, nobody sponsors the *Reader's Digest*.

The most recent example of lack of imagination on the part of the broadcasters is the rash of carbon copies of the late Jack Paar program and its successor, the Johnny Carson show on NBC.

This olla podrida of questionable entertainment interspersed with an incredible number of commercials, both network and local, has sprouted no fewer than six other programs that are indistinguishable from it in any artistic way.

---

* I have not said anything about daytime programming. It is a hodgepodge of silly game programs, unbelievable soap operas and reruns of old domestic comedies and even older moving pictures, and is best left strictly alone.

In each, the master of ceremonies, who is either Carson himself, or Joey Bishop, Merv Griffin, Mike Douglas, Dick Cavett, Woody Woodbury or the perennial Steve Allen, in the order of their appearance in the new pattern, sits at a practically identical desk on a practically identical platform, and with a straight man (Ed McMahon, Regis Philbin, Arthur Treacher, *et al.*) and an orchestra, and proceeds to introduce and interview and call upon a series of guests, most of whom make practically identical contributions to the several shows.

It can only be that there is a considerable number of people in the land whose inability to go to sleep causes them to prefer almost anything to counting sheep.

I wouldn't care were it not for the fact that through several of these late-evening shows, patterned on nightclub entertainment, television is becoming a medium for highly suggestive discussion and barely disguised dirty jokes. That the audiences quite obviously enjoy their familiarity with so much of this questionable material makes no difference. This is something television could better do without. *Playboy* in print is playboy enough. It is a case of hitting below the belt. The television operators continue to flaunt the Marquis of Queensberry rules, and while I am quite aware that in this they are only following the movie magnates, it seems a poor excuse, and no place at all in advertising.

There is nothing in the history of American business that matches the rapacity with which the entrenched broadcasters have attacked pay-TV. The situation is precisely what it would be if the railroads had prevailed upon Congress sixty years ago to ban the manufacture and distribution of automobiles despite the earnest pleas of the Federal Trade Commission and never changed their stand. The National Association of Broadcasters is a bald-faced lobby which pretends, like the National Rifle Association, to be acting in the public interest. But its stated opposition to pay-TV is based upon three false and misleading premises.

In the first place, say the lobbyists, pay-TV would make set owners pay for much of what they now see on their sets free of charge. The fact is that the Federal Communications Commission has already set up rules that would prohibit pay-TV from showing any sports events customarily shown free on stations now. And they prohibit pay-TV from showing any moving pictures more than two years old; the huge backlog is left to the regular broadcasters.

Second, say the broadcasters, organized labor opposes pay-TV. But the fact is that the AFL-CIO expressed approval of pay-TV years ago, and their position has never changed.

Third, says the NAB, pay-TV will favor the wealthy, discriminate against the poor. The fact is that a person in modest circumstances can show his entire family a first-run moving picture for a single small charge — about $1.50. (He also can invite all the neighbors his living room will hold.) The facts were established over a period of years in Hartford, Connecticut, where the Zenith Radio Corporation developed a workable system of subscription television more than seventeen years ago. Thus, pay-TV is not a dream.

In addition to the FCC, the great majority of the country's newspapers are in favor of pay-TV. Virtually every television columnist and critic is in favor of pay-TV. In short, almost everyone who knows anything about television wants pay-TV, because of the quality and diversity it could bring to programming.

Almost everyone except the broadcasters, who would simply deny the public the right to choose for itself whether to watch their free channels or whether to tune them out from time to time and pay a small fee for programs the members of the NAB say they cannot afford and do not offer: Broadway hits, first-run movies, travelogues, championship fights, opera. The broadcasters, by their opposition, are forcing the public to see *their* kind of television: hour after hour of mediocre entertainment, jammed with commercials. The possibility that they might lose some of the revenue that currently accrues from those commercials is unthinkable to the NAB members.

In the same way, I would hope that every encouragement is given to CATV (cable television) operators. No one, I think, could reasonably object to any improvement in television reception in hard to reach places; behind high mountains or across great open spaces.

The trouble is, cable antenna stations may be capable also of originating programs, and so competing with some of the established broadcasters. This they do not like. But their selfish interests should not be considered.

Television is no place for monopoly.

It is sometimes said in jest that many television commercials are more interesting than the programs they interrupt; and if we compare them minute for minute with the insipid game shows and the rebroadcasting of fifteen-year-old situation comedy that wasn't very funny to begin with, then I suspect that even the commercials for headache remedies and boluses for bad breath and upset stomach may, indeed, be more entertaining.

Here I should confess that I am intrigued with the classic colloquy between the man and his disembodied stomach in the interest of Alka-

Seltzer; I enjoy every repeat showing of the hard-boiled, hulking parking station attendant whose indifference causes an Excedrin headache in an exasperated customer whose car has been lost; and I consider the exotic scenes through which a parade of rugged individuals
walk a mile for a Camel to be superior television on every count. I
only wish that the program producers would do as well.

John O'Toole, who is head of creative planning for Foote, Cone &
Belding, points out that "new techniques and new uses of film had to
be devised to communicate what a product does, why it does this
better, what kind of person it is for, and where you get it — all in
ninety feet of 35-mm film. Extreme close-ups violate the traditional
rules of cropping. Sudden cuts are used for time transitions, instead
of long dissolves. Scenes are dropped in for as little as a fraction of
a second (as in the flashing shower scenes in Dial soap commercials).
New relationships are conceived between soundtrack and picture.
Sound becomes important, dialogue less so. Many commercials now
contain no more than six or seven words right at the very end — simply
to underline the graphic communication."

What really has brought about the striking increase in the wit and
polish of today's best efforts in television advertising has been the
eagerness of the advertising people themselves to explore the possibilities in the medium far beyond anything the broadcasters have yet
undertaken. They have refused to be satisfied with the stodgy advertising merely because it works in so many cases. They find the old
patterns, still adhered to by some of the soap companies and many
of the manufacturers of proprietaries, no fun to live with.

They want to do something different. They have discovered how
much more interesting people are when they look and talk like people
who have never had a film test or heard of method acting. (The
truth is, most of these people *are* professional actors, but they are
character actors, not near-stars or starlets, and they play their minute
spots for all they are worth.)

Falling in love with pure entertainment is the principal hazard on
the horizon for the commercial makers. For the most part, the new-
style commercials depend upon humor, and nothing is more difficult
to control. It is at its best in advertising when it is subtle, as when
a sculptor with a thick accent explains patiently how man's imper-
fectly designed face practically demands a new kind of razor, designed to get around the various obstructions — demonstrated on a
plaster cast. The comedy is in the plaster of paris. The razor is presented straight.

Two generations of advertising people have established the rule that sound advertising always delivers a worthwhile message. If it doesn't do this, no matter how entertaining it may be to bored television critics and commentators, it is worthless.

Unless advertising makes important selling points clear and easy to remember, fun and frolic in television should be left to the programmers.

The same thing is true of printed advertising. While it is a fact that wild-eyed women whisked out of their laundries by fast-cleaning action in their washing machines, tornadoes in turbid sinks washing dishes, and pistols shot at impenetrable plastic sheets to simulate the hard finish of floor waxes never quite made it into print because they required animation, printed advertising has not been immune to all of the bad influences of television. Those remarkable people who suffered black eyes for their loyalty to Tareyton cigarettes, and their silly neighbors who happily ate their hats as a fair price to pay for the revelation of a new taste in Lucky Strike cigarettes, brought new inanities to the printed page.

Again, there is nothing wrong with such advertising in the sense that it is evil. It may even be preferable to a number of advertising campaigns of the past which made outrageous claims for all manner of products. On the other hand, such idiocies are inexplicable to ordinary, sensible people. For if the best advertising is always that advertising which most closely resembles a personal solicitation, a proposition made under conditions as representative as possible of real life, there is no sensible reason for anything else.

In fact, there is no reason at all; except that there is a small group of people in advertising who are not truly advertising people, who have attached themselves to it in mistaken belief that advertising is a branch of show business.

Here I would remind the successors to the men on the cover of *Time* that for every successful item of entertainment there are scores of attempts that fail, and fail abysmally: widely heralded plays and movies and songs and television programs that are born and flutter briefly and die. And however little this may affect show business in the long run, it is surely not a good enough ratio for advertising.

Theatricality in advertising assumes the reader to be in an aisle seat, as it were, having paid his way in, wanting to find out what the show is all about. And what could be more absurd?

Few people among us have nothing more important or more amusing to do than leaf through the pages of a newspaper or magazine to seek out the points of obscure advertising. There is no captive audience for advertising in print; and nothing that I can imagine is much easier to do than to turn the page on a meaningless advertising message.

Let me repeat: advertising is to tell somebody something; no one should use it to play games with.

Without a promise that seems both plausible and with the strong probability that it will be kept, advertising must fail. This is something that most opponents of advertising find difficult to understand. But this is the way advertising is; the values and the vices that are attributed to it are more often than not contingent upon personal assessments of its purposes and its propriety.

The contemporary record is filled with the values just as the archives are filled with vices; and it is possible to dismiss these only if one denies that there are any virtues at all in a society where free choice supports the economy. As it is, our economy requires large amounts of information if it is to remain free, and advertising plays a major role in providing that information.

To this I suspect that Arnold Toynbee and John Kenneth Galbraith, who are among the severest critics of advertising, would counter that whatever else it may do, advertising exercises a carefully contrived hypnotic effect upon the public that wastes its material substance.

In arguing the point I have tried not to become involved in a defense of all advertising, for advertising has its sordid sides, as everyone knows, and it can be both mildly irritating and highly objectionable. But to argue that advertising is either hypnotic or subliminal is ridiculous. I hope I have made it clear that the business is not nearly that sophisticated. That it is wasteful is a condition beyond doubt. But so is freedom. Otherwise, who is to be told, "You can't manufacture another television receiver or soup or shaving cream because we don't need another television set or soup or shaving cream; the ones we have will do us well enough!"

The possibility that this could happen is something that some of my associates and some of my friends look upon with growing alarm. I am much less apprehensive. I am aware of the vague unease and restlessness that manifests itself in spirited articles on all kinds of institutions solely because they represent things as they are. One of these institutions is advertising.

Among a growing number of young people who have never heard of either the historian Toynbee or the economist Galbraith, advertising is condemned as a tool of competition, which it is; and competition is viewed as something that should be shunned in a brave new world of noninvolvement. But it is not the way of most young people to be uninvolved for very long, nor is it the way of most young men and women to renounce competition. Their way is just the opposite.

I believe that competition in business will continue just as long as it remains a driving force among architects, engineers, lawyers, doctors, teachers and clergymen, for it is what gives everyone a chance. That the way may be riddled with pitfalls changes its value not at all.

The alternative that is suggested by noninvolvement is empty and selfish and, above all, dangerous. The overwhelming majority of people must accept the responsibilities of a free society if only to keep it free.

Decent advertising is one of the means. How well it is used in the near future will be up to the successors.

Index